So
Communities

Sociolinguistic Variation in Speech Communities

Edited by Suzanne Romaine

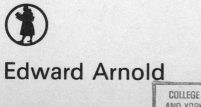

Edward Arnold

© Edward Arnold 1982

First published 1982 by
Edward Arnold (Publishers) Ltd
41 Bedford Square, London WC1B 3DQ

British Library Cataloguing in Publication Data

Sociolinguistic variation in speech communities.
  1. Language and languages—Variation—Addresses,
essays, lectures
  2. Sociolinguistics—Addresses, essays,
lectures
  I. Romaine, Suzanne
  401'.9   P41

ISBN 0-7131-6355-0

Set in 10/11 pt Times Monophoto
by Willmer Brothers Limited, Birkenhead, Merseyside
Printed in Great Britain by
Richard Clay (The Chaucer Press) Ltd, Bungay, Suffolk

Contents

Notes on Contributors

Dr Jenny Cheshire is Lecturer in Linguistics in the School of Modern Languages, University of Bath. Her research interests are mainly in the field of language variation and sociolinguistics. Her publications include *Linguistic and Sociolinguistic Variation in an Urban British English Dialect* (forthcoming).

Professor Nancy C. Dorian is William R. Kenan Jr Professor of Linguistics at Bryn Mawr College where she teaches Linguistics and German. Her main research interest is in the study of linguistic extinction. Her publications include *Language Death, the Life Cycle of a Scottish Gaelic Dialect*.

Dr Richard A. Hudson is Reader in Linguistics at University College, London. His publications include the textbook *Sociolinguistics* and his main research interest is in the theory of language structure.

Dr Nader Jahangiri teaches in the Department of English at the University of Mashad, Iran and is actively involved in a major literacy campaign. He was previously employed on the dialect survey of the Iranian Academy of Language.

Professor Robert Brock Le Page is Head of the Department of Language at the University of York. He previously taught at the University of Malaya and the University of the West Indies. His main research interests are creole languages and sociolinguistics. His publications include *Dictionary of Jamaican English* (with F. G. Cassidy), *The National Language Question* and two volumes of *Creole Language Studies*.

Dr John Local is Lecturer in Linguistics at the University of York. He was previously employed on the Tyneside Linguistic Survey. His main research interests are in psycholinguistics, with particular emphasis on variability in intonation and child language acquisition.

Dr Damian McEntegart was Research Assistant to Professor R. B. LePage, Department of Languages, University of York. In October 1980 he took up a permanent position as Statistician for Cleveland County Research and Intelligence Unit.

Dr James Milroy is now Head of the Department of Linguistics and Director of the Language Laboratory at the University of Sheffield.

He was previously with the Department of English at the Queen's University of Belfast. His publications include *The Language of Gerard Manley Hopkins* and *Regional Accents of English: Belfast*.

Dr Lesley Milroy is Senior Lecturer teaching phonetics and linguistics at the Ulster Polytechnic. Her main research interests are in the theory and methodology of research into language variation. Her publications include *Language and Social Networks* and, together with James Milroy, *Authority in Language* (forthcoming).

Dr Suzanne Romaine is Lecturer in Linguistics at the University of Birmingham. Her main research interests are in sociolinguistics and historical linguistics. Her publications include articles on sociolinguistic variation in Scottish English, methodology and *Socio-Historical Linguistics. Its Status and Methodology*.

Dr Joan Russell is Lecturer in Linguistics and Swahili at the University of York and has previously published *Communicative Competence in a Minority Group*.

Dr Mats Thelander is Research Assistant at the Department of Scandinavian Languages at the University of Uppsala where he teaches Sociolinguistics and Bilingualism. He has published numerous articles in both English and Swedish.

Introduction

Suzanne Romaine

Since the publication of Labov's *Social Stratification of English in New York City* (1966), which launched a series of empirical investigations into the sociolinguistic structure of urban speech communities, great progress has been made in the study of sociolinguistic variation and methods of quantitative analysis. The significant body of work which has emerged from this research has been crucial in the development of what one might broadly call 'a sociolinguistic theory'. Such a theory attempts to make a coherent statement about the relationship between language use and social patterns or structures of various kinds.

By and large, the great majority of this research has been based on urban varieties of English (and these largely North American ones) and English-speaking communities. The restriction of the data base for sociolinguistic theory to these cases has had both advantages and disadvantages. One immediately obvious advantage, of course, is the tremendous increase in our knowledge of the range of sociolinguistic variation in English. Sociolinguistic studies on varieties of American and British English now complement research within the already well-established tradition of regional dialectology on both sides of the Atlantic to give us a more complete picture of the linguistic situation than may exist for other languages elsewhere; in fact, it would probably not be claiming too much to say that more is known about more kinds of English than about the varieties of any other language in the world.

Another distinct advantage in operating initially within a theoretical perspective based on exiguous and not very varied data is that it allowed sociolinguists, in particular Labov, to lay a solid methodological foundation for the study of language in its social context. This methodology generated a set of empirical findings or principles, which Labov (1972b) has called 'sociolinguistic patterns'. These can be regarded as testable hypotheses concerning the basic principles underlying the organization, social differentiation and change of speech communities. One of the first places in which Labovian methodology was applied outside the United States was Britain. Of necessity, much of this early work was programmatic, and thus, not strikingly original in either design or execution. Trudgill's (1974b) study of Norwich and Macaulay's (1977) of Glasgow represent however, important pioneering attempts to replicate Labov's methods and findings in two very different urban British settings. Macaulay's work and subsequent research on varieties of northern British English in particular, pointed out clearly the detriment in trying to construct a coherent and comprehensive sociolinguistic theory on such narrow foundations. The problems encountered in applying Labovian methodology in what are essentially a range of more linguistically diverse Old World communities (as opposed to North American ones, which are clearly less varied), led to extensions and inevitable modifications to existing methods, and in some cases to significant innovations.

The papers in this collection are representative of 'post-Labovian sociolinguistics' in a primarily European (or non-North American) setting. This designation does raise at least one important question: to what extent can one justifiably speak of the emergence of a distinct and more broadly based variety of sociolinguistic methodology and theory based on the data from non-North American speech communities? If we conceive of 'sociolinguistics' broadly, as Labov (1972b) and Trudgill (1978: 11) do, i.e. sociolinguistics is itself a methodology or a 'way of doing linguistics', then I think it is fair to say that there *is* a distinctive character to the approach being taken by the contributors to this volume. The papers here reflect a number of distinct and innovative trends in the analysis of the use and function of sociolinguistic variation in a range of speech communities, which are recognizably different to the lines of enquiry being taken in recent North American sociolinguistic work. One might reasonably speak of a 'post- or neo-Labovian sociolinguistics', which is founded on an attempt to break away from the exclusively status-based theory and straightforward correlational methodology of Labov. But it is perhaps somewhat misleading to speak of this development as exclusively post- or neo-Labovian. Despite the obvious indebtedness to Labov, the departure from his status-based approach on this side of the Atlantic owes much to the theoretical insights of Le Page as well as to the fact that Labovian models and methods were not directly transferable in all respects to varieties of urban British English. The papers here focus special attention on a number of aspects of sociolinguistic methodology and theory, e.g. the role of the individual, problems of quantifying and analysing variables and the integration of social factors into linguistic description. Taken as a whole, they reflect a movement away from the prevailing theoretical assumption that the patterning of sociolinguistic behaviour is to be explained by reference to social class or status.

That is of course only one way to look at the relationship between social and linguistic differentiation. Labov found, for example, in New York City that higher social class groups were closer to the norms of the standard language in their use of certain linguistic variables (as defined in terms of relative deviation on a continuum from an ideal prestige standard to non-standard vernacular), and women in each group more so than men. The shifts which each group underwent in more formal situations were 'explained' in terms of the effect of upward social mobility on language use.

Part of the difficulty posed by the kinds of speech communities dealt with here in assuming such a model stems from the relationship between varieties within one language (e.g. dialect vs. standard) on the one hand, and between languages on the other, which may reflect a long and complicated history of linguistic contact. Many of the communities discussed by the contributors to this volume are just not socio-linguistically organized in a way familiar to us from Labov's description of New York City. These are just as likely to be English-speaking (e.g. L. Milroy and J. Milroy on Belfast) as non-English speaking communities (e.g. Thelander on Burträsk Swedish, Russell on Mombasa Swahili, Jahangiri and Hudson on Tehrani Persian, and Dorian on East Sutherland Gaelic). I have suggested in my own paper that the notion of 'speech community' as Labov defined it with specific reference to New York City (1966: 7) quickly breaks down elsewhere.

Jahangiri and Hudson, for instance, find that almost any member of the highest-ranking group (in terms of educational level) can be taken as a model of standardness on almost any variable; but this is not the case for the lowest-ranking. Thus, they suggest it would be misleading to regard Tehran society as anchored between two norm-defining groups, i.e. standard and non-standard Tehrani Persian. It is anchored instead only at the top; Tehran society consists of a range of social groups, each of which defines its own norms for each variable. Thelander similarly feels that the conception of Burträsk as a 'bi-dialectal' community where people switch between local dialect and standard Swedish is seriously undermined by the observation that (micro-) variables behave so differently. He believes one must acknowledge the existence of an intermediate variety, i.e. regional standard. In her paper Russell cites the long-standing history of linguistic heterogeneity in Mombasa as the source of earlier reports that Swahili speakers there speak a language which is neither pure Mombasa nor pure Zanzibar. A number of the papers point to the limited usefulness of variable rule-governed grammars in the modelling of sociolinguistic variation in speech communities (e.g. Romaine, Dorian and Thelander). J. Milroy introduces the notion of 'shape of speech communities' and argues on the basis of the sociolinguistic patterning of certain complex variables that Belfast is a triangular (rather than linear) speech community.

It is not just organization which is at stake here, but also the competence one must have to be part of such varied speech communities. Dorian, for example, stresses the need to look at individual speakers along a proficiency continuum, which represents various stages in a community-wide shift from Gaelic to English monolingualism via bilingualism. There the notion of passive ability in Gaelic must enter into an adequate definition of speech community, i.e. 'semi-speakers' have passive skills of a native speaker, but still feel very much a part of the community. One needs to strike a distinction between the requirements necessary for participation as opposed to membership in a speech community. It seems that in East Sutherland one can have very limited productive skills and still count as a member as long as one has a repertoire of formulaic expressions, whose value is primarily inter-actional rather than informational. Hymes (1974) has observed that a large part of any speech community's repertoire is made up of such formulas and pre-packaged social routines. Fillmore (1976) has also stressed the central role of formulaic expression in second language learning. She found, for example, that language learners are able to use language in meaningful social settings long before there is evidence of rule learning. One might say that speakers are able to 'perform without competence'. Since these formulaic expressions are among the first skills to be acquired and from what Dorian says, among the last to be lost, we may have another interesting adjunct to the Jakobsonian (1941) principle of irreversible solidarity. But perhaps more important from a theoretical perspective is the fact that very little of the verbal activity of semi-speakers is generated by application of the formal rules of grammar in a productive and creative way. To the extent that most current models of grammar describe only rule-governed productive linguistic behaviour, these would not be appropriate in a situation where most of the output of a community (or sub-section of it) is highly formulaic.

Not surprisingly, a rather parochial view can result from an exclusive concentration on English-speaking communities (even if one takes these to include British and American varieties of English as well as English-based creoles). If we want to make progress towards a more general sociolinguistic theory of the kind suggested by Hymes (1974) and Le Page (1978), then contributions of the kind found in this volume provide extremely critical and important tests of existing methodology and theory. I doubt the usefulness of a restricted theory which deals only with special synchronic cases and uses of language (cf. also Weinreich 1966: 399 for a similar comment on restricted semantic theories). Maybe a more fundamental question is whether we are willing to accept theories which cannot handle all the uses/forms in which language may manifest itself in a given speech community over time. A viable social theory of language must present a coherent account of how particular uses, functions and kinds of language develop within particular speech communities. This will require the testing of methodology on new and different kinds of data.

Although all the papers in this volume present novel data, I personally feel that they are innovating in more than just this sense. More specifically, the contributors are attempting to develop a more integrated and coherent account of the manner in which real communities of speakers use language in a socially meaningful way (cf.

McEntegart and Le Page). This concern manifests itself in a desire to study individuals and/or linguistic tokens in more insightful ways, in some cases by means of sophisticated quantitative techniques. The papers by Jahangiri and Hudson, and Thelander suggest quantitative techniques for taking into account syntagmatic aspects of the distribution of linguistic variants. Jahangiri and Hudson's paper also tries to look in detail at the types of patterns found in the data, rather than to report bare findings about the influence of age, sex and education on variables in Tehrani Persian; (though the latter are surely interesting in their own right, since these are some of the first sociolinguistic data to appear on Persian). Thelander, on the other hand, suggests that a distinction between micro- and macro-variables needs to be drawn on the basis of the differential sensitivity to extra- and intra-linguistic constraints. After dividing all instances of a certain variable into linguistically defined sub-categories, only those which exhibit similar patterns of social variation should, in his opinion, be aggregated. This is surely an important refinement to the concept of linguistic variable; the requirement that social constraints on linguistic variables be considered on an equal footing with linguistic ones has been much neglected in recent American sociolinguistic work. Unless our analyses are equally responsive to both social and linguistic factors in an integrative fashion, then we run the risk of presenting a lopsided view of a speech community as a whole. Such piecemeal analyses cannot claim to be truly sociolinguistic (cf. also Romaine 1979a).

In fact, too much emphasis on analytical innovations and devices for dealing with linguistic constraints on variation has characterized North American sociolinguistics, where a decided emphasis has been given to the development of more sophisticated varieties of probabilistic variable rule analysis. The papers in a recent volume by Sankoff (1978) reflect this trend. The great amount of sociolinguistic research which has developed under Labov's influence has been addressed much more specifically to linguistic issues, e.g. constraints on optional rules, implicational relationships among variable constraints. This concentration on the organization of internal linguistic variation has of course allowed significant advances in our understanding of language variation. However, this kind of quantitative work has now assumed such a commanding position, that for many, this *is* sociolinguistics (cf. for example, Trudgill 1978: 11). This advance in analytical precision has unfortunately often been at the expense of the emergence of a coherent model for the analysis of language use and social structure. McEntegart and Le Page's paper is painstakingly honest in its detailed appraisal of the relative success and failure of statistical methods used in the sociolinguistic analysis of multilingual communities in the Caribbean. Many of the assumptions about the identity of linguistic units to be counted and the comparability of data and situations across a large number of informants, though taken for granted elsewhere, just don't hold in this case. The complexities of the emergent social structure and cultural matrix of ethnically diverse creole communities defy compartmentalization into the neat social and linguistic categories, which quantiative sociolinguistic analysis generally takes as a relatively unproblematic starting point.

A formal approach isn't exclusive of course to 'quantitative sociolinguistics'; linguistics itself as a discipline is founded on a formal approach to grammatical description. The direction taken by the contributors to this volume doesn't rule out formal grammars of variation by any means. But much of the recent analytical formalism in North America, e.g. variable rules, appears to be too heavily tied to transformational grammar (and an early model of TG at that). What the papers here suggest is that formalization is a useful conceptual aid, but it is not a goal to be pursued for its own sake, especially in the absence of accompanying treatment of qualitative phenomena. Thelander, in particular, points out the danger in 'over-quantifying' sociolinguistic data. These two approaches, qualitative and quantitative, go hand in hand and represent two different perspectives on the same socio-linguistic phenomenon (cf. also McEntegart and Le Page). We cannot hope to make a contribution to understanding the use and function of variation in speech communities solely through formalism. The investigation of the sociolinguistic structure of speech communities should not be tied exclusively to a single model of grammar on the one hand, nor should it necessarily entail an organization of linguistic means as restrictive as an abstract grammar of a single speech community using a set of variable rules in the same way, on the other (cf. the papers by Romaine and J. Milroy).

Labov (1972b: 183–4) has said he believes that the validity of socio-linguistic research is to be measured in terms of its ability to relate sociolinguistic data to the central problems of linguistic theory. Surely, this is too narrow a conception of the role of sociolinguistic research. The social and linguistic differentiation which forms the data of empirical work in sociolinguistics remains uninterpretable (and even paradoxical) within such a narrow conception of grammar on the one hand and the goals of sociolinguistics on the other. In other words, formalism in and of itself is not sufficient to support a theory of language which will account for sociolinguistic phenomena in an integrative and illuminating fashion.

Emphasis on the integration of social factors into sociolinguistic description and analysis on the part of the contributors here has not resulted in a neglect of analytical procedures. None of us would be content to count tokens and correlate these mechanically with groups etc. In fact, Local's paper stands out here as an example of how one must extend the concept of variation and methods of analysis of quantitative data beyond those adequate for segmental phonology in order to deal with intonation. Local demonstrates that non-segmental systems exhibit regional and social differences similar to those found in vowel and consonant systems, lexis and syntax etc., and that intonational varieties are non-discrete. Local argues convincingly that children must acquire the rules for using intonational systems appropriate to the adult community in order to be sociolinguistically competent. There is of course a sense in which one could think of children as comprising a speech community in their own right (or at least an important sector of the adult community). It is significant that differences in the context of elicitation along a formality dimension don't seem to affect the realization of non-segmental phenomena. In this respect then intonational varieties differ from other varieties. Local's findings suggest that one needn't worry too much about controlling settings, isolating contextual styles etc., which is a major concern for Labov, given the rather gross effect context has on segmental variables. As I have suggested, such extensions provide crucial tests of methodology and theory. I take it that one important purpose of varying our observations and extending the theory to cope with variation at different levels of the grammar and in different communities is to see how far it will go before we are required to alter basic descriptive categories and hypotheses. Otherwise, we must content ourselves with a sociolinguistic theory which is very restricted both in scope and application.

Many of the findings reported here need to be seen in larger terms as a more general manifestation of what Le Page (1978) has referred to as 'speech as an act of identity' on the part of the individual. His approach has validated the individual as a respectable starting point for sociolinguistic analysis and demonstrated that the study of individual linguistic behaviour is not to be equated with chaos, as Labov, for example, has suggested (1966: 6–7). Labov of course is basically interested in the construction of 'community grammars', since he has assumed that the speech of any social group will be less variable than the speech of any individual. This assumption of isomorphism between individual and group grammars has of course been questioned by others (e.g. Bickerton 1971) and furnishes the basis of criticism in some of the papers here (cf. Romaine, and J. Milroy). Jahangiri and Hudson, for example, find that only one speaker was consistently above or below average. Thus, they suggest a negative answer to the question of whether some social groups (or individuals in them) are more consistent than others in terms of their usage of variables.

Le Page's multidimensional approach has developed within the context of his work on language use in multilingual communities in the Caribbean (cf. for example, Le Page *et al.* 1974), where it has been necessary to take account of a number of sources of influences on a person's speech. He is keen to stress that speakers choose to bring into play the variable linguistic resources available to them in a community as a means of identifying with different groups. A group approach simply covers this up. Since several of the papers here draw explicitly on these ideas and attempt to apply them in diverse settings using network analysis (e.g. L. Milroy in Belfast and Russell in Africa), it is especially useful for comparative purposes to have McEntegart and Le Page's assessment of the difficulties involved in modelling these hypotheses about a speaker's perceptions of his role in a group or speech community using cluster analysis. It is clear that certain significant findings emerge here only through a careful consideration of the role of the individual. For example, it is true in both Tehran and Belfast that different variables have different social functions as group differentiators and markers of various social identities (cf. L. Milroy and Jahangiri/Hudson). Jahangiri and Hudson make a contribution towards developing statistical means of measuring the relative homogeneity of groups and variables. And Thelander, for example, finds that it is necessary to speak of individual differences in 'relative bi-dialectalism', just as Dorian examines individuals in terms of a relative proficiency continuum.

Although the individual has not occupied a place of importance in North American sociolinguistics (cf. however, the recent collection of papers in Fillmore *et al.* 1979), this has not always been the case. A number of the papers in this volume might reasonably be referred to as 'post- or neo-Labovian' to the extent that they hark back to early work by Labov on Black English Vernacular in Harlem (1968) and on Martha's Vineyard (1963) and to the qualitative approach of Blom and Gumperz (1972). In all these studies the effect of peer group, in particular in-group and out-group identity, was found to have a significant effect in enforcing community norms. While much of this ethnographic type of research seems to have fallen by the wayside in the United States, it has occupied a prominate place here; the influence of these early community studies is very much in evidence in Russell's, Thelander's, Cheshire's and L. Milroy's papers. Cheshire for example, finds that that the extent to which speakers participate in vernacular culture is reflected in the frequency with which adolescents in Reading use certain non-standard linguistic forms. L. Milroy and Russell show that identification with various social and cultural groups is just as important a source of influence for adults in two diverse situations, i.e. Belfast and East Africa respectively, as it is for teen-age adolescents.

All of the studies here appear to suggest in one way or another that one must look at the place of the individual speaker as a particular level of abstraction in linguistic analysis. This points to the following hierarchy:

individual
network
social group
speech community
language

As L. Milroy (1980: 201) has recently pointed out, status-based approaches which start from the social group and solidarity-based approaches relying on the concept of network are not mutually exclusive. The findings reported in a number of the papers here don't so much alter or contradict Labov's basic sociolinguistic patterns, but rather put them in a different and often more intelligible perspective. For example, if we examine the phenomenon of sex differentiation from the perspective of the individual and his network (rather than in terms of categories such as 'middle-class women' and 'working-class men') we can deepen our understanding of what is otherwise a rather static and unsatisfactorily explained correlation between language and sex. L. Milroy's paper shows that there is a close relationship between sex of the speaker and network scores for many of the variables in Belfast; and furthermore, that network scores are sharply differentiated in areas with the largest amount of sex differentiation. Thus, sex and network interact to produce some very interesting and intricate sociolinguistic patterning. Cheshire discusses the differential structure of male vs. female peer groups and its effect on the use of linguistic variables. That is, some features mark adherence to the vernacular culture and others don't; and there are differences in the use of these by boys and girls.

Many of the papers in this volume also have important implications for language change. In particular, J. Milroy's contribution underlines the fact that diachrony and synchrony intersect in any given speech community. This has a number of practical consequences; among these is the complexity of determining word class membership at any given time. The difficulties in Belfast appear greater than in other English-speaking communities. It is interesting that Russell too notes such fluctuation in her Swahili-speaking informants. Another practical consequence of this heterogeneity arises in the construction of variable scales and deciding what to count; one can't simply assume that the relevant word class for the variable in question is the same as in the standard language. Different lects within the same speech community may have different inputs to these lexical sets that are eligible for change and variation (cf. also McEntegart and Le Page). One cannot therefore give an adequate picture of the synchronic social stratification of speech variants without also paying attention to the diacronic dimensions of the gradual diffusion of lexical items from one word class to another. Jahangiri and Hudson also find that the chances of occurrence of non-standard variants differ radically from one lexical item to another and can't be predicted on phonological or morphological grounds.

Milroy's conclusion (like that of Dorian) is that any model which doesn't take into account differential speaker competence and social evaluation of variables in the community is inadequate. A similar point comes out clearly in Russell's work, where variability in ways of speaking Swahili continually shifts its locus; though it is women (rather than men, as in L. Milroy's study), who are preserving the more obvious markers of the community. Cheshire's finding that in Reading English the non-standard forms *ain't* and *in't* do not correspond exactly to their supposed standard English equivalents (*aren't* and *isn't*) provides more evidence for the conclusion that non-standard variants cannot automatically be assumed to stand in a simple relationship with the standard. Her work too has diachronic implications, for it suggests that the variant *in't* (which occurs as an invariant form in non-standard tag questions), is not related to the 3rd person plural present tense form *in't* other than historically; and that it is now instead a marker of the vernacular themes of aggression and hostility.

The role of the individual in linguistic change is of course a perplexing question, not just for the contributors here; as Romaine's paper suggests, the Neogrammarians raised this question a long time ago. Jahangiri and Hudson's paper poses a new dimension to the dilemma by asking how it is possible, given that individual speakers in many cases are unreliable sources of group norms, that norms are passed on from generation to generation without disintegrating into chaos. A number of the papers here suggest insights on the process of redistribution over time of variants as markers of various social identities within the developmental and historical continua of speech communities. Local, for example, documents the redistribution of pitch movements over stable syntactic structures in the speech of children who are in various stages of acquiring particular kinds of localized intonation systems. It is significant there, just as in J. Milroy's and Dorian's papers, that individuals can be placed at different points along the continuum of change and variation.

The linguistic consequence of the continuation of local community and network becomes paramount in the light of L. Milroy's work in Belfast, where change in network structure is implicated as a contributory factor in linguistic change. While change in network structure alone doesn't appear to be a sufficient condition for change towards a standard, it is significant that one consequence of the break-up of close networks may be the blurring of sex differentiation in language. Thus, when codes and variables lose their symbolic function, i.e. as markers of various social identities, the way for linguistic change is paved. The finding that localized network structure can be correlated with the adherence to a non-legitimized norm puts in a more concrete perspective a result which has remained somewhat paradoxical within the Labovian framework—namely, why do people continue to speak low status vernaculars in the face of pressure from more socially prestigious standard varieties/languages?

All the papers here raise exciting prospects for future empirical work in other speech communities, particularly now that such a variety of testable hypotheses has emerged which relate to the organization and change of ways of speaking. In particular, however, Le Page's notion that the same kinds of processes operate on speakers from different cultures and of different statuses to provide a highly focused set of linguistic norms needs wider testing. In fact, the value of his theoretical perspective lies in its general applicability to both multilingual and multilectal settings. He suggests that cultural and linguistic focusing may take place at any level of society where social conditions are favourable; that is, this can happen in such diverse settings as Belize and working-class areas of Belfast as well as it can among the members of Harlem street gangs or teen-age peer groups in Reading described by Labov and Cheshire respectively. L. Milroy (1980: 180f) has recently pointed out that within British society, focusing is characteristic of both upper and lower groups. In other words, RP (received pronunciation) speakers operate with closed, multiplex networks just as much as lower-class vernacular speakers do. In both cases, network structures may function powerfully to maintain a highly focused set of linguistic norms intact. Other speakers, however, whose networks are more open and broadly based (e.g. women in Belfast and men in Mombasa), i.e. whose members are socially and geographically more mobile, are in Le Page's terms more 'diffuse' with regard to patterns of language. This pattern of greater focusing of linguistic behaviour at the edges of society also appears to be in evidence in Jahangiri and Hudson's finding that the most consistent and constraining groups in Tehran society are at the extremes.

There is one final point I would like to emphasize here; namely, that one needs to look at sociolinguistic phenomena from several different vantage points. Certain levels of analysis, e.g. individual, network, social group, speech community, may prove to be more telling in particular situations than others. Of course the large task which remains for a sociolinguistic theory is the clarification of the interface between these various levels of abstraction. If the quality of the research which has emerged so far within the context of European sociolinguistics can be taken as indicative of future trends, then one has every reason to expect further substantial contributions to our understanding of these crucial issues.[1]

[1] I would like to acknowledge all of the contributors, who provided me with such stimulating and carefully prepared papers. My introduction by no means covers all the questions they raise about sociolinguistic variation in speech communities. I'm especially grateful to Lesley Milroy for discussing an earlier version of this introduction with me and for focusing my attention on specific issues. Any remaining diffuseness in thought is my own responsibility.

1

What is a speech community?

Suzanne Romaine

It may seem counter-productive, if not even disrespectful, to question a concept like speech community, or to suggest that there is a problem here. Since Gumperz (1968) defined it as a sociolinguistic entity and a fundamental unit of analysis, the literature is rife with references to the speech community. My point of departure here will be Gumperz's notion of a speech community as a group of speakers (not necessarily of the same language) who share a set of norms and rules for the use of language(s). Thus, Labov (1966:7), for example, says about New York City:

> That New York City is a speech community, and not a collection of speakers living side by side, borrowing from each others' dialects, may be demonstrated by many kinds of evidence. Native New Yorkers differ in their usage in terms of absolute values of the variables, but the shifts between contrasting styles follow the same pattern in almost every case.

This type of speech community goes hand in hand with unidirectional variation organized along a continuous sociolinguistic dimension. Labov's work has concentrated on situations of this sort. To take a specific illustration, Labov (1963) has argued that centralization on Martha's Vineyard has a social meaning. A speaker who uses the more centralized variants of two diphthongs is asserting local solidarity in a strong way through positive identification with life on the island. The variation in this case can be ordered along a continuous linguistic dimension (specifically, a phonetic one which represents differing degrees of centralization) as well as a social one which corresponds to the speaker's strength of identity with the local community of fishermen. The implication of this pattern of variation is that speakers vary in their use of /aw/ and /ay/ only to the extent that certain groups carry the change further along than others. What is implied then is a relationship of relatively greater or lesser use of the same variable.

It seems reasonable to suppose, however, that in different speech communities social and linguistic factors are linked not only in different ways, but to different degrees, so that the imbrication of social and linguistic structure in a given speech community is a matter for investigation and cannot be taken as given. In fact, I am coming to the conclusion that speech communities in which sociolinguistic variation is organized in the monotonic and straightforward way that Labov describes must be the exception rather than the rule. I think others might agree (cf. also Dorian, this volume).[1]

For example, Milroy and Margrain have difficulty in making sense out of the classic definition of speech community, even when trying to describe the behaviour of one group of speakers in Belfast. They say (1978: 25–6):

> These results show that even in a single speech community—and it would be plausible to describe Belfast vernacular speakers in that way—there are many differences in the manner in which speakers take hold of 'pieces' of the language and use them as symbols of community loyalty.

Their conclusion is that 'sociolinguistic structure is woven in a complex way throughout the community, with different phonological elements being associated with various social groups' (Milroy and Margrain 1978: 31).

Milroy does not find the results surprising; nor would most creolists working within the dynamic paradigm, which takes the individual as the starting point of analysis, largely to avoid this problem of defining group boundaries (cf. especially Bickerton 1971: 487–8). In fact, both J. Milroy (1978) and I (Romaine 1979a) have suggested that a number of the most interesting cases of variation in both Belfast and Edinburgh respectively are those in which variation behaves non-continuously (as, for example, in the alternation between *hame* and *home* in Scots). This type of variation is often characteristic of diglossic and post-creole continuum situations which are perhaps better described in terms of coexistent grammars.

It could be argued that I am exaggerating the difficulty involved in defining a speech community by picking the most awkward examples. It is no doubt true that as English-speaking speech communities go, Belfast and Edinburgh are very heterogeneous; but, as it turns out, even fairly homogeneous speech communities may display more than one direction of change and variation, and subgroups within the community can be characterized by bimodal distributions with respect to the use of the same variable, i.e. they use it *different* ways.

Guy (1977), for example, reports that within one group of speakers the same constraints on the rule of t/d deletion are not in effect to the same extent. There do not seem to be any extra-linguistic factors which will account for the bimodal distribution; for some speakers, the most important constraint on the application of the rule is the presence of a

[1]These kinds of communities are what Le Page (1979b) has referred to as 'highly focused'. He has commented (1979b: 9):

> There *are* [emphasis in original SR] highly-focused societies whose linguistic systems can be represented as more-or-less uniform—albeit only by gross abstractions, but they are the exception rather than the rule.

monomorphemic form (e.g. *last*), while for others, it is the presence of an irregular past tense verb form (e.g. *told*). This finding is particularly interesting because t/d deletion seems to be a stable process and is not undergoing change.

One conclusion which might be drawn from these few examples I have discussed is that speech communities do not know how to behave; or else, linguists do not know what speech communities are or how they behave. And I think linguists should take the 'blame' here. We scarcely know how heterogeneous some speech communities are.

Certainly, once we abandon the assumption that all dialects or lects must have the same underlying forms, or stop describing non-standard varieties in terms of their divergence from an idealized standard, then the picture becomes messier. As I have pointed out elsewhere (cf. Romaine 1979b), there does not seem to be any reason for assuming that black speakers, for example, start out with the full forms of the copula, as Labov claims that white middle class speakers do, and then delete them. The primary justification is is a descriptive one; it allows us to say that the differences between black and white speakers are quantitative, and not qualitative.

I suppose my original question should be revised as follows: What is a speech community if all of its members do *not* use the rules of a grammar in the same way? Or better yet—*Are* there really speech communities which use the rules of grammar in the way in which Labov would have us believe? I believe the latter is a more profitable starting point.

The search for the illusive homogeneous speech community is well documented in Gauchat's (1905) and Hermann's (1929) study of the Swiss village of Charmey. Gauchat's work does not seem to have aroused much interest (apart from Hermann's follow-up investigation), until its mention by Labov (1963) and Weinreich *et al.* (1968), probably because Gauchat's findings were so controversial at the time of the study. In any case, I think Gauchat's study must now be seen as a superb piece of sociolinguistic research. In fact, it is probably the first demonstration of the importance of age-grading as a mechanism in the transmission of linguistic change.

Gauchat found that there was fluctuation among the middle generation of speakers with respect to the use of old and new norms as shown below; the case in point being a change from [λ] to [j] (Gauchat's /l'/ and /y/).

Data from three generations of Charmey speakers (Gauchat 1905: 205)

Generation	I (90–60 years)	II (60–30 years)	III (under 30)
	l'	l'-y	y

In 1929 Hermann concluded that Gauchat had obtained a record of sound change in progress in this observation of age-grading differences by comparing the differences between Gauchat's records and his own later ones.

Gauchat's results were striking for a number of reasons. Firstly, they challenged the homogeneity of the idiolect; and secondly, they indicated that one way in which change within the system could take place was by oscillation between old and new norms. The latter finding challenged the Neogrammarian view of a linguistic system as a set of uniform and homogeneous rules which changed discretely from generation to generation.

Gauchat's conclusions were all the more damaging to Neogrammarian ideas about sound change since he had chosen Charmey for the study precisely because the conditions there seemed most likely to support the existence of a homogeneous speech community.[2] Thus Gauchat observes (1905: 222):

> Cependent il importe de constater qu'à Charmey, où toutes les conditions sont plutôt favorables à l'unité, la diversité que je ne le serais imaginé après une courte visite ... L'unité du patois de Charmey après un examen plus attentif, est nulle.

Despite the Neogrammarian belief that language was a property of the individual (cf. for example, Paul 1920), individuals did not have a part to play in transition from one stage of the language to the next. The locus of change lay in the discontinuity of different generations of speakers in the community, and one way in which change originated was through the imperfect acquisition or imitation by children (i.e. *Einübungstheorie*). Both Gauchat and Hermann found evidence which contradicted the notion that idiolects remained stable after childhood; but Gauchat, in particular seemed puzzled by the role of the individual in transmitting sound change. He says (1905: 230–2):

> Nos materiaux nous obligent à chercher les motifs immediats d'une loi phonetique *à l'intérieur d'une* génération [emphasis in original SR]. La part active de l'enfant consiste à Charmey à généraliser un fait qui parait capricieux dans la bouche de l'individu et se généraliseraient dans les conditions favorables ... mais alors, comment s'explique le changement de l'articulation des debutants et comment faut-il que ces debutants soient faits pour devenir influents? Faut-il être un enfant de riche ou de maître de'école pour jouer un rôle dans l'évolution linguistique? ... Nos matériaux n'offrent aucune trace d'influence personelle. La formule *dow pã (du pain)* peut devenir *du pã* dans la bouche de n'importe quelle personne. La faute *du pã* ne devient loi qu'après avoir été faite indépendamment par un très grand nombre de personnes. Seules les fautes génériques ont des chances de

[2]One way out of the dilemma in Charmey would have been to explain the behaviour of the second generation as dialect mixture or borrowing (or even internal borrowing, i.e. the middle generation could 'borrow' a form from the older or younger generation). Gauchat, however, claimed that there were no external influences in Charmey; the village had been selected precisely for its supposed homogeneity. Hermann (1929: 198) nevertheless challenged Gauchat's belief that Charmey was a likely spot to look for homogeneity; his opinion was: 'die Mundart von Charmey bildet also einen Ausnahmefall; denn sonst ist eine Mundart nach allen Seiten von derselben Sprache umgeben'. According to Hermann, then, Gauchat had had 'eine falsche Vorstellung über die Abgeschlossenheit Charmeys'.

s'imposer ... Enfin l'état des choses que nous avons observé à Charmey ne donne pas raison a croient encore à l'infallibilité des lois phonétiques. Les personnes ne jouent pas un rôle très important dans la transmission de la langue, mais bien les mots.

The problem which bothered Gauchat was how to define the origin of change if the individual himself could not change the language. By equating selection with origin, the transition factor was shifted onto society, i.e. individuals vary, but the group changes the language by selecting among variants. This is also the position taken by Weinreich *et al.* (1968: 187):[3]

> Linguistic change is not to be identified with random drift proceeding from inherent variation in speech. Linguistic change begins when the particular alternation in a given subgroup of the speech community assumes direction and takes on the category of orderly differentiation.

Thus the introduction of a new variant into the speech use of an individual does not constitute change. A whole group has to show change before it is considered real change. This suggests that changes or innovations have to keep recurring within individuals until they are selected and the transmitted. Paul (1920: 39) believed that change occurred in the idiolect by selective adaptation to other idiolects during social interaction. The theory of biological evolution provided an analogy for linguistic evolution in the principle of natural selection as a proposed explanation for change and diversity.[4]

The biological metaphor is still productive in current views on language change which emphasize the role of the individual; for example, Stross (1975:24) comments:[5]

[3]Sapir's (1921: 165–6) often-quoted statement about language drift incorporates the notion of linguistic evolution consisting of two processes, variation and selection:

> What significant changes take place in it [i.e. language SR] must exist to begin with as individual variations ... the drift of a language is constituted by the unconscious selections on the part of its speakers of those individual variations that are cumulative in some special direction.

The conflation of origin and selection obscures the exact point of spatio-temporal actuation of a change in Labov's theory, but not Bailey's. Of course, it is highly unlikely that such a point would be recorded (except maybe by accident); we would only recognize such an innovation in an individual as the origin of a sound change in retrospect anyway.
[4]The parallels between the theory of biological evolution and linguistic change were recognized by Max Müller (before Darwin), and by Schleicher (1863), i.e. origin from a common ancestor; but it was Darwin, in fact, who in a sense completed the analogy by arguing for the principle of 'the survival of the fittest', which he had read in the work of Müller.
[5]Cf. also Longmire (1976), who suggests that /s/ deletion in Spanish is a 'reappearance' of an innovation which began in Early Latin. She discusses the problem of how to bridge the gap between language as a property of the individual and that of the group apart from the individual. She (like Sapir), seems to be saying that languages have inherited tendencies transmitted either known (?) or unknown to their speakers, which can then reappear (Note also Mendel's idea that the reappearance of traits within organisms after several generations constituted the transfer or inheritance of a trait).

Generation, transmission, and extinction of particular variants is essentially an individual phenomenon, but variation can also be viewed from the perspective of the speech community in terms of competition and selection. Variants compete for dominance in the community repertoire as the pressures of natural selection acting upon the human bearers of variants tend to remove some variants from the repertoire while allowing others to continue the struggle for survival and dominance.

As an explanatory principle, however, the concept of natural selection is meaningless unless some independent criterion for survival can be established; there does not seem to be a convincing argument in favour of the adaptive function of linguistic diversity and change.[6]

It may seem that I have digressed from the question at hand by bringing in the issue of language change and the role of the individual/group in its transmission, but it will become apparent in the following discussion that Labov's conception of the mechanism of change depends upon coherent notions of speech community and sociolectal grammar. If the latter are not tenable, then Labov's view of change as occurring in the grammar of a speech community becomes increasingly difficult to maintain. In fact, I will now argue that it is impossible for change to occur at all in the type of speech community Labov describes.

Labov's theory of language differentiation and change focuses specifically on speech communities where all the social groups use the variable concerned in the same way, though not necessarily to the same extent. Labov's claim is then that the locus of the grammar is in the community or group and that the speech of any social group will be less

---

[6]Lass (1980) has given a detailed discussion of some of the functionalist arguments used in theories of language change in order to show their explanatory inadequacy. He cites the particular difficulty in defining the locus of a function, i.e. individual or collective; in order for a change to be propagated, the function must be propagated along with it.

In fact, a better case (or one equally as good) can be made for the *maladaptive* function of linguistic change and diversity, if one examines the socio-political consequences of linguistic heterogeneity (cf. for example, Fishman 1968). The Neogrammarians, of course, claimed that sound change was dysfunctional (but cf. Weinreich *et al.* 1968: 101). In view of a number of facts it would have to be concluded that it looks bad to speak more than one language or variety of a language. For example, countries in which more than 85 per cent of the population speaks one language have a higher gross national product, higher life expectancy, more education for more of the population, lower death rates, and are, in general, more highly developed economically speaking.

Thus, it can be reasonably argued that serious social consequences are often associated with linguistic heterogeneity. In spite of this, however, there is also evidence to support the observation that dialect diversification is continuing, even in the face of expanding communications. A strict interpretation of evolutionary theory requires that diversification and complexity be seen as an advance, since functionally speaking, this allows an increase in the range and variety of adaptations to the environment (cf. however, Jespersen's 1894 idea of 'progress' in language, which is connected with simplicity, rather than complexity). The notion of simplicity/complexity of language as a hallmark of advanced evolutionary status runs into trouble with special cases like pidginization, decreolization and language death.

variable than the speech of any individual. Variable rules describe group behaviour rather than individual behaviour; thus, individual and group grammars are isomorphic.

Bailey, however, and the proponents of the so-called 'dynamic paradigm', who take the individual rather than the group as the starting point for analysis, have a somewhat different view. Not every member of the community necessarily operates with the same set of rules, with the result that community and individual grammars are *not* isomorphic.

As I mentioned earlier, Labov's model of variation and change is unidirectional and is tied to the concept of a speech community which shares both rules of grammar in the form of variable rules and norms for using them. Henceforth, I will refer to such communities as 'prototype variable rule communities' (cf. also the discussion in J. Milroy this volume). The cohesion of these prototype variable rule communities is manifested perhaps most obviously in patterns of style shifting. In discussing these, Labov says that each group of speakers shows regular style shifting in the same direction. The groups are different in the sense that they use the variable to differing extents, but they are all moving in the *same* direction. Even though a higher level group, socially speaking, will be nearer the norm, the other groups will shift towards that norm in the same circumstances in which the upper group moves even closer to it.

Since the lower social groups are further removed from the norm in their ordinary speech, they shift to a much greater extent than the upper social group. This is one reason why greater variability is generally observed among the lower working class than the middle class. Another reason is that most of Labov's studies have concentrated on the linguistic behaviour of the working rather than the middle class.

In a prototype variable rule community then, all the speakers share not only the variable rule in question, but also its constraints. In other words, in order for speakers to share a rule of community grammar and use it in the same way, they must also share the same constraints or factors affecting the application of the rule; and this means that these factors will be ordered or weighted in the same way. As I pointed out initially, this has not always been the case. Some of Labov's data show clear interactions between social and linguistic constraints from individual to individual and group to group.

Labov (1975: 118–9) himself cites the following irregularity:

> The basic t/d constraints appear to be binding on all dialects, motivated by general phonetic and semantic principles. But when there is no clear linguistic motivation for one constraint or another predominating, we have the possibility of dialect differentiation.

He is referring here to the observation that the effect of a following pause on the rule of t/d deletion differs from dialect to dialect as well as from individual to individual. As I indicated earlier, Guy (1977) observed an anomaly in the rule's application with respect to the grammatical conditioning factor, i.e. monomorphemic vs. past tense forms.

Let's examine the consequences of deviations from the ideal behaviour of individuals and groups in the prototype variable rule community. If the constraints of a variable rule are reordered for one individual or group as opposed to another, then either the whole group or community must move in the same way. Furthermore, if there is a shift in the feature weight of one context or environment of a variable rule, this brings about a change in other contexts, i.e. reordering or reweighting. Now if change typically begins as an increase in the frequency of application of a variable rule in one environment, as Labov (1969: 742) has suggested it does, this entails a change in the weighting of other contexts, thus, a reordering of a constraint hierarchy in a variable rule.

We now come to a logical impasse. In order for change to take place at all in a prototype variable rule community, the community *must* go through a stage in which it does *not* share the same constraints on the application of a rule. In this case, then, the grammar of a speech community *cannot* be described by one variable rule which all speakers use in the same way. Kay (1978) has observed that the notion of speech community grammar is contradicted in a number of places by Labov's own data, and that Labov's conception of the mechanism of linguistic change depends on the interaction of linguistic and social constraints. He has therefore questioned whether variable rules are useful in modelling situations of linguistic heterogeneity in which there is on-going change. I do not think the model really applies adequately in the case of stable communities. The rule of t/d deletion is a case in point; if we assume it to be a relatively stable rule, i.e. one which is not undergoing change, then the observation that differing constraint hierarchies obtain from one group to another in the same community would force us to conclude (erroneously) that a linguistic change *was* taking place, at least within Labov's theory.

The variability of individual idiolects, or their lack of isomorphism with the group is a problem, or at the very least an embarrassment which a number of sociolinguists (cf. for example, Guy 1974) have tried, but not successfully, to explain. But the real difficulty in maintaining the prototype variable rule community as a viable entity lies in the fact that the assumption of isomorphism between individual and group grammars and between groups with respect to rules of grammar and their use places a constraint on change in the system by defining transition as impossible. The way Labov chooses out of this dilemma is to obliterate the distinction between origin and propagation of a change (cf. Weinreich *et al.* 1968: 186–7).

This conflation of the origin and propagation of a change into one factor shifts the search for 'explanations' of change from the individual to external forces in society. In fact, as far as Labov is concerned, there no longer seems to be any argument about whether social factors are involved in linguistic change, but *how deeply* they are involved. There are, however, a number of inconsistencies in the 'explanations' Labov has offered for social dialect differentiation and language change.

A number of sociolinguistic studies have illustrated the embedding of linguistic change in social class (cf. for example, Labov 1966 and Trudgill 1974b). So far, examples seem to be of two types, which are described by Labov (1966: 328) as change *from below* and change *from above*. Each illustrates a process in which social pressures and attitudes come to bear on linguistic structure. Although change does not seem to be unidirectional, i.e. from the upper down to the lower classes, what does seem to be characteristic is that the originating group is neither the lowest nor the highest in the social hierarchy. Change originates from within the system rather than on the periphery.

Change from below is initiated by a group which is near the bottom of the social class scale; it spreads until it becomes more generalized in the speech of groups higher up, where social reaction may fasten on to it and suppress or reverse it. Such change is typically below the level of conscious awareness. Change from above, by contrast, comes from the upper social stratum and is generally noticed because it is associated with a high prestige group. This change may then be adopted by groups lower in the social scale. During the earliest and latest stages of a change there may be little correlation with social factors, but Labov (1972b: 292) has commented that in every case that has been closely studied, 'one social group or another has been found to lead strongly in the development of a linguistic-change'.

I think it is fair to say that Labov's theory is based on the assumption that the spread of linguistic innovations depends on the social prestige attached to them. He has proposed the notion of *covert prestige* to account for the spread of change from below, i.e. from the lower-middle or working class. Overt prestige, on the other hand, emanates from the upper prestige groups. If however, each group's norm has its own prestige, then why do we not find that change originates in any group? Why, for example, is there no change from the very lowest social groups? Labov argues that this group is the least affected by prestige norms, although if the above account is true, then they must attach prestige to their own norm (cf. J. Milroy and Dorian, this volume for a discussion of differential social evaluation of variables).

Labov does not really offer an explanation for the differences in mechanisms of change which originates from above or below in the hierarchy. Must change from above motivated by overt prestige of the upper classes always be conscious and must change from below always be unconscious? According to Labov, the dominant group affects change either by inhibiting change from below, or borrowing from external groups, while the lower social groups initiate change through internal borrowing, either of the variants already existing within the group, i.e. centralization of /ay/ and /aw/ on Martha's Vineyard, or of the prestige norms of groups higher up, mainly by hypercorrection. One empirical finding of Labov's that has gone largely unchallenged is the peculiar behaviour of the middle class; and this observation is particularly relevant to the discussion here. Middle-class speech is seemingly characterized by less internal differentiation and less complex phonetic conditioning than that of the working class (cf. also Berdan 1975a: 38 and J. Milroy's discussion of phonological simplification in middle-class speech, this volume). There does not seem to be any reason why this should be so other than the possibility that this result is the artefact of a methodology which has concentrated almost exclusively on working-class speech, which Labov has claimed is the most consistent (cf. also p. 19). Therefore, most of the vowel shifts discussed in Labov *et al.* (1972) originate in working-class vernacular. There is also the added fact which I mentioned earlier (cf. p. 15) that the speech of the lower classes is typically defined in terms of its deviation from the standard speech of the middle class, and change is assumed to take place for all individuals and groups in the community in that direction.

Once we acknowledge the existence of different norms of speaking and prestige attached to them as coexistent *within the same* speech community, then the notion of the prototype variable rule community describable in terms of its usage of a linguistic variable controlled by a single variable rule breaks down. The idea that a speech community can move as a whole like a physical body in a certain direction appears to be too simplistic and unconvincing (cf. also Romaine 1981).[7]

An examination of recent sociolinguistic studies reveals that a number of linguistic changes seem to be accomplished by competing pressures from two social groups in the speech community which do *not* use the language in the *same* way (cf. for example, Irvine 1978 and Romaine 1978). These sorts of competing changes represent cases in which norms of speaking associated with different groups in the *same* community are crucial in providing an account of differentiation and change in the system. Covert prestige (if there is such a thing), can be just as powerful a factor in the maintenance of vernacular norms as change, as Milroy and Margrain's (1978) account of pressure towards preservation of vernacular norms in Belfast demonstrates. It also seems that the norms of upper and lower groups may coincide in certain cases (cf. again Romaine 1978 and also J. Milroy, this volume) which does not seem interpretable as change from above by conscious imitation of a prestige norm, or as conscious movement towards a more standard form of speech.

Irvine's (1978) findings in particular serve to emphasize some of the points in my argument as they contradict some of Labov's predictions about the mechanism of linguistic change. She discovered that a spread

---

[7]In his criticism of historicism, Popper (1961: 124) has commented on the 'holistic confusion' apparent in the belief that society like a physical body can move as a whole along a certain path and in a certain direction.

of the innovating tendencies in the Wolof noun classification system (which is associated with the upper class of nobles), is moving the system towards the norm of high-status speaking. In Wolof the latter is characterized by a reduction in surface elaboration. The linguistic outcome of the change is a familiar one, i.e. ostensible simplification, but the social mechanism or agent which is responsible for carrying it out, i.e. the highest ranking social group, is not what Labov's theory would lead us to expect. Labov's work shows that the lower classes typically lead in simplificatory processes; but in Irvine's case, it is the lower class that is more linguistically conservative. This group is tending towards elaboration of the system and maintaining it intact.

What conclusions can be drawn from all this? If there are prototype variable rule communities (and I think it must be accepted that these are abstract entities), then they are doomed to extinction because they cannot change, at least within the model Labov has defined. I suppose the thrust of my argument is against the specific descriptive device, the variable rule (cf. also Romaine 1981);[8] it seems too rigid to accommodate a truly integrative view of linguistic differentiation and change, which I would assume is one good reason for rejecting it as a foundation for a sociolinguistic theory. It furthermore leads us to a rather monistic conception of language.

A systematic relationship beween two or more coexistent grammars in a speech community does not entail identity of deep structure rules and underlying sameness of superficially different variants. No grammar, however, exists in isolation. It has 'arrived' from somewhere and is 'headed' somewhere, but not in the same direction, or on the same track in all cases. The process of decreolization is good witness to this statement; the target is not always the matrilect, and there are changes other than from basilect to acrolect. Washabaugh (1975) for example, discusses the deletion of *fi* complementizers in Providence Island Creole as an instance of a competing rule, i.e. it exists in addition to a rule whereby *fi* becomes *tu*. The latter rule reflects true vertical movement towards the acrolect, while deletion is neither more or less basilectal than *fi*. Creole situations are of course full of such cases.

In conclusion, I would not recommend dispensing with the concept of speech community as a group of speakers who share a set of norms and' rules for the use of language, but I raise finally the question of whether it is possible to share the norms and rules of a language without using the language in the *same* way. I think the answer to this is yes; and this need not be a contradiction.

We need to recognize, as Hymes (1974: 46–51) has suggested, *kinds of language* on the one hand, and *uses of language* on the other, and accept that there will probably not be a one-to-one mapping of these for

---

[8] I have argued my case more fully in Romaine (1981), where I have treated the problem of individual/group grammars in more detail.

different members/groups in a speech community. Access to the uses of language available to the community as a whole will differ; individuals may share the same *Sprachbund* without necessarily sharing the same *Sprechbund*. What a sociolinguistic theory needs to concern itself with is how people manage the relationships between kinds and uses of language. Here I think we might profitably make use of an additional term, *social network*, which can be taken to represent a level of abstraction below the speech community (cf. for example, Milroy and Margrain, 1978 and the papers by Russell and L. Milroy, this volume).

Surely speech communities share a socially based organization of linguistic means which is not necessarily cast in the highly restrictive form of a community grammar consisting of variable rules. The system must undoubtedly be more open-ended with respect to use than Labov allows. A sociolinguistic theory which places such tight constraints on the organization and uses of language as Labov's does cannot provide a reasonable account of language change.

2

Defining the speech community to include its working margins

Nancy C. Dorian

For a Highland district, eastern Sutherlandshire has a relatively long history of use of English. Early in the twelfth century a prominent Moray family of proven loyalty to the Scottish crown was granted lands there to challenge Norse power in the northeast and establish a significant Scottish political presence (Crawford 1976–77). This family, which took the name de Moravia, was probably of Flemish origin (White 1953; Pine 1959); in any event they certainly did not stem from any Celtic or Pictish line native to the northern Highlands. Ennobled as early as the second Sutherland-based generation, they constituted a point of entry for English in a wholly Gaelic area. Their two principal seats of power, Dunrobin (site of the House of Sutherland's castle) and the royal burgh of Dornoch, can be shown to have fostered the use of English long before that language was in use elsewhere in the district (Dorian 1981: 14–15, 52).

Although the shift to English in East Sutherland has been slow, it is now almost complete. Most present-day natives of the district are monolingual in English, the sole exception being the descendants of a distinctive ethnic group, the East Sutherland fisherfolk. Fisherfolk descendants are bilingual in English and Scottish Gaelic. They constitute a speech island, in that they are surrounded by English monolinguals and are not in contact with any other dialect of Gaelic. Furthermore, their Gaelic is of a distinctive East Sutherland variety which is unlike other Gaelic dialects.[1]

Since all Gaelic-speaking fisherfolk descendants are bilingual, they belong simultaneously to two speech communities, whereas their monolingual fellow-villagers belong only to one. This is the picture one arrives at by adopting Gumperz's definition of the speech community: 'any human aggregate characterized by regular and frequent interaction by means of a shared body of verbal signs and set off from similar aggregates by significant differences in language usage' (1971: 114). But while this definition allows clear-cut recognition of two readily

[1]The Gaelic of the fishing villages of Easter Ross showed the greatest resemblance to East Sutherland Gaelic, in all likelihood (see Watson 1974 and Dorian 1978: 143–4). The Gaelic of the Easter Ross fishing villages is all but extinct, however (Watson, personal communication).

identifiable groups—monolingual members of an English speech community, and bilingual members of both an English and a Gaelic speech community—it does not so clearly accommodate a third group which can be shown to exist in the region: low-proficiency 'semi-speakers' and near-passive bilinguals in Gaelic and English.

Semi-speakers are individuals who have failed to develop full fluency and normal adult proficiency in East Sutherland Gaelic, as measured by their deviations from the fluent-speaker norms within the community. At the lower end of the proficiency scale they are distinguishable from near-passive bilinguals by their ability to manipulate words in sentences: reminded of a forgotten Gaelic noun or verb, for example, they can nearly always build it into an intelligible Gaelic sentence, whereas near-passive bilinguals can rarely do so (although near-passive bilinguals know a good many lexical items and short phrases). At the upper end of the proficiency scale, semi-speakers are distinguishable from even the youngest fully fluent speakers of East Sutherland Gaelic by the presence in their speech of deviations from the local grammatical norms (recognized as 'mistakes' by fluent speakers), and by the frequency of such deviations, as well as by the presence of a marked degree of analogical levelling and a tendency to eliminate syntactic redundancies (Dorian 1977 and 1980). Semi-speakers differ among themselves in their grammatical and phonological abilities in Gaelic, however, and also in their manner of delivery. Some speak quite readily, though usually in short bursts; despite their phonological and grammatical deviations, they are generally known and accepted as Gaelic speakers of a sort. That is, they are considered part of the local pool of Gaelic-English bilinguals by the fully-fluent speakers (who did in fact name most of them when asked to identify local Gaelic speakers). Others of the semi-speakers use Gaelic relatively little (and in one case, scarcely at all). They speak in a halting manner, and often leave sentences incomplete. Such semi-speakers are usually of low proficiency; but so is the occasional short-burst semi-speaker who uses Gaelic much more freely. That is, the amount of Gaelic actually spoken and the manner of delivery are not perfectly correlated with levels of grammatical proficiency.

It is the low-proficiency semi-speakers who speak very little Gaelic, and also the near-passive bilinguals (whose verbal output is mainly short phrases and single-word utterances), that are of interest here, because they challenge the definitions of the speech community which have prevailed in recent years. In terms of their active use of Gaelic, they can not easily be included in the East Sutherland Gaelic speech community. They speak only English with any readiness, and they speak mostly English in their day-to-day living. Some of them rarely make any active use of Gaelic. One young woman in this group claimed not to speak Gaelic at all, in fact, although when persuaded to undergo a battery of translation tests she proved to control Gaelic grammar slightly *better* than a relative very near her in age who is an enthusiastic, even eager, short-burst semi-speaker. The reluctant semi-speaker, like some of the near-passive bilinguals, cannot really be said to be 'set off from [other] aggregates by significant differences in language usage', if language usage is taken to mean active use of a speech variety by the individuals in question.

Because some properties commonly taken to be important to membership in a speech community are absent among low-proficiency semi-speakers of East Sutherland Gaelic and among near-passive bilinguals in the same community, their claim to inclusion in an East Sutherland Gaelic speech community needs to be carefully considered. They can usefully be compared both with English monolinguals, who are readily excluded, and with fluent speakers of East Sutherland Gaelic and with high-proficiency semi-speakers, who are readily included.

There is first and foremost the issue of language use and the norms that govern it in a given group. Fishman's definition of the speech community, like Gumperz's, includes this notion: 'A speech community is one, all of whose members share at least a single speech variety and the norms for its appropriate use' (1971: 232). Labov's concept of the speech community abandons any notion of uniformity in usage, but rests on a shared *evaluation* of patterns of usage: 'The speech community is not defined by any marked agreement in the use of language elements, so much as by participation in a set of shared norms; these norms may be observed in overt types of evaluative behaviour, and by the uniformity of abstract patterns of variation which are invariant in respect to particular levels of usage' (1972b: 120–1). Thus Labov can perceive New York City's complex native population as a single speech community because it shares regular patterns of subjective reaction to phonological variation: 'it seems plausible to define a speech community as a group of speakers who share a set of social attitudes towards language' (1972b: 248).

Since low-proficiency East Sutherland Gaelic semi-speakers and near-passive bilinguals do not conform at all well to the prevailing fluent-speaker norms for use of East Sutherland Gaelic, and are quite insensitive to many breaches of grammatical and phonological norms produced either by themselves or by others (e.g. by foreign learners of Gaelic), they would not seem to qualify for membership in the local Gaelic speech community by these criteria. Yet in certain important respects they are entirely unlike the English monolinguals who represent the clear-cut excludable group. The first is their outstanding receptive control of East Sutherland Gaelic, and the second is their knowledge of the sociolinguistic norms which operate within the Gaelic-speaking community.

The fisherfolk descendants of East Sutherland number just under 100 at present[2] and are distributed over three villages. The Gaelic speakers

---

[2]The number was about 200 when I began fieldwork in East Sutherland in 1963–64.

in any one village are complexly interrelated to one another, and there are also kin ties across villages; this is the result of about a century of forced endogamy among the fisherfolk. Kinship networks are also often friendship networks, so that relatives representing a variety of ages interact a good deal. Families also traditionally ran rather large, so that siblings sometimes span more than a decade in age ranges. As a result of these two facts, interaction networks which include both fully-fluent, Gaelic-dominant bilinguals and low-proficiency semi-speakers or near-passive bilinguals, and even young English monolinguals, are fairly common. In one household, for example, four unmarried children, all adult, lived in the home of their Gaelic-dominant mother, while two somewhat older (and married) children lived nearby in the same village (village A). The three oldest siblings were fully-fluent bilinguals, the next two were high-proficiency semi-speakers, and the youngest of the siblings was a near-passive bilingual. Relatives who visited regularly in this household, often spending entire evenings there, included both fully-fluent bilinguals and English monolinguals. In another village (village B), various relatives gathered irregularly in the home of their eldest kinswoman, a fully-fluent woman who is now a nonagenarian. Most of them were likewise fully fluent, but the nonagenarian's high-proficiency semi-speaker daughter was often present, and also a low-proficiency semi-speaker kinswoman who was a next-door neighbour. Most of my remarks about the claims of low-proficiency semi-speakers and near-passive bilinguals to membership in the East Sutherland Gaelic speech community are based on long-term participant-observation of these two networks and another one composed of East Sutherland exiles from village A residing in and around London, plus less intimate knowledge of other similar networks. The networks I have observed and participated in—these three as well as others—have been altered by the deaths of one or more members over the 17-year period that I have known them; therefore I use the past tense to describe them even though they continue to exist in reduced form.

The most striking feature of the cross-generational interaction networks among fisherfolk descendants was the ability of the low-proficiency members to participate in Gaelic interactions. Despite their very limited productive skills, they were able to understand everything said, no matter how rapidly or uproariously. They never missed the point of a joke or failed to grasp a significant tidbit of gossip. They occasionally supplied a translation of something difficult to hear or something poorly enunciated for the linguist-guest who spoke a far more grammatical and likewise more fluent East Sutherland Gaelic than they did.

The second notable feature of the participation of low-proficiency network members was its sociolinguistic 'fit'. What they actually said might be very little, and some of their utterances were always grammatically deviant. But since their verbal output was semantically well integrated with what preceded in the conversation, and since it conformed to all the sociolinguistic norms of the dialect, the deviance could usually be overlooked. Often the semi-speaker or near-passive bilingual did not even have to finish the sentence; some fully-fluent member of the group could step in, if there was a marked hesitation, and supply the anticipated conclusion. Low-proficiency members of these networks, unlike the linguist-guest, were never unintentionally rude. They knew when it was appropriate to speak and when not; when a question would show interest and when it would constitute an interruption; when an offer of food or drink was mere verbal routine and was meant to be refused, and when it was meant in earnest and should be accepted; how much verbal response was appropriate to express sympathy in response to a narrative of ill health or ill luck; and so forth.

Two approaches to the speech community which seem more adequate, in the sense that they do not define out of membership those who have low productive capacity but high receptive capacity and who conform to the sociolinguistic norms, are provided by Hymes (1974) and Corder (1973). Hymes proposes that the social group, rather than the language, be taken as the starting point, and that we then consider 'the entire organization of linguistic means within it' (1974: 47). This would enable us to start with the participants in Gaelic verbal interactions, in East Sutherland, including the low-proficiency semi-speakers and near-passive bilinguals, and define the speech community so as to include them. Their inclusion would be appropriate not simply because they are participants (so, after all, was the linguist-guest), but because they are highly successful participants whose receptive skills and knowledge of the sociolinguistic norms allow them to use their limited productive skills in ways which are unremarkable (that is, provoke no comment).[3]

Corder takes the self-perceived group as the basis for the speech community: 'A speech community is made up of people who *regard themselves* as speaking the same language; it need have no other defining attributes' (1973: 53; italics in original). This approach has the advantage of according well with the well-integrated position in the Gaelic interaction networks of some individuals with extremely poor active skills. The very low-proficiency semi-speaker who lived next door to the (now) nonagenarian fluent speaker in village B expressed the complete ease she felt when her visits to her neighbour coincided with those of another relative, this one a verbally gifted, notably articulate fluent speaker:

[3] I have noted that semi-speakers' East Sutherland Gaelic is grammatically deviant in ways that are labelled 'mistakes' by fluent speakers, which is true enough. But when left to their own devices, so that they can speak when they wish to, briefly and in the structures they are most comfortable with, semi-speakers are often able to reduce the deviance to the point where it can be overlooked, especially in the flow of a general conversation. Semi-speakers are sometimes also 'rescued' by a fluent speaker from the necessity of finishing more adventurous sentences which they may have begun and in the middle of which they then hesitate.

Semi-speaker: J., she's fluent—Gaelic speaker. But any—any time she's in, if she does [speak Gaelic], you know, I don't—I just take it in my stride, as—just as if it's English, you know? It doesn't worry me in any way. Or I don't get mixed up, an' I know what they're—I can join in the conversation, because I know everything they're saying, you know. I haven't to stop and think or anything.
Investigator: Yes. Uh-huh. And if you joined in, would you join in in English or Gaelic?
Semi-speaker: I would join in in Gaelic, you know. As best I could, y' know.[4]

When this woman's active skills were first tested, in the same year (1974) the above interview was taped, the testing was done in her fluent next-door neighbour's home where she spent so much time. It proved a distressing experience for all participants: neither of the women, though neighbours for years, had realized how little active control of the dialect the younger woman had; nor for that matter had I, or I would not have exposed her to the embarrassment of 'public' testing . She proved to be one of the very weakest speakers in my sample, yet none of us had noticed her failings as an active speaker, thanks to her skillful use of what proficiency she had and to her outstanding receptive skills and sociolinguistic knowledge. Although it's clear that she acknowledges some weakness in her speaking abilities ('as best I could'), it's also clear that she feels included in the interaction ('I know everything they're saying').[5] At least until the testing took place, her neighbour certainly considered her an adequate member of the Gaelic speech community. That was precisely why the testing proved so distressing to all of us—it showed plainly that she was actually less than adequate in productive East Sutherland Gaelic skills. But she regarded herself, and was in turn regarded by fluent speakers, as a speaker of East Sutherland Gaelic.

What is interesting about this case (and others in which low-proficiency semi-speakers and near-passive bilinguals participate successfully in Gaelic interactions) is that it highlights the minimum requirements for membership in a speech community. Fluency is not required, nor grammatical and/or phonological control of the speech variety common to the participants. The foreign learner can achieve those things and still be only a *participant* in a speech community and not a *member* if he or she does not also fully master receptive skills and sociolinguistic norms. As Hymes has so often insisted, communicative competence depends not only on knowing how to say something, but also on knowing how to say it appropriately (1964a, 1964b, 1967, 1971,

[4]This interview was conducted in English and is quoted here verbatim. It proved extremely difficult, almost impossible even, to interview this semi-speaker in Gaelic, since the presence of the tape-recorder produced a nervousness which compounded her difficulties with Gaelic.
[5]A young man in Berks County, Pennsylvania, a low-proficiency semi-speaker of Pennsylvania Dutch, expressed exactly the same sense of inclusion in interactions with fluent Pennsylvania Dutch speakers, for the same reasons.

1974, for example). In fact it seems that knowing how to say relatively *few* things appropriately is more important than knowing how to say very many things without sure knowledge of their appropriateness.

Low-proficiency semi-speakers, not to mention near-passive bilinguals, meet none of Fillmore's criteria for fluency (in the sense of speaking one's language well; Fillmore 1979: 93). In my experience their only productive skill which is even close to normal is control of what Fillmore calls formulaic expressions (1979: 91–2, 94). There are a great many formulaic expressions which can be trotted out on suitable occasions; knowledge of their forms and their suitability enables the user to participate actively in the verbal interaction and helps to keep the interaction going forward smoothly, and thus earns the user a measure of social approval.[6] Observation of semi-speaker success with these items offers support for Fillmore's belief that 'a very large portion of a person's ability to get along in a language consists in the mastery of formulaic utterances' (1979: 92).

I noted at the outset of the discussion of low-proficiency semi-speakers and near-passive bilinguals that any definition of the speech community which implied productive control of the language in question would eliminate these apparent members of the East Sutherland Gaelic speech community, and likewise any definition which required sensitivity to the social evaluation of usage patterns. In connection with the latter criterion, I stated that these marginal East Sutherland Gaelic speech community members are insensitive to even fairly gross breaches of the local grammatical and phonological norms. Even if they were not insensitive in this respect, however, Labov's notion of 'a set of social attitudes toward language' as a defining feature of the speech community would not apply in East Sutherland in anything like the way he found it to apply in New York City, where people who used certain forms at very different levels could assign social values to them quite uniformly (cf. also L. Milroy, this volume). The reason is that East Sutherland Gaelic is singularly lacking in patterns of social (as opposed to grammatical) evaluation of linguistic structures. A great deal of variation is characteristic of the dialect, morphophonemically, morphologically, and syntactically. Comment on this variation is confined almost wholly to patterns that correlate with a particular village, not with social groups within or across villages. That is, regional variation is the obsessive interest of East Sutherland Gaelic speakers, not social variation. Every East Sutherland Gaelic speaker is on the alert at all times for the intrusion of a variant characteristic of one of the other villages, and I myself provided endless material for this preoccupation

[6] In the absence of strong skills in the use (as opposed to the form) of formulaic expressions, my own strategy has been to master a good many East Sutherland Gaelic proverbs. It is clearer on the whole when they are appropriate, and they also earn the user strong social approval for the same set of reasons noted in semi-speaker use of formulaic expressions, as well as for control of highly valued traditional material.

because of the fact that I travelled regularly from village to village and often carried 'alien' forms along with me through inability to switch cleanly enough from one village's forms to the other's as I went.[7] A very large amount of morphophonemic, morphological and syntactic variation *not* correlated with geography passed without notice among East Sutherland Gaelic speakers. I pointed much of it out to the more thoughtful of my informants over the years, and invariably they said that they had never noticed it. In fact, I had a hard time *getting* them to notice it even when I produced two variants of the same structure in a row for them, so as to highlight the difference. Often I had to repeat the variants several times before they could spot the variation in question.[8] When they did become aware of the variation, they had no strong feelings about the alternatives: they made no social judgements in connection with them and generally had no sense that one was more correct or suitable than another.

The chief reason for the absence of social evaluation of linguistic variation must be the fact that the East Sutherland fisherfolk constituted until very recently an undifferentiated social group: all followed the same occupation, all were poor, all were members of a stigmatized ethnic group, none who remained in East Sutherland had more than the legal minimum of education. Intra-group status distinctions rested on skills or moral character, not on differences in occupation, education, or wealth. All present-day bilinguals grew up in active fisherfolk households, and all share the same status in the local social hierarchy as a result.

How deep low-proficiency semi-speakers' and near-passive bilinguals' knowledge of regional variation is, I cannot be sure. Everyone in the Gaelic-speaking group, regardless of level of proficiency, can produce on request a short list of regional variants which are local stereotypes, much discussed and frequently imitated for the purpose of poking fun. But among fluent speakers, despite the fact that all produce the same small list of stereotypes when asked about regional variation, there is *awareness* of many more variants than they typically offer. If asked about words not among the stereotypes, they can often come up with the 'alien' forms used in other villages, and when they listen to tape recordings made in another village they spot the regional variants readily, without any prompting. They are eager to discuss them, in fact, and will concentrate on them to the exclusion of content, oftentimes. I have neglected to press the low-proficiency semi-speakers and near-passive bilinguals to the limits of their skill in these matters, so that I am unable to say whether they can match the fluent speakers' knowledge.

[7]It was not uncommon for me to be in all three villages in the course of one day, and I was simply unable to monitor my speech carefully enough to guarantee only the correct forms for whatever village I was in at a given time.

[8]Control of the phonology is one of the stronger points in my own East Sutherland Gaelic, so that foreign accent is not an explanation for this outcome.

Another issue on which I cannot at present shed any light is the position of true passive bilinguals in the speech community. I know that there are such people—individuals who understand what is said, but cannot produce Gaelic speech—since I once heard a young woman whose inability to pronounce East Sutherland Gaelic words was both evident and self-admitted translate a Gaelic conversation for the benefit of a foreign visitor. Unfortunately I have not myself worked with any true passive bilinguals, and so I have little notion of the actual extent of their passive abilities. Their existence is acknowledged by the bilinguals, who complain that one can't count on keeping a secret through use of Gaelic if these people are about. Although they are sometimes 'participants' in Gaelic interactions by dint of injecting English comments and responses into a Gaelic interchange which they have understood, I have never heard anyone deliberately address a Gaelic remark to them (except as a direct challenge to them to reproduce it—a test of their abilities), nor have I ever heard anyone refer to them as Gaelic speakers. In both these respects they differ from semi-speakers of any proficiency, and even from the near-passive bilinguals, who are frequently spoken to in Gaelic despite their severely limited productive skills. Provisionally, then, I would exclude them from the East Sutherland Gaelic speech community. The behaviour of fluent speakers towards low-proficiency semi-speakers and near-passive bilinguals, on the other hand, indicates that the East Sutherland Gaelic speech community needs to be defined so as to include these marginal speakers.

3

Probing under the tip of the iceberg: phonological 'normalization' and the shape of speech communities[1]

James Milroy

Most of the basic analytic work in quantitative social dialectology that has been carried out since 1966 has depended rather directly on the methods developed in Labov's New York study (1966). In brief, these methods seek accountability to the data by (1) isolating a 'variable' (usually a phonological one), (2) quantifying a large number of tokens of the variable, (3) presenting the mathematical result either in terms of a binary percentage score or as a 'weighted index' score, and (4) demonstrating co-variation between group scores and such social parameters as socioeconomic class. From the patterns so discovered, Labov has gone on to draw certain theoretical conclusions, e.g. regarding linguistic change. Although there have been criticisms of the Labov methodology, e.g. on the grounds that it is not linguistically sophisticated enough (Knowles 1978), and although some urban dialect work still being published proceeds without the benefit of its insights (e.g. Heath 1980), I prefer to regard it as an extremely important methodological innovation which has, moreover, a considerable potential for theoretical advances.

I should like to focus in this paper on the problem of what I call the *complex* variable and the difficulties involved in giving a correct and illuminating quantificational account of such a variable (for a discussion of some of the complexities involved, see Milroy 1977). I shall attempt to show that the methodology on which we have been mainly dependent is, in some respects, too limited or insufficiently flexible and that one of the results of this may be an incomplete, or possibly false, account of what is

[1]The data reported on in this paper are chiefly from a random sample survey of 42 households in the city of Belfast carried out as part of the project 'Sociolinguistic Variation and Linguistic Change in Belfast' which is supported by the Social Science Research Council and directed by J. and L. Milroy. The fieldwork was carried out by John Harris, Zena Molyneux and Linda Policansky. The data in Table 1 are from the inner-city project 'Speech Community and Language Variety in Belfast' carried out in 1975–7 and also supported by SSRC. I am grateful to all my co-workers, but particularly to Zena Molyneux for transcription of the /a/ data, and to Sue Margrain for advising on statistical work and carrying it out.

actually happening in speech communities. For reasons of space and clarity, I shall not be able to deal with all the difficulties in detail (e.g. the very important question of the correct lexical input to any variable), but will content myself with probing a small distance under the tip of the iceberg by presenting and discussing some aspects of our work on short (a) in Belfast. I shall also briefly indicate some of the theoretical questions that may arise.

In Labov's early work, variables that could be viewed as consisting of three or more variants were quantified by using a weighted index score, i.e. a score ranging from 1 to, say, 5 was assigned to each variant (e.g. of a vowel) as it occurred in a phonetic continuum, e.g. from low to high or high-mid in phonetic space. The total scores of individuals would then be found to fall at various points in the continuum, and these scores in turn would be shown to co-vary with a socio-economic class hierarchy (as individuals were grouped by their SEC). It is clear that there are some mathematical objections to this method (see Berdan 1978). To simplify: in a three-way variable assigned scores of 1, 2, 3, it may happen that speaker A favours variant 2 100 per cent of the time, whereas speaker B may favour variant 1 50 per cent of the time and variant 3 50 per cent of the time. In such a case both speakers will have the same index score, although their speech-habits are quite different. The Belfast data on short (a) will show that this kind of situation is not as unlikely as it might appear. Here, the many speakers who focus on the middle of the range might have similar scores to those who range very widely. But the assumption of a phonetic continuum is also open to objections—this time on phonetic rather than mathematical grounds. With the variable (eh) (i.e. short /a/) in New York City Labov chose to quantify mainly in terms of vowel-height, even though there appeared to be variation also in vowel-length and diphthongization. He demonstrated that it was possible to treat the variation meaningfully and successfully by assuming that the dimension of height was the important one. Yet it is likely that in a particular case (not necessarily New York (a)) several different parameters of phonetic variation might be shown to be important to a greater or lesser extent. Therefore, in terms of accounting adequately for the facts of phonological variation, the early methodology is not highly sophisticated.

In our own work, variables that are more or less co-terminous with a whole phoneme class appear for the most part to be *complex* in that a number of different parameters of phonetic variation seem to be present in them. Laferrière (1977) indicates in an informal way that this may be true of short (a) in Boston—in that rules of fronting and backing are both present in the system. The Belfast (a) system, however, seems to be more complex than Boston. Not only do we have variation in fronting and backing, rounding, lengthening and diphthongization, it also appears that different possibilities of change and variation attach to different sub-sets in the system and that probabilities of, e.g. backing are different for different sub-sets. Thus monosyllabic items with preceding [k] alternate between [ε] and [ɑ] with something approaching a quantum jump across phonetic space; items with following velars favour front vowels, with backing more or less prevented; other items allow backing, but in different proportions. For example, some sub-groups in the population do not have backing before voiceless stops. In general, backing is less likely before voiceless stops than before other obstruents and nasals, and whereas some sub-sets cannot back-round to [ɔ], other sub-sets (e.g. nasals) can and frequently do. One way of dealing with such complex variation is to subdivide into, e.g. velar sets, voiceless stop sets, etc. (cf. also Thelander, this volume). If we were to do this for every complex variable, however, we would obviously have rather too many variables, and some of them might not give high enough quantities for reliable conclusions to be drawn. Another possibility is to devise quantificational methods to deal with complex variables as wholes (on the assumption—not a difficult one to justify—that native speakers 'know' such variables as systems). Work is now proceeding on Belfast short (a) on these lines, and a report on a similarly complex case—'short' (ɔ)—will appear shortly (Harris and Milroy, forthcoming). In this paper, the work reported is much simpler.

Considering that the New York methodology was quite limited, one might have expected that an early development in the quantificational paradigm would have been to explore methods of dealing with phonologically more complex variation. The main development, however, has been the Variable Rule (VR) methodology, which does not focus mainly on how the data are to be prepared in the first place, but takes the linguistic input and method of analysis for granted. Similarly, one might have expected the development of a more sophisticated kind of social theory, involving, for example, the consideration of social variables other than socio-economic class (for advances in this area see now Sankoff and Laberge 1978) and the possible interaction effects existing amongst these variables. On the whole, this has not begun to happen until recently (see L. Milroy 1980), partly as a result of the fact that VR models have not allowed for interaction effects (as acknowledged by Sankoff 1978 and pointed out by Kay 1978).

VR models have been criticized from various points of view (cf. Romaine 1981 and also this volume), but I am not interested in these general criticisms here (e.g. whether it is reasonable to express probabilistic 'rules' in terms of a generative grammar that is anti-probabilistic in its basic conceptions). What is important in the present argument is that VR models have been in one important sense (not in every way of course) more limited in what they can express than Labov's New York methods were. They have until recently been able to deal only with binomial data, i.e. data coded as binaries. Thus they have been used, for example, to express the probability of final-stop deletion (as in *hand, fast, wild*) applying in different environments and rank the linguistic constraints on the rule in an ordered hierarchy of constraints. The best-known VR work has dealt with binaries such as stop-deletion (e.g. Fasold 1978), complementizer *que* deletion in Montreal French, copula deletion, and so on. It has not so far been feasible to deal with multivalued variables such as (a) in New York City or (i) in Glasgow (Macaulay 1977) by VR programs to any extent (cf. however, Sankoff 1979). This means that many of the variables studied in the wake of Labov's work (e.g. in the British Isles by Macaulay 1977, Trudgill 1974b; Milroy and Milroy 1978) have not been studied in terms of VR models. In addition, the requirement that variable rules are stated in terms of generative rules imposes decisions as to the correct input to, or structural description of, a rule—*for the whole community*—when our experience suggests that there may be variable 'competences' within the community. There is probably a great deal of socially significant complexity which, owing to limitations in the methods, has not really been touched. None of these statements is intended to detract from the merits of the VR methodology or to deny that VR methods do demonstrate important things about variation. It is simply that there may be more under the tip of the iceberg than we know about.

At least two doctrines that have arisen from the current paradigm are in danger of becoming articles of faith. The first is the doctrine of common evaluation of variants throughout a 'speech community', i.e. all members of the community are believed to evaluate variants in terms of status or prestige in the same way (cf. Dorian, this volume) (thus, presumably, members of a variable *h*-dropping community all 'know' that *h*-dropping is stigmatized). Obviously, if such common evaluation is constant, it is difficult to see how socially motivated linguistic change can take place. The second doctrine is that of 'uniformity of constraints' in the speech community. This means that for any variable, the phonological constraints affecting it will be ordered, from strongest to weakest, in the same order for all the speakers in the community. While it is probable that this is often so, it does not seem to me to have been demonstrated that it is *always* likely to be so (cf. Romaine, this volume). The data to be discussed from Belfast may be held to throw some doubt on the reliability of the first doctrine. As for the second, the important point arising from the Belfast data seems to be that at certain points in the community, the linguistic constraints affecting a variable are actually lost completely. Thus, it may be further suggested that rule-loss or loss of constraints on rules is observable in the speech community, which is to imply that native-speaker competence may differ at different points in the community, and also to imply that some phenomena observed synchronically in a speech community are formally identical to diachronic phenomena.

Phonological complexity of kinds that have not so far been handled by standard techniques are particularly likely to be observed in speech-communities in northern areas of the British Isles. In cities like

Newcastle, Edinburgh and Belfast the range of variation from the most 'non-standard' to the most 'standard' is much greater than in most North American communities. If, in these British cities, we simply apply the classic techniques and demonstrate that certain variables co-vary in a single phonetic parameter with some social variable such as socio-economic class, we run a real risk of superficiality. In Glasgow, for instance, Macaulay (1977), using Labov's methods, was able to study only a few variables relevant in relatively 'standard' speech. There is probably a great deal of variation in Glasgow that is much more interesting than this; however, to study it would have required extensions to the classic New York techniques. As it was, the limitations of the method forced some limitations on the investigator.

If we want to deal with variation in Belfast using an unmodified version of the methodology, we are forced to pick those variables that fit neatly into the system, or to adopt certain strategies limiting the sub-sets that we study. Either way, we simplify, and we may miss generalizations that are theoretically important. Perceiving that the sociolinguistic structure of the community is more complex than that of, e.g., New York as reported, we have to extend and develop the methodology. This may in turn force us to take a rather different view of the sociolinguistic shape of a speech community than is suggested by the Variable Rule-Speech Community doctrine.

In approaching a study of the Belfast speech community there is a preliminary difficulty. Although it is extremely important, we can only comment briefly here. The difficulty is that we do not necessarily know beforehand what is the correct lexical input to any variable (cf. also McEntegart and Le Page, and Russell, this volume). For instance, if we study the historical phonology of Northern British dialects, we find that they usually have failure of historical rounding of /a/ after /w/. Thus, items like *wasp*, *watch*, *want*, should have [a] in Belfast. However, such items in Belfast are variably subject to correction in the direction of the standard, by backing and rounding. Many other short /a/ items, e.g. *man*, *hand*, *bad* are also subject to backing and rounding (see Table 1), but in this case the backing/rounding is a vernacular characteristic and not a correction. This is plainly very awkward, but rather typical.

As for the shape of the speech community, there are two important facts about the sociolinguistic structure of Belfast that are not easily captured within the classic paradigm. First, phonetic continua (e.g. from low to high) do not necessarily co-vary hierarchically with socio-economic continua in that phonetic variants do not necessarily pattern in a unidirectional order against the social-class hierarchy. Second, it appears that low-prestige varieties display a much wider range of allophonic or phonologically conditioned variation than do high-prestige varieties. The very extensive vernacular range for short /a/ is clearly shown in Table 1.

To consider the first point: it is quite common to find that some low-prestige vernacular form is similar to a very high-prestige form (possibly influenced by RP), whereas the in-between 'medium prestige' form (if we can reasonably call it that) is not like the high-prestige form. There are indications (see Patterson 1860) that the Belfast vernacular (a) system is swinging away from front-raised realizations towards central and back realizations (Milroy and Milroy 1978; J. Milroy 1976). Front-raised realizations (especially before velars, but sporadically elsewhere) are stigmatized. This has the odd result that pronunciations that sound like RP are avoided by most of the community. At the highest level (in the RP-influenced speech of television announcers, for instance), vowels are fronted again and frequently front-raised to match RP pronunciations. Thus, the pattern is not a unidirectional one (as for (a) in New York): it goes from mid-front to low-front to low-back and then moves in the opposite direction from back to low-front and mid-front again. This suggests that there are different patterns of prestige at different levels in the community. Working-class speakers are tending to stigmatize front and front-raised realizations: middle-class speakers are avoiding the most extreme back realizations (but see below), and tending to front again. There are other similar cases.

In a rather different way, the short (a) data in Tables 2 and 3 display the fact that a unidirectional phonetic continuum does not co-vary regularly with a social class hierarchy. Instead, the form regarded (at least by middle-class speakers) as the prestige form converges on the middle of the continuum. These tables also demonstrate the second important fact about the shape of the speech community, viz. that low-prestige varieties have a wider range of (apparently) phonologically conditioned variation than 'higher' varieties. The rules of the /a/ system are difficult to capture fully in a formal rule statement. Informally, note that following velars may front and raise, but in any case resist backing: following voiceless stops can be front, and may be backed, but resist back-raising and rounding; other following obstruents and nasals allow full backing and rounding in monosyllables; disyllables resist the fullest backing and rounding, except that inflected disyllables are treated as monosyllables (compare *passing* with *passage* in Table 2). In addition, although this is not clear from the data in Tables 1 and 2, there are points at which two rules are in competition within the /a/ system. For example, there is a rule for front-raising of /a/ to [ɛ] after /k/ when in a monosyllable closed by an obstruent (other than voiceless stop) or nasal. Many speakers pronounce the word-list item *cab* as [kɛb]. In Tables 1 and 2, however, the speakers opt for the rule backing /a/ before obstruents and nasals and may be said to have lost the fronting rule. The fronting rule, though present in the community, is recessive, and the backing rule is gradually winning out.

It is remarkable that, as Table 2 shows, the vernacular rules are not lost in careful styles, where we might expect attempts at standardization. In word-lists, in which Labov argues that a great deal of attention is paid to speech, the rules are quite carefully observed. Therefore, since most

Table 1: /a/ range for a working-class Belfast speaker: casual conversational style (from a community study). Figures in brackets indicate number of occurrences.

ɛ	æ	a	ɑ	ɔ
bang (5)	Bangor	Castlereagh (2)	bad	past
crack (2)	jacket	barracks	Strathearn	plaster
Kojak	back	that (3)	have	palace
avenue	cracking	snap	wrap	hand
		cracking	happen	Belfast (2)
		Albert	Belfast	stand-by
		avenue	Catholic (2)	handsome
		baton (2)	Castlereagh	can
		camera	happy	strand
		Shankill (2)	handsome	
			candid	

Table 2: /a/ range for a working-class Belfast speaker: word-list style (from random sample survey)

	ɛ	æ	a	ä	ɑ	ɔ
bag	+					
back		+				
cap			+			
map				I		
passage				+		
cab					+	
grass					+	
bad					+	
man					+	
castle			+			
dabble			+			
passing					+	
Index score of convergence on [a]				:	24	
Range score				:	5 (maximum)	

Table 3: /a/ range for a middle-class Belfast speaker: word-list style (random sample survey)

	ɛ	æ	a	ä	ɑ	ɔ
bag			+			
back			+			
cap			+			
map			+			
passage			+			
cab			+			
grass			+			
bad			+			
man			+			
castle			+			
dabble			+			
passing			+			
Index score of convergence on [a]			:	0 (max. convergence)		
Range score			:	0 (min. range)		

Belfast speakers exhibit some range of conditioned variation here, it follows that they must 'know' that the different sub-sets within the system have different target vowel realizations. Depending on our version of phonology, we may claim that these sub-sets are derived by low-level rules from an underlying phoneme, or that they constitute two, three or more separate lexical sets, each with different target vowels and different potentialities for change.

The data in Table 3 form a dramatic contrast to the vernacular speech represented in Tables 1 and 2. The difference between the working-class and middle-class speakers is not one of relative degrees of backing, fronting or raising of all relevant items: what Table 3 shows is the end-point of a process in which allophony is gradually reduced as one moves up the socio-economic class hierarchy. At this level, one might still expect to find some residual signs of fronting in velar environments and backing in, e.g., nasal environments. Sometimes this is the case; yet, in other cases middle-class speakers seem to be able to give slight fronting to more or less any item on the word-list in an apparently random way (possibly by influence from RP). If these speakers do have any intuitive 'knowledge' of velar and other constraints in the vernacular, they seem to have suppressed that 'knowledge'. In the comparison of Tables 2 and 3, we are observing what can be loosely called a process of standardization. A characteristic of this process is phonological simplification—reduction of allophony or loss of low-level rules and constraints on rules.

This trend towards simplification is not confined to /a/. In describing other vowels and consonants in a forthcoming account of Belfast phonology (J. Milroy 1981), I have repeatedly had to indicate that vernacular speech usually has more variants than 'standardized' speech. For /ɛ/, as in *get*, *less*, etc., we can distinguish at least four clearly differentiated variants: a short low vowel, a short mid vowel, a long mid vowel, and a mid vowel with an inglide. Middle-class speakers tend to reduce the range to two, avoiding the low vowel and the diphthong. A complete quantitative analysis of the word-list data from the survey clearly supports this. Therefore, while it can be argued that vernaculars tend to *reduce* distinctions at the level of morphology (e.g. the common reductions in the strong or irregular verb paradigms in English), whereas standard forms tend to maintain distinctions—the converse applies at lower phonological levels. Vernaculars maintain allophony, and standardization reduces it.

So far, the argument has been based on evidence *selected* from the corpus. As we are under an obligation to demonstrate that the observations hold good for all the data, and not just for selected parts of it, quantification is necessary. In our random sample survey of the city we had word-list data from 60 speakers. The problem was to devise quantificational methods that would clearly demonstrate any trend towards normalization that might be present in the data.

Two simple methods of quantification were used and the results were then subjected to statistical testing. The first method was the weighted index, adapted in such a way as to measure the degree of convergence on low-front [a], presuming this to be the 'norm'. (Note that an index based on front to back would wholly distort the prestige patterns.) A score of 1 was counted for each [a], scores of 2 and 3 for the two degrees of deviation towards mid-front and scores of 2, 3 and 4 for the three degrees of deviation towards the back. The score was then totalled and 12 subtracted from it (this is the number of items on the word-list). Thus, the data in Table 3, which show no deviation, appropriately score 0, whereas Table 2, in which there is considerable deviation, scores 24. In general, a score of about 13 or more indicates considerable deviation from the presumed norm, whereas lower scores indicate a tendency to normalization.

Once the index scores had been calculated, a three-way analysis of variance was used on the data. This test was selected as I wanted to know, amongst other things, whether there were any interaction effects, e.g. whether sex or age differences might affect in some way the socio-economic scores. For example, it could happen that the scores for two social classes turned out to be the same; yet within these two groupings, the usage of the two sexes, or two different age-groups, might be totally different. These differences would be submerged on a simple social-class score.

For a number of reasons our random sample of 60 Belfast speakers throughout the city was divided into only two class groups, one (24 persons) representing (roughly) the LWC and the other (36 persons) representing MWC-MC. Other statistical methods might have allowed smaller groupings, but this would have carried a greater risk of misassignment of individuals to groups. As few MC people live within the city boundaries, only 9 of our sample of 60 could be assigned unambiguously to the true MC (in terms of housing and occupation). The assignment to classes was of course made independently of any knowledge of linguistic variation. Using the index score of convergence on (a), the difference between the two class groupings is very highly significant. The mean deviation score for the lower group is 15, whereas that for the upper group is 10.8. In the lower group 2 speakers (8 per cent) have scores of 10 or below (these are both older females), whereas in the upper group 18 speakers (50 per cent) have scores of 10 or below (i.e. they tend much more to converge on [a]). The difference between 8 per cent and 50 per cent is obviously considerable. The probability statistic (0.0006) indicates that the class distribution is very likely indeed to be real and reliable: the probability of the distribution being the result of chance is 6 in 10,000. There can be no serious doubt that the method used has confirmed the view that as one goes up the socio-economic class continuum there is a strong tendency to reduce allophony and converge on [a].

The statistic for difference between male and female speech (p. 0094) is also highly significant (better than .01). This means that, taken over the whole sample, females normalize on [a] significantly more than males do. Loosely speaking, we can say that this tends to support the now widely accepted view that women are more inclined to 'correct' than men. The statistic for 'age' is not quite significant (p. 0678), but indicates a strong tendency for older speakers to normalize on [a] more than younger speakers do.

The interaction between sex and class, which is nearly significant (p. 0683), means that the different sexes tend to behave differently in the two class groups, i.e. there is little difference between men's and women's usage in the lower group, whereas females in the upper group normalize much more than males do.

It may be thought that quantitative analysis using an index score has been wholly successful, and that we may reliably say that my initial observation—viz, that MC speakers (and many females of different classes) lose low-level rules and converge on [a] has been clearly confirmed. In general, this is correct, but it may be that the figures, based as they are on a large number of speakers, conceal other interesting facts about variation in the speech community. See the criticisms of weighted index scores on p. 36. For example, there is no reason to suppose that normalization always results in convergence on one particular area of vowel space. It could happen that for different speakers and groups the process focuses on different areas of vowel space, and a weighted index could conceal such differences. This appears to be the case in Belfast.

There is a small group of speakers, all young, male and middle-class, who normalize on back [ɑ] rather than front [a]. Their type of pattern is represented in Table 4. Obviously, the index score representing

Table 4: /a/ range for a middle-class Belfast speaker showing convergence on [ɑ]: word-list style (random sample survey)

	ɛ	æ	a	ä	ɑ	ɔ
bag		+				
back		+				
cap					+	
map					+	
passage					+	
cab					+	
grass					+	
bad					+	
man					+	
castle					+	
dabble					+	
passing					+	
Index score of convergence on [a]				:	21	
Range score				:	2	

The range shows normalization in all environments except pre-velar.

deviation from front [a] is for these speakers just as high as the score for WC speakers who range from [ɛ] to [ɔ]; yet, their pattern is quite different, and they normalize (in their case on [ɑ]) just as people who converge on front [a] normalize. I can think of different ways of analysing and quantifying the data in order to take account of this fact. What I have done up to the moment is to produce a *range* score for the data to stand beside the index score. This has the advantage that it does not assume a unique direction of normalization; thus, speakers like those represented in Table 4 have a low range score, which properly shows the fact that they normalize quite strongly, even though the normalization is not on front [a]. However, they can be said to retain one vernacular constraint, which can be expressed as prevention of backing when a velar consonant follows the vowel (see Table 4).

The range score is very simple to calculate. The number of columns through which the tokens range are counted, and 1 is subtracted. Thus, the maximum range is 5 (Table 2) and the minimum is 0 (Table 3). The lower group has a mean range of 2.83, and the upper group the much lower mean of 1.97. This and other details are given in Table 5. The difference between the mean range scores of the two groups (upper and lower) is very highly significant (p. 0003). As the likelihood of this difference having occurred by chance is in the order of 3 in 10,000, we can be confident that the tendency to reduce allophony (reflected in progressively lower range scores) increases as we go up the social scale, regardless of whether the tendency is to converge on low-front or on low-back.

More sophisticated mathematical methods could no doubt be used, but the range score has the advantage of counteracting possible criticisms that can be made of weighted index scores. Although the weighted index score used in this research has aims that are different from those of Labov's New York work, it is subject to one of the same criticisms viz. that one particular area of vowel space (defined in strict phonetic terms) has to be presumed as a 'norm'.

Table 5: Range

Average range scores (maximum 5):		
Lower group	(LWC-MWC):	2.83
Upper group	(UWC-MC):	1.97
No. of speakers with range of 1 or less:		
Lower group	1	(4 per cent).
Upper group	11	(31 per cent).
No. of males and females with range of 1 or less:		
Males	3	(10 per cent).
Females	9	(30 per cent).
No. of speakers with range of 3 or more:		
Lower group	16	(66.7 per cent).
Upper group	10	(27.7 per cent).

My observations in this paper have a number of implications, both methodological and theoretical. Methodologically, I have used simple quantificational techniques to demonstrate a pattern of variation of a kind that has not so far been approached (or, as far as I know, noticed). I have also used standard statistical methods to assess how much confidence can be placed in the conclusions. In this case the degree of confidence is very high indeed: we can place much greater confidence in claims of the kind made here than we can in many of the substantive claims made in linguistics in general—for example, the E Mod E vowel system presumed by Chomsky and Halle (1968), claims regarding rule-orderings in some poorly attested dialect, and so on. Whatever reservations may be advanced about probabilistic methods and about what arguments can, or cannot, be based on proof of co-variation of linguistic and social data, it is not reasonable to reject findings that are fully accountable to the data (many linguistic findings are based on more selective and more dubious data), and which are plausible anyway.

The shape of the speech community demonstrated here is triangular or pyramidal rather than linear. Working-class speech (even when it is careful speech) is rich in low-level phonological variation: middle-class speech appears to suppress this variation. While it would be premature to claim that this is a universal, I believe it will turn out to be generally true of large urban speech communities where there have been long histories of dialect diversification in rural hinterlands and recent urban growth. It may be less easy to demonstrate this pattern in long-established urban dialects or in rural forms. When it is observed, it may be argued that the simplification pattern is an aspect of the process of standardization. Standardization, it seems, is intolerant of wide variation in low-level phonology, overlapping of phonemes in phonetic space, and so on. One of the effects of 'change from above' may therefore be to reduce allophony, reduce overlapping between phonemes, and prescribe uniformity in target realizations within phonemes; thus, amongst other things, standardized accents are likely to conform to the phonemicists' bi-uniqueness condition.

The likelihood that non-standard segmental phonology is more complex than standard phonology carries with it a number of implications for standard theories and models. Do all the speakers in the speech community described really 'know' that they 'ought' to realize /a/ consistently as a low-front vowel? If they know it, why then do they observe the allophonic variation of the vernacular so regularly in careful styles? Why should we suppose that individuals at different social levels make the same social evaluations of the possible variants? If basic 'speaker competence' is different at different levels with processes like rule loss and even rule inversion operating in the community, then in what sense is it a single 'speech community'? The implications for historical linguistics are also quite important. If twentieth-century speakers observe great complexity of regular variation in /a/, then what is the status of characteristic historical 'findings' of the kind that say 'E Mod E /a/ was fronted to [æ] in the seventeenth century'? Surely the language was not simpler in the past than it is now? It seems as if the data-base of prevailing theories—e.g. British phoneme theory (e.g. Gimson 1980) and North American generative phonology—is still standardized and normalized speech, to a much greater extent than it should be. Thus, if we want to show what native speaker competences really are like and if we hope to explain linguistic change, we shall have to probe further under the tip of the iceberg than we have to date.

4

Patterns of variation in Tehrani Persian[1]

Nader Jahangiri and Richard A. Hudson

Introduction

The data to which we shall refer in this paper are a set of tape-recorded interviews made by the first author in Tehran, and we shall report on the ways in which 10 linguistic variables in these recordings are related to one another and to the social differences between the speakers. It is intended partly as a contribution to the growing literature on socio-linguistic variation in Persian,[2] but partly too as a contribution to the theory of speech variation in general. We shall show that variation patterns can differ considerably (a) as between linguistic variables, (b) as between social groups and (c) as between individual speakers. This seems to us to be an important finding, though not entirely unexpected, as it suggests that the techniques for dealing with variability need to be even more sophisticated than those at present available. More importantly, it suggests that we need to be very much aware of such differences when we interpret the results of an empirical study in terms of some theoretical model such as a grammar containing variable rules, or a pragmatic model of variation (cf. Romaine, this volume).

At least at the time when the data were collected in 1977 (before the Iranian revolution) there were considerable social differences of many kinds among people in Tehran, but our hypothesis was that one of the main influences on a person's speech was education—specifically, the level of education which he or she had attained. Some of the results which we obtained seem to confirm the importance of education, since quantity of education turns out to be a very good predictor of a speaker's score on some of the linguistic variables. However, we also decided from the start to simplify the research design by keeping other

[1] We have benefited greatly from the comments of William Beeman and another, anonymous, reviewer of an earlier version of this paper, and also from comments which we received when we presented part of the material at the Sociolinguistics Seminar in Walsall in September 1979. We should also like to thank Brian Parkinson and Barry Blakely for help with the statistical analysis.
[2] See Beeman 1977 and the references given there. Since writing this paper we have heard, through an anonymous reviewer, of a University of Kansas dissertation by Yahya Modaressi on a very similar topic, but have not yet been able to obtain a copy of this. Further details of our data are to be found in Jahangiri 1980.

social variables either constant or as closely as possible in step with the educational variable. Thus we included in the sample only speakers who had been born in Tehran and who had native speakers of Persian as parents, and we selected speakers whose level of education was matched by their occupation, where they lived within Tehran, and their father's level of education. In other words, on the basis of what we knew about Tehran social structure,[3] our speakers were prototypical members of groups defined in terms of education, so that the factors of occupation, place of birth and so on are not independent variables whose influence on speech can be studied in our data. This means, of course, that what we shall refer to as educational groups are really much more complex in their definitions than might appear from this label, so where we refer to the influence of education this is to be taken as meaning 'the influence of education when other social factors are as one might expect given the speaker's level of education'. In order to know what influence, if any, other social variables have on speech, we should need to do further research in which level of education was kept constant and factors such as occupation were varied. As far as the present report is concerned, the consequence of this decision about the sample is that we can be fairly confident that little or no variation in our results is due to factors other than education and the other two factors which we consciously controlled.

Apart from level of education, we selected speakers to represent variation on two other social variables: sex and age. The age variable was only partially represented in fact, since we allowed it to vary only for half of the sample, those at the two extremes of the educational range. Moreover, we distinguished only two age-groups: school-children between 14 and 16 years of age[4] and adults over 28. We distinguished four levels of education (university, secondary, primary and none), so the distribution of our 60 speakers is as shown in Table 1. In the following we shall pay most attention to the results for the older speakers, since only these allow all four educational groups to be compared, but we shall be able to refer to the figures for the younger speakers as well in order to ask whether any of the variables appear to be in a state of change.

The data were all gathered in structural interviews following the model of those used by Labov (1972b) and Trudgill (1974b), but we shall again concentrate here on the figures for the unscripted parts of the interviews, to the exclusion of the parts where the informant was reading

[3] The first author had lived in Tehran for many years, although he is himself a native speaker of Gilaki, an Iranian language from the north of the country; his knowledge was confirmed by information on Tehrani society obtained from other sources such as the official census figures; see Jahangiri 1980: 13–30 for further details.

[4] The 'educational' classification of the school-children was based, for obvious reasons, on factors which normally correlate with educational level, notably the parents' educational level, the area of their home, and the nature of the school attended.

Table 1: Distribution of speakers on three social dimensions

	Male		Female	
	Young	Old	Old	Young
university	5	5	5	5
secondary		5	5	
primary		5	5	
no educn.	5	5	5	5

a prose passage or a list of words. It would be wrong to claim that this keeps the variable of 'situation' constant, of course, since what is objectively the same situation is almost certain to influence different speakers in different ways. In particular we are aware of the danger of assuming that even the most carefully 'stage-managed' interview produces behaviour approximating to that which the informant would produce in genuinely casual circumstances.[5] Moreover, a person's behaviour (including his speech) are very much influenced by his hierarchical social relations *vis-à-vis* other participants,[6] so it is likely that the less educated speakers showed more deference in their speech to the interviewer (Jahangiri) than did the more educated. Beeman (1976a, 1977) has in fact suggested that four of our linguistic variables ((man), (r), (h) and (?)) are used for showing different degrees of respect, and this seems quite plausible, as an extra possible variable. Thus it may be that where we find differences between the educational groups in their use of some variable, this is to be explained in some cases via an intervening variable of respect. Without further research it is hard to tell to what extent this variable is relevant, but we can at least be sure that it is not responsible for all the variation between educational groups, since different linguistic variables were sensitive in different ways to educational differences, as we shall see below.

The ten linguistic variables which we studied are shown in Table 2.[7] It is probably unnecessary to add to the information given in this table, except to make a comment about the effect of differences between lexical items. We have clear evidence for at least two of the variables ((be) and (st)) that the chances of a non-standard variant occurring vary radically from one lexical item to another, and that such differences cannot be attributed to the effect of phonological or morphological differences.[8]

[5]See Milroy (1980) for an excellent discussion of some alternatives to the interview. We could scarcely claim even that our interviews were ideally stage-managed, since many of them had to be conducted under very formal conditions, in the offices of the Iranian Academy of Language, in order to allay suspicions that the subject's political inclinations were under investigation.

[6]See Beeman (1976a, 1977) for graphic discussion of many examples, including specific reference to certain areas of language. Chapter 4 of Jahangiri 1980 contains a detailed discussion of the way in which choice of lexical items for pronouns and verbs is influenced by power and solidarity relations between participants.

[7]As already mentioned, four of these variables are discussed in Beeman 1976a and 1977.

[8]The evidence is given in detail in Jahangiri 1980, but some of it is also presented briefly in Hudson 1980: 170.

Table 2: Linguistic variables referred to in this paper

Variable name	Constant	Variants standard	non-standard	Examples
(man)	meaning: 'I'	(man).... ..verb+am	(mɑ:).... ..verb+im	(man) raftam (mɑ:) raftim } 'I went'
(be)	prefix in imperative, subjunctive, etc. verbs	/be/+verb	/bV/+verb (V assimilated to first V of verb)	/bekoš/ /bokoš/ } 'kill'
(ha)	plural suffix on nouns	noun+hɑ:	noun+ɑ:	/šahrhɑ:/ /šahrɑ:/ } 'cities'
(ɑ:)	...V Nasal	/ɑ:/	/u:/	/tehrɑ:n/ /tehru:n/ } 'Tehran'
(st)		/st/	/ss/	/daste/ /dasse/ } 'handle, group'
(ey)		/ey/	/e/	/seyl/ /sel/ } 'flood'
(h)		/h/	Ø	/šahr/ /šar/ } 'city'
(?)		/?/ or vowel-length	Ø	/ma?dan/ /madan/ } 'mine'
(d)		/d/	Ø	/čand/ /čan/ } 'how much'
(r)		/r/	Ø	/xorde/ /xode/ } 'little'

For example, some of the most common verbs almost always have the assimilated (non-standard) variant of the *be*-prefix, whereas there are other verbs which hardly ever have it; thus, 'do!' was pronounced /bekon/ only 9 per cent of 331 occurrences in our data, the remainder being /bokon/ (or some partially assimilated version); whereas 'cut!' was pronounced /bebor/ on no fewer than 97 per cent of the 124 occasions on which it occurred, with only 3 per cent of the non-standard assimilated or partially assimilated version. Such lexical variation is of course interesting as evidence for lexical diffusion, but it raises methodological problems since it is easy for a particular lexical item to occur very much more often in one text than in another, depending simply on what the subject of discussion is, and this may seriously distort the figures for the two texts. In order to cope with this problem, we applied the principle that we would never count more than the first three occurrences of any one lexical item in each text. All the figures quoted below were produced in accordance with this principle, so we think influence of lexical differences can be discounted as a possible source of variation.

One final point which is worth mentioning in connection with the data and the analysis is that the figures for all the 10 variables are based on a complete analysis of the whole of each interview (excluding the reading part), which means about 40 minutes of speech. This produced total figures for most variables around 50 per speaker, but (d) was rarer, with about 8 per speaker, and (r) only occurred about 20 times per speaker, on average. The (ɑː) variable was very frequent, with about 150 per speaker as an average. The (man) variable already stands out from the others in the range of variation in the total numbers per speaker: the lowest number was 26, and the highest 442. This is not too surprising, given that the figure depends on the number of times the speaker chooses to refer to himself or herself. In the following we shall refer to this as a 'semantic variable', in the sense that what is constant is an independent semantic element, and what varies is the morphological realization of this element. None of the other variables was of this type, since they involve only the levels of phonology and morphology. We shall see in the next section that there is an even more fundamental difference between the kind of variation found in the (man) variable and that found in the other variables.

Syntagmatic relations among variants

A question which has only occasionally been raised in the literature on variation[9] has to do with the syntagmatic relations among variants of a variable within the same text: is a speaker's choice of a variant influenced by the last choice he made for the same variable? (cf. also Thelander, this volume). For example, when a Persian speaker is about to say a word containing a potential /r/, is he more likely to pronounce the /r/ if he selected this variant on the most recent occasion that he used a word subject to the (r) variable than he would have been if he had dropped the /r/ on that occasion? We might broaden the question to apply to the influence of earlier choices before the most recent one, but we may assume that if the answer is negative for the most recent instance, then it will also be negative for more distant occurrences. As we shall see, the answer is negative in most cases, so we shall not bother to pursue this broader question here.

We were encouraged to ask this question because of the way in which we had recorded the analysis of our texts. This allowed us to reconstruct the order in which variants occurred within a text, and thereby to count the number of transitions between one variant and the other. For example, one hypothetical text might contain 50 instances each of the standard and non-standard variants of some variable, in the order: all 50 standard variants, followed by all 50 non-standard ones, with therefore just one transition between the two variants. It this case, it would be clear that the variants were occurring in 'blocks', and the selection of

[9]The references of which we are aware are Berdan (1975b) and Sankoff and Laberge (1978), both of which present valuable data and insights.

variant on different occasions was not independent. Of course, there would still remain the question of how to describe the phenomenon, whether by referring to the influence of one occurrence on the next, or by referring to some external factor (such as the influence of situation) which influences the probabilities of the two variants. The main point, though, is that it would be wrong simply to say of such a text that the two variants each had an equal probability of occurring, without saying anything at all about the blocking behaviour. In contrast, there might be another text which also contained 50 instances of each of the same two variants, but in a very different kind of distribution, all mixed up together. If there was no more chance of a standard variant being used whether the previous occurrence of the variable was represented by a standard or a non-standard variant, then we should expect about 50 transitions between standard and non-standard,[10] so if this was roughly what we found then we could be fairly sure that separate choices of variant on the same variable were independent of one another. Thus, in order to measure the degree to which occurrences of a variable are independent of one another, all we need do is compare the number of transitions between different variants which we actually found with the number to be expected on the assumption that there is no influence from one occurrence to the next.

When we applied this test to our data, we found that (man) behaves quite differently from all the other variables, in that only (man) shows evidence of 'blocking' behaviour. If we divide the number of transitions observed by the number to be expected on the null hypothesis (i.e. no influence between occurrences) we find that (man) only exploits slightly more than half of its potential expected transitions (0.53), whereas the same figure for all the other variables is between 0.82 and 1.0.[11] It seems

[10]Let us represent the total occurrences in the text of the two variants by S and N (for 'standard' and 'non-standard'). On any given occasion, the chances of a standard variant occurring is $\dfrac{S}{S+N}$, on the assumption that there is no influence from the previous occurrence of the variable; and similarly the probability of its being non-standard is $\dfrac{N}{S+N}$. Now we can calculate the probability of a transition from a standard to a non-standard variant, simply by multiplying the number of standard variants (S) by the probability of a non-standard variant occurring, giving $\dfrac{S \times N}{S+N}$. Similar reasoning gives the same formula for transitions in the opposite direction, from a non-standard to a standard variant, so the total number of transitions to be expected is $\dfrac{2 \times S \times N}{S+N}$.

[11]It is also possible to approach the problem from the other end, by asking how many transitions we might expect on the assumption that there *is* some influence between occurrences. Obviously we can only calculate this if we have some idea how strong the influence is, but it seems reasonable to assume that the influence of one variant on the next

reasonable to conclude, then, that as far as (man) is concerned, there is a tendency for variants to occur in blocks, but that this is not the case for any other variables in our data.

Why should (man) behave so differently from the other variables? We have already prepared for the answer which we want to suggest: it is because (man) is the only variable which relates a semantic element to two alternative morphological realizations (it is the only 'semantic' variable). In support of this explanation, we should like to refer to the findings of Sankoff and Laberge (1978) concerning Montreal French. These workers report clear evidence of influence between occurrences of three variables: the alternation of *on* with *tu* or *vous* to refer to 'one', its alternation with *ils* to refer to 'them', and its alternation with *nous* to refer to 'us'. These three variables are clearly very similar to our (man) variable,[12] in being semantic variables involving alternative pronouns with the same referent. What we find interesting is that the only clear evidence for syntagmatic influence involves semantic variables, so we should like to suggest the following hypothesis:

> All and only semantic variables tend to have variants which occur in a run of one variant followed by a run of the other variant; i.e. for such variables the chances of a given variant occurring vary according to whether or not the most recent occurrence of the variable concerned was also an instance of that variant.

We have still only started to move towards an answer to our question by suggesting that (man) behaves as it does because it is a semantic variable. We now have the more interesting question of why semantic variables should behave like this (on the assumption that our hypothesis above is correct). One possible explanation is that all such variables are evidence of code-switching, but this seems unhelpful unless we can find evidence of other variables which co-vary closely with each other and which could be described meaningfully as involving two different 'codes'. So far as we know this has not yet been shown, and we have no evidence from our Persian data that any other variable co-varies with

---

selection will be proportionate to that variant's own probability of occurrence, so that a very frequent variant will have a lot of influence, and a very rare one will have very little. On this assumption, the formula for predicting the number of transitions for a text is $\dfrac{S \times N}{S + N}$, which, it will be seen, leads us to expect just half the number of transitions compared with the number predicted on the null hypothesis. The figure of 0.53 found for (man) compares well with the figure predicted on the assumption just stated.

[12]Sankoff and Laberge concentrate in their paper on the interesting question whether the influence of one instance of a variable on the next instance of the same variable is stronger or weaker according to the nature of the intervening material, and they find that this is indeed the case. For example, if the two instances are in separate sentences the first instance has much less influence on the second than if they are both in the same sentence. We could not test their hypotheses against our data, but we have no reason to think that they are wrong.

(man). If (man) is the only variable which defines the difference between two stretches of text, it is clearly wrong to say they involve different 'codes' without emptying this word of the little meaning it has.

Another possibility is that the variants have separate contextual meanings, so that each corresponds to a different way of conceptualizing the situation, on the lines of the well-known markers of power and solidarity. For instance, by referring to himself by the word which normally means 'we' a speaker would show that he was seeing himself simply as a representative of some larger group (cf. the habit of many authors of referring to themselves as *we*, as though they were a collective of some kind). It would be natural if such variables showed blocking behaviour, since we should expect a speaker to be consistent in his way of presenting the same referent from one pronoun to the next. On the other hand, we should also have reason to think that whenever he changed from one pronoun to the other he had changed his view of the situation, or the way he wished the hearer to view it. As far as our Persian data are concerned, it is not always plausible to suggest such a conceptual change when there is a change on the (man) variable, but very often a change on this variable coincides with some kind of change in the situation—for example, with an interruption by the interviewer, or a change in the topic. At least some such cases involve a change in the way in which the speaker is presenting himself, as in the following passage (given in translation, with (S) for 'singular' to indicate *man* and its related forms, and (P) for 'plural' to indicate *ma:* and its related forms):

> I (P) had a wife who took all my (P) possessions; whatever I (P) had she took, and left me (P) homeless and penniless in the streets; I (P) slept in the streets in the night—six months, yes six months I (S) was in terrible condition, in this Tehran I (S) was hungry for days, I (S) could work, but I (S) was driven crazy because of anxiety.

It seems likely that the speaker started to feel particularly sorry for himself at about the point indicated by the gap, and that he then stopped using the relatively personal singular form to refer to himself rather than the distancing and impersonal plural. It has been suggested[13] that the plural form is used to express humility, so this could explain why the speaker started off the above passage by using the plural form, out of deference to the interviewer.

Whatever the explanation for the behaviour of (man), however, the important thing to note is that the behaviour of all the other variables is quite *different*, so it would be quite wrong to generalize from (man) to them in developing a general theory of variation. For example, it has been suggested by Beeman (1977) that (d), (r) and (?) have a similar function to the one just described for (man), but we have seen that they

---

[13]See Beeman 1976b: 465, quoted by Beeman in a personal communication.

do not show blocking behaviour, so *a fortiori* they do not provide transitions between blocks which coincide with those for (man). This is not to say that such variables are not related to changes in the situation; on the contrary, we have clear evidence that they are sensitive to differences, say, between unscripted speech and reading aloud. Rather, it is to say that we must develop a theory of variation which allows different types of relation between situation and linguistic variable, and which specifically distinguishes between semantic and non-semantic variables in this respect.

The symbolic functions of linguistic variables

All of the ten variables contrast a 'standard' variant with a non-standard one, and in every case speakers with more education use more of the standard variant than do speakers with less education. However, as we might expect from the literature on variation, there are important differences among the variables in their relations to the social variables to which we can refer. On the one hand, different linguistic variables are not all sensitive to the same social variables, and on the other, they differ in the accuracy with which they reflect the relevant social variables.

Table 3 gives the group averages for our 10 variables. For each variable, we calculated the percentage of non-standard variants used by each speaker, so the group averages shown here are simply the mean of the five individual percentages of the members of each group. Table 3 includes the figures for the four groups of school children, to which we shall refer briefly below, but most of the discussion will centre on the scores of the adults. In each case, the scores are given in the order shown in Table 1—i.e. female to the left of male, and university graduates above secondary school graduates above those with just primary school education above those with no education. The circles bring together adult scores which differ by no more than 6 percentage points. We shall call such scores 'similar'.

One point which emerges clearly from this table is that each variable is unique in the way it divides the population, though there are also similarities between variables. For example, it will be seen that (a:) and (r) ignore the speaker's sex in the top two groups, but distinguish these two groups from one another, whereas (h) distinguishes sex in these groups but does not distinguish the two educational groups. At present there appears to be little more to say about these qualitative differences between the variables, though it would be interesting to know why each variable recognizes the particular distinctions that it does.

Another difference is a quantitative difference, in the number of adult scores that are similar to some other score. At one extreme we have (be), where there are no similarities at all among the scores, and at the other extreme we have (r), where every score is similar to at least one other.

Table 3: Group averages for use of non-standard variants on ten variables

(man)	4	(4 12) 16	(be)	31	5 13 33	(ha)	68	33/54 56
		6 21			24 32			60 57
		9 57			41 53			77 81
	24	(23 53) 61		48	65 79 63		82	77 86 88

(a:)	45	(36 37) 44	(st)	29	12 24 41	(ey)	21	(16/22) 22
		50 49			40 47			25/34
		62/70			55/74			61 62
	73	76/81 74		49	74/86 80		60	65/73 60

(h)	28	18 33 26	(?)	66	67 47 45	(d)	78	53/77 85
		19 38			58 56			79 79
		42/72			69 65			89 95
	60	55 76 65		76	69 71 78		96	89 95 90

(r)	69	(61 64) 75
		81 77
		88/94
	92	97 97 92

Here there does seem to be a potentially interesting generalization to be made: the variables with the fewest similarities among their scores are the ones which show the greatest differences between old and young. To calculate the age difference for a variable, one very simple measure is the sum of all the differences between each young group and the corresponding old group. For example, for (be) the young females of the top educational group scored 31, which differs by 26 from the figure for the adult females of this group; and the sum of all the relevant figures for this variable is 77. The sum for (st), the other variable with little similarity among its scores, is 65, but no other variables have sums higher than 45. Even this figure, for (d), is due mainly to a change in just one group (females of the top group), and the same may be said, regarding again the same group, of the score of 44 for (ha). If we disregard these two variables as in some sense a special case, we find that none of the variables other than (be) and (st) have change-scores higher than 32. Moreover, the variable showing the least change, (man) with just 13, is the one with the most complex similarities among its scores.

Before trying to understand this apparent relationship between similarities among groups and the amount of change taking place, we should make it clear that the kind of change which contributes to the high scores for (be) and (st) is what we may call *convergence*—the young members of the two extreme educational groups are more similar to one another than their adults are. There are problems in interpreting these results in terms of long-term changes, since it is known that middle-class adolescents sometimes adopt relatively working-class speech patterns just during their adolescence,[14] so their contribution to the high change figure may not represent a permanent change. In contrast, the two variables with scores of 44 and 45 for change, (d) and (ha), both seem to be changing in favour of the non-standard variant, since all but one of the groups of youngsters use more non-standard variants than their adults do. Thus it may be that the connection to be established is between *a high degree of convergent age-difference* (however we interpret this in terms of change) and *a low degree of similarity among groups*.

It is intriguing to speculate about the reasons for this connection, if it is real. One possible explanation is that young speakers are aware that these variables are particularly clear indicators of a speaker's group-membership, and that this makes them concentrate on these variables in their attempt to align themselves with a different group from their parents. Thus educated children of uneducated parents would use fewer non-standard variants in order to show their education, and those of highly educated parents would (for some reason) use more of the non-standard variants in order to dissociate themselves from their parents. Whatever the explanation, it seems likely that it will have something to do with the high discriminating value of the variables with little similarities among groups. Of course, it is even more intriguing to speculate about what the next generation of children will do if the changes turn out in fact to be permanent, and not just adolescent aberrations, since the effect of the changes is precisely to reduce the discriminating value of these variables, by reducing the differences between the educational groups. Rather than continue with such speculations, we finish this discussion with a general hypothesis:

> Variables with high discriminating value will be used more than other variables by adolescents whose speech differs from that of their parents in showing reduced differences between social groups.

One possible objection to the above discussion is that our measure of 'discriminating value' was too crude, since it involved nothing but counting the number of group-averages which were less than 7 percentage points different from other group-averages. There are two weaknesses of this measure: the figure of 7 points is arbitrary, and the measure ignores the extent of variation within the groups. Thus in principle two sets of data could both yield the same group-averages but

---

[14]See for instance Wolfram 1969: 124.

could in fact represent very different distributions of scores between groups, one with a great deal of overlap between groups and the other with little overlap. We developed a somewhat more sophisticated measure of discriminating value in order to overcome these difficulties, and we shall refer to this as the 'discrimination index'. We based this index on the standard deviations of the variable scores for each group[15] and also took into account the total spread of scores, from the highest group to the lowest. The index is designed to show how much of this total spread is taken up by the normal members of the groups, so that if the index is less than 1, this shows that there are gaps between the groups, and if it is over 1, it shows that the groups overlap in their scores.

If we apply this measure to our variables, we find once again that (be) comes out as a good discriminator, since it has a score of 0.84. This means that all but 15.87 per cent of scores for this variable may be expected to fall within areas of the percentage range defined for the separate groups which themselves only take up 84 per cent of the total range between the extreme groups, leaving 16 per cent of this range to be used by the remaining 15.87 per cent of cases. We have already seen that the group averages are all clearly different from each other on this variable, so we may claim that there is hardly any overlap between the scores of individuals in one group and those of individuals in other groups.[16] In contrast, all the other variables, including (st), have discrimination indices above 1, and some of them are very far above 1. (The extreme is (r), with an index of 3.82, which means that it hardly has any discriminating value at all; that is, if we know a speaker's score on this variable we could not predict which of up to four groups he belonged to, since he would fall within the normal range of all of them as defined by their standard deviations.) This conclusion is somewhat awkward, since we assumed above that (st) was a good discriminator, along with (be). On the more sophisticated measure, it has an index of 1.72, which is higher than two other variables ((h) with 1.42 and (ɑ:) with 1.60)), but we saw that there was far more difference between young and old in the scores for (st) than for either of these variables. We are not sure how to reconcile this finding with our hypothesis, as it seems unlikely that the cruder measure is a better indicator of how members of the community see the discriminating value of variables. At least we have found that (be) is the best discriminator by either measure, and this after all is the variable with the most age difference.

[15]The standard deviation of a group of scores is a measure of the dispersion of the scores around their mean. It is calculated on the assumption that the scores recorded belong to members of a larger class, though some of them may not be typical of this class, and it allows one to predict that all but 15.87 per cent of the larger class's members will have scores falling within 'one standard deviation' of the group mean. Thus the standard deviation may be used as a reasonable measure of the spread of scores in a group: the larger the standard deviation, the less homogeneous is the group.

[16]The individual scores on this variable are given in Hudson (1980: 164).

Norms and their setters

If we assume that speech patterns are learned, it would be interesting to know whether there are any individuals or groups in a society that act as particularly helpful models for the learner. For example, are some university-educated females more consistent models than others are for someone wanting to find out how a typical university-educated female speaks? And are some social groups more consistent than others as far as their members' speech is concerned, allowing them in some way to act as models for the rest of society? Such questions are important not just as part of our attempt to understand how society works, but also from a methodological point of view. For example, if we find that some people are more consistent representatives of their social group, it might be possible to identify such speakers and use them as informants when studying variation. It is possible to give a tentative answer to them on the basis of our data.

To answer the question about individual speakers as typical members of their groups, we may ask whether any speakers in our sample have average scores for their group on all of the 10 variables. In order to have a criterion for what counts as average, we shall use the standard deviation of the group, so that any score within one standard deviation of the group's mean will count as 'average'. Similarly we may distinguish between 'above average' (i.e. more non-standard than average) and 'below average' scores, and ask whether any speakers are consistently above or below average on all 10 variables. The answer is disappointing for the researcher, and surprised us. Of the 40 adult speakers, only *one* (a male university graduate) was consistently average for his group on all variables, and *none* were consistently above or below average. Thus 39 out of 40 speakers were inconsistent, in sometimes being average, and sometimes being above or below average. Moreover, over half of the speakers (22) departed from the average in both sometimes being above average and sometimes below. In other words, none of our speakers is a better or worse example of the class that he represents than any of the others. One conclusion from this is, of course, that our method of selecting speakers and of defining their social classes was a good one, since we have no misfits. A less comforting conclusion, however, is that it is hard to imagine how a speaker identifies the norm for his group, since there are no individuals whom he can rely on to be average in all respects. We feel we are a long way from understanding how variation works.

In order to ask the corresponding question about groups, we must naturally develop a different measure of consistency. This time we shall measure the total range of variation for each group, across all 10 variables, and ask if any groups have more variation than others. This is easy to do, since we already have a measure for each group on each variable: the standard deviation. The total variation for the group is measured by adding together all the 10 standard deviations, so if a group is relatively consistent, in the sense that its members do not vary much from the group average, then it will have a small total figure. When we apply this test to our results, we find that one group stands out as relatively *in*consistent—females with no education—but that all the others have similar scores. (Whereas uneducated females have a total of 90.8, all the other groups have scores between 64.3 and 76.6.) Thus it seems that in Tehran society no social group has any special advantage over the others for anyone in search of a consistent model with a small range of variation among its members; but he would be particularly unwise to take the group of female illiterates as his model.

To end on a somewhat more positive note, there is some evidence that the group of university-educated females has advantages over other groups as a model of standard Persian, although as we have just seen there is just as much variation among speakers for this group as for any other. The evidence to which we refer comes from a simple measure of the rank of each speaker on each variable. For any given variable, we

Table 4: Assignments of members of eight social groups to eight rank groups

| | | rank-groups | | | | | | | |
		A	B	C	D	E	F	G	H
univ.,	female	(35)	5	4	1	1	2	1	1
	male	(13)	(13)	11	9	4	0	0	0
second.,	female	8	11	(14)	8	4	3	2	0
	male	2	10	(14)	11	8	4	1	0
primary,	female	1	2	3	12	(16)	8	4	4
	male	0	1	2	4	10	(14)	13	6
no educ.,	female	0	0	2	6	8	10	(15)	9
	male	0	1	1	1	4	9	15	(19)

may rank our 40 speakers from those with the lowest score for the use of non-standard variants to those with the highest score, and we can then bring together the rankings of each of the members of a group on all the 10 variables as a kind of group profile. In order to make the comparison easier, we assigned speakers on each variable to one of 8 groups of 5, labelled A (for the 5 most standard speakers) to H (the 5 least standard speakers). For each group we can then count the number of times any of its members were assigned to each of the rank-groups from A to H. If some group consistently occupied the first five rank places on every single variable, it would score 50 (5×10) assignments to the A group, and so on for all the other rankings, but no group came near to a score of 50 in any one rank-group, with the exception of the university-educated females, who had 35 assignments to rank-group A. The figures are shown in Table 4, from which it can be seen that all the other social groups had a maximum of between 13 and 19 assignments to one rank-group. The circles show the highest scores for each social group.

In conclusion, we have shown that there are considerable differences among linguistic variables on a number of important dimensions, notably whether or not their variants tend to occur in runs, and whether or not they have good discriminating value for social groups. On the other hand, we have found surprisingly little difference either among individual speakers, or among groups of speakers, in the extent to which they present a consistent norm in their speech.

5

A qualitative approach to the quantitative data of speech variation

Mats Thelander

Among the features which I have been studying in an investigation of speech variation in the northern Swedish community of Burträsk I should first like to comment on the alternation between /dɔmm/ and /dɛmm/ for 'they'.[1] Out of a total of 1,373 instances of this variable in my material, 747 have the form /dɔmm/, i.e. the variant of spoken standard Swedish. This means that the variable (THEY) in my recordings from Burträsk is employed in its standard variant in 54 per cent of all cases; the s% of (THEY) equals 54. Now this could of course be interpreted in a number of ways and I would like to isolate, in turn, three possible explanations.

The observed mixture might be a result of what Labov (1969: 728) has termed *inherent variability*, that is to say a rule in present-day Burträsk which prescribes this proportion of /dɔmm/ and /dɛmm/ in any speech produced in an extralinguistic context similar to my recording situation. Such a rule quite adequately accounts for the figures and it need not be assumed that the corpus is non-homogeneous with respect to speakers or speech situations. No matter which part of the recording was to be examined individually, the relative frequency of /dɔmm/ (as against /dɛmm/) would still remain 54 per cent.

Secondly, the mixture could be a consequence of having a *non-homogeneous corpus*. A total of 56 Burträskers make up the recorded material. Thirty of them were born before 1930. Suppose these people all say /dɔmm/ and never /dɛmm/ and suppose the rest of the speakers, i.e. 26 persons, always say /dɛmm/ and never /dɔmm/. Provided there is no systematic difference between the two age groups in their use of the over-all variable (THEY), this categorical distribution of /dɔmm/ and /dɛmm/ over speakers born before and after 1930 would produce exactly the observed proportion of variants, 54 per cent /dɔmm/ and 46 per cent

[1]An earlier version of this essay was read at the Sociolinguistics symposium in Birmingham, 19–21 September, 1979. My participation in the symposium was made possible by a grant from the Bank of Sweden Tercentenary Foundation. The research reported on was to a large extent financed by the Swedish Humanistic Research Council. I am indebted to Martin Naylor BA for revising the language in my paper.

/dɛmm/. Naturally this heterogeneity of the material would reveal itself as soon as the speakers were subdivided into any groups in which older and younger persons were not evenly represented.

Thirdly, the outcome 54 per cent /dɔmm/ and 46 per cent /dɛmm/ could be a reflection of the fact that I have been studying a *non-homogeneous linguistic variable*. In spoken standard Swedish the form /dɔmm/ is used both as subject and object. Among the people of Burträsk, however, /dɔmm/ could be confined to subject usage (= *they*) whereas /dɛmm/ might be exclusive in object position (= *them*). Assuming further that these two functions of (THEY) are distributed in the ratio of 54 to 46, these are the relative frequencies of /dɔmm/ and /dɛmm/ which must be expected. This categorical rule would not become transparent from subdividing the material into extralinguistically defined groups, since each speaker is likely to adhere to it individually. The heterogeneity of the variable will, however, appear when we compare intralinguistically defined sub-sets between which the different syntactic functions of the variable are unevenly distributed.

My reason for discussing this trivial example at some length is to point out that although quantitative results may not initially lend themselves to a qualitative interpretation they need not, on the other hand, exclude such solutions altogether. It is justifiable to retreat to the first—truly quantitative—of the above explanations only after the second and third have been effectively refuted. For various reasons I think it is important not to over-quantify sociolinguistic data. With reference to the results from Burträsk I intend to propose methods for handling quantitative data without overlooking qualitative tendencies in them. One of the aims of my research has been to investigate in what way code-switching and coexisting speech varieties combine with the variation of isolated features, known as linguistic variables (Labov 1963); or to use my own terminology: the problem has been to reconcile the notion of *macro-variation* with that of *micro-variation*.

Micro-variation in language is often influenced by factors both in the extralinguistic and the intralinguistic context. The alternation between for example the dropping and retaining of postvocalic /r/ may be conditioned both by the age and sex of the speaker and by the phonetic environment in which the variable occurs (for variation in Scottish English cf. Romaine 1978). Macro-variation on the other hand can be affected only by extralinguistic factors since alternating between two languages or two dialects normally involves a complete change of linguistic environment.

Suppose we have a corpus consisting of pure speech in two languages L_1 and L_2 and suppose these languages cover 60 per cent and 40 per cent respectively of all that is being said. An examination of linguistic features a, b and c—which differ between L_1 and L_2—would make clear that the quantitative relations between a_1 and a_2, between b_1 and b_2 and between c_1 and c_2 are also 60 as against 40 per cent provided of course that each variable a, b and c is comparable between L_1 and L_2 as to its relative frequency. The numerical relation between English *and* and its Swedish counterpart *och* will reflect the relative use of English and Swedish only on condition that the use of *and* in English is exactly as frequent as the use of *och* in Swedish. In other words, to make sure that the proportion of two variants a_1 and a_2 will mirror correctly the relative use of L_1 and L_2 in the same material, there must be complete independence between variation in form (between a_1 and a_2) and variation in the relative frequency of the variable (the number of a-occurrences in relation for instance to the total number of words).

Now, let's look at this from a slightly different angle. The observation that three binary variables x, y and z are distributed between their two variants in similar proportions would seem to be indicative of macro-variation taking place at some levels above that of the isolated features. But in order to allow this common pattern of variation to emerge, each variable must be freed from any dependence on intralinguistic factors. We want variables to be independent of variation in linguistic environment, since that influence is likely to be specific to each single variable, making a possible similarity in their co-variation with extralinguistic factors less obvious. All variables must be made to oscillate in one dimension only if we wish to interpret the fact that any or all of them move in phase as an indication of macro-variation. By studying the variables in the same material we have made sure they are all affected by exactly the same extralinguistic forces (cf. also the discussion in Jahangiri and Hudson, this volume).

Linguistic variables sensitive only to extralinguistic influence can be created strictly inductively. After dividing all instances of a certain variable into linguistically defined sub-categories, only those categories which exhibit similar patterns of social variation should be aggregated. What was originally considered to be one sociolinguistic variable may in this way be transformed into two or more variables, each defined by a specific set of intralinguistic constraints. I call them *micro-variables* and they constitute the minimal units of sociolinguistic variation. A correctly demarcated micro-variable will not permit a subdivision by intralinguistic criteria such that the proportions of the variants will differ significantly between sub-sets.

At this point I would like briefly to return to the example which I started with, the various possible explanations of an apparent mixture of /dɔmm/ and /dɛmm/ in the Burträsk material. Three interpretations were mentioned, viz. inherent variability, a non-homogeneous corpus and a non-homogeneous variable. Because (THEY) in fact meets the requirements of a micro-variable, the third interpretation is eliminated. The use of 54 per cent /dɔmm/ and 46 per cent /dɛmm/ for (THEY) does not correspond to any known difference in the distribution of the variable across linguistic sub-categories. Before taking a closer look at the second explanation—suggesting that the mixture of /dɔmm/ and

/dɛmm/ is due to a non-homogeneous speech corpus—some further information on the Burträsk survey must be provided.

The site of investigation is a small community in a traditionally agricultural area of northern Sweden. It is situated 25 miles from the nearest city, Skellefteå. Of approximately 6000 inhabitants in the former county (*kommun*) of Burträsk, ¼ live in the town itself. Despite the fact that Skellefteå is not far off, the town of Burträsk has been able to maintain a high level of service and commercial activity, making the whole district relatively self-sufficient. Most of my field-work was carried out in 1973. That year was also the last in which Burträsk constituted a separate administrative entity. In 1974 Burträsk was incorporated into a larger county, with Skellefteå as centre.

The original dialect of Burträsk has characteristics which are of an archaic nature, making it unintelligible for Swedes from the central parts of the country. An important reason for selecting Burträsk as the place of investigation was the fact that the old dialect, *Burträskmålet*, is among the best documented in Swedish dialect literature.

In many respects Burträsk resembles Hemnesberget, the Norwegian community where Blom and Gumperz (1972) made their well known study of bidialectalism and symbolic code-switching. Important impulses for the investigation of Burträsk certainly originate in their anthropological study. This investigation is, however, closer in method to Labov's quantitative analysis of variation in urban speech. Some of the problems which I have already touched upon have no doubt emerged as a consequence of applying Labov's exacting micro-techniques to data from a speech community where some element of bidialectalism must be expected.

The bulk of empirical data for the study was drawn from the linguistic analysis of 28 hours of recorded group discussions and 2 hours of recorded interviews. With one or two exceptions the 56 speakers were all born and resident in either the town of Burträsk (= B) or in its immediate surroundings (= b). The selection of informants can best be described as a judgement sample within the age bracket 14 to 65 years.

Informal group discussions were chosen for the main series of recordings to secure a fair amount of intra-individual speech variation (cf. Gumperz 1972: 208). Each of the 14 group sessions lasted for two hours and included four speakers. Ten groups were self-recruited (*closed groups*) whereas the remaining four were composed at random (*open groups*). All discussions took place in a relaxed atmosphere either in the home of one of the members or in a home-like setting on neutral ground. The speakers knew that they were being recorded. However, half of the groups were told that the purpose of the recordings was to collect natural colloquial speech (*language orientation*) while the other half were told that the recordings were made to collect opinions about the impending consolidation of Burträsk into the county of Skellefteå (*subject orientation*). In reality all group discussions revolved around similar topics.

For the purpose of generating a controlled shift of speech situation the informants were joined after one hour of talking on their own (*the A-situation*) by a stranger who took part in the second half of the discussion (*the B-situation*). He or she was introduced as a member of the research staff which, it was expected, would make the speakers associate him or her with activities not belonging to the local sphere. To make sure that the informants did not refrain from using their dialect for reasons of intelligibility, care was taken in each instance to engage a person from the north of Sweden to play the part of 'stranger'. Individual interviews were made with nine persons out of the 56 who several months earlier had participated in group discussions. Another four of the speakers were recorded twice in group sessions, once as additional members of regular groups of four. Each of the 56 individuals was recorded in two or three different speech situations. The material, therefore, can be divided into a total of 125 *speakers' situations*, by which I mean the complete speech of one informant in one of the controlled speech situations.

The linguistic features selected for closer investigation were originally meant to serve as accessible indicators of an assumed shifting in Burträsk between the local dialect and standard Swedish. Therefore the variables were chosen among features for which the dialect of Burträsk and standard Swedish have easily distinguishable variants. The contrast between /dɔmm/ and /dɛmm/ for (THEY) has already been mentioned. The other eleven variables were likewise selected from the morphological and morphophonemic levels.[2] In order to simplify the analysis only features that could be treated as binary variables were chosen. For each variable one standard variant (*s-variant*) and one dialect variant (*d-variant*) have been specified. Speaking standard Swedish requires the use of standard variants for all variables whereas speaking *Burträskmål* would imply a choice of dialect variants throughout. Since a large number of features were under study the majority of them have not been excerpted from the entire material due to limitations of time. The description of these variables is based on their variation in a random sample of utterances and clauses from the corpus. As ultimately defined each variable can be regarded as a micro-variable.

[2]Some designations of micro-variables are not immediately comprehensible. These are: (INF): long-stemmed infinitives which have the ending -*a* in standard Swedish but lack ending in the dialect, e.g./resu'ne:ra/cf./resu'ne:r/ ('reason'). (IT$_n$): the neuter pronoun in various syntactic functions. (IT$_{nn}$): the non-neuter pronoun with inanimate antecedent. Standard Swedish/dɛnn/ (for both the masculine and feminine genders) is an innovation whereas the dialect has retained /hann/ for masculine, /hunn/ for feminine references. The pronouns /hann/ and /hunn/ are reserved in standard Swedish for animate antecedents. (PRES): the present tense of certain verbs where standard Swedish has the inflexion -/ər/, *Burträskmål* -Ø, e.g. /'stikkər/ cf. /stikk/ ('sting'). (SC): subject complement with a plural subject; the standard Swedish forms /*fri:a/, /*tvungna/ in this position correspond to the dialectal uninflected forms /fri:/, /*tvungən/.

Table 1

Micro-variable	n	Standard variant	n	Dialect variant	n	s%
ARE	487	ær	335	ˣvara	152	69
INF	282	-a	146	-Ø	136	52
IT$_n$	1114	de	391	he	723	35
IT$_{nn}$	919	dɛnn	173	$\left\{\begin{array}{l}\text{hann}\\\text{hunn}\end{array}\right\}$	746	19
KV	503	kv-	255	kw-	248	51
NOT	858	ˣintə	215	int	643	25
PRES	268	-ər	39	-Ø	229	15
SC	502	-a	193	-Ø	309	38
SV	428	sv-	292	ʃw-	136	68
THEY	1373	dɔmm	717	dɛmm	626	54
TV	605	tv-	452	çw-	153	75
WERE	197	var	106	ˣvuur	91	54
total	7536		3344 -		4192	44

To attain that end certain linguistic positions or lexical categories were excluded from the domain of some variables. Since the proportions of standard and dialect variants are fairly consistent between the remaining linguistic environments an observation of non-categorical use of either variant will then suggest inherent variability or a non-homogeneous speech corpus or both.

In Table 1 some general characteristics of each micro-variable are given. The leftmost column lists all variables in alphabetic order. The first column of figures represents the total frequency of each variable in my material. These tokens are distributed between the standard and dialect variants according to the numbers in the second and third column of figures. The rightmost column gives the percentages of standard variants in relation to the total numbers of variable occurrences. It can be noted that s% ranges from 15 (for PRES = present tense) to 75 (for TV = word initial *tv-*).

The great disparity of s-percentages between different micro-variables introduces a new problem into the search for categorical speech norms in Burträsk. Had each micro-variable been an indicator of the alternation between standard and dialect one would expect the relative frequencies of standard variants to be much the same between variables. As illustrated by Figure 1 the wide range of s% cannot be dismissed as the mere effects of chance. Because sex differences are insignificant the dotted and the broken lines can serve as an expression of the reliability of the data. The order of the variables according to average s% shows a rank correlation of 0.93 between male and female speakers.

Figure 2 compares the three speech situations with reference to average s% for each micro-variable. The variables are reordered according to decreasing s% in the A-situation. Although there is an increase in the relative frequency of standard forms when speakers move

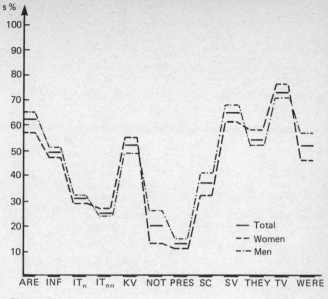

Figure 1

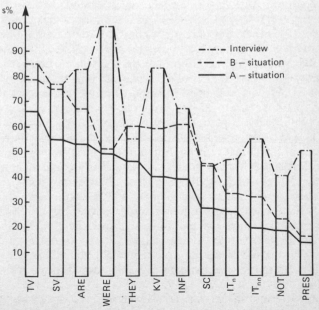

Figure 2

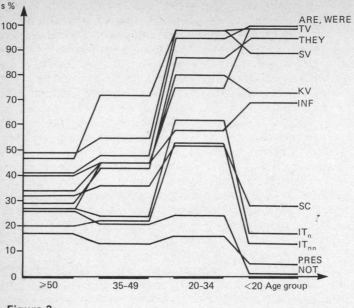

Figure 3

from less formal to more formal situations there is in no case a difference great enough to evoke the notion of code-switching.

Figure 3 deserves special attention. It shows the co-variation between speakers' age and the relative frequency of standard variants. The oldest informants (50 years or above) tend to use approximately the same share of standard variants for all variables. With declining age the dispersion of the variables increases to reach a maximum among speakers below the age of 20. While the youngest informants show almost total absence of dialect variants of certain features, they at the same time almost totally avoid standard variants of other features. All micro-variables clearly fall into one or other of these categories. As illustrated on a map in Thelander (1979a: 115) the most powerful basis for determining the vitality of a dialect variant in present-day Burträsk would seem to be its geographical dispersion in northern Sweden. The forms which are rarely used by Burträsk youngsters (e.g./çw/for TV and /*vara/ for ARE) are at the same time those which are most limited geographically. Moreover, the dialectal phenomena in Burträsk speech which hold their own against standard counterparts (e.g. /hann/ for IT_{nn} and /int/ for NOT) are common for most dialects in northern Sweden. This may be an important aspect of the mechanisms by which local dialects give way to regional dialects.

The conception of Burträsk as a bidialectal community where people use either *Burträskmål* or standard Swedish is seriously undermined by the observation that micro-variables behave so differently. As parallel indicators of an assumed shift between two speech varieties they could be expected to produce a comparable s% making it possible to aggregate all of them into one single variable without loss of descriptive power. I use the term *macro-variable* to designate such an aggregation of a set of uniform micro-variables. The reason is that this set would be capable of signalling a shift between speech varieties rather than just a shift between linguistic variants.

The fact that all 12 micro-variables do not constitute one homogeneous macro-variable means that the data do not support a model of two coexisting speech varieties in Burträsk. This does not, however, exclude other models of macro-variation. In theory each micro-variable could form a macro-variable of its own, all of them being related through *implication*, as outlined by DeCamp (1971) in his description of Creole varieties in Jamaica. This would result in a total of 13 categorical norms in Burträsk specified in Figure 4, where the variables are ordered with reference to average s% for all speakers. This model, however, fits the actual data even less well (see Thelander 1979b: 47).

But between models with *one* macro-variable (producing two speech varieties) and those with *twelve* macro-variables (producing 13 speech varieties) there are several other models which deserve consideration. And recalling the way micro-variables tended to split into two natural classes in the speech of young people (cf. Figure 3) there is one model which appears to be particularly promising.

Manual statistics—for details see Thelander 1979b: 46–52 and 134–5—have indeed confirmed that this model of two separate macro-variables provides the best categorical approximation to data. I refer to the two aggregated sets of micro-variables as *dialect indicator* (= DI) and *standard indicator* (= SI). The dialect indicator comprises seven

Microvariables												Speech variety
TV	SV	ARE	THEY	WERE	INF	KV	SC	IT_n	IT_{nn}	NOT	PRES	
d	d	d	d	d	d	d	d	d	d	d	d	V1
s	d	d	d	d	d	d	d	d	d	d	d	V2
s	s	d	d	d	d	d	d	d	d	d	d	V3
s	s	s	d	d	d	d	d	d	d	d	d	V4
s	s	s	s	d	d	d	d	d	d	d	d	V5
s	s	s	s	s	d	d	d	d	d	d	d	V6
s	s	s	s	s	s	d	d	d	d	d	d	V7
s	s	s	s	s	s	s	d	d	d	d	d	V8
s	s	s	s	s	s	s	s	d	d	d	d	V9
s	s	s	s	s	s	s	s	s	d	d	d	V10
s	s	s	s	s	s	s	s	s	s	d	d	V11
s	s	s	s	s	s	s	s	s	s	s	d	V12
s	s	s	s	s	s	s	s	s	s	s	s	V13

Figure 4

micro-variables with high percentages of standard variants (ranging from 51 to 75 s%). The standard indicator comprises five micro-variables with low percentages of standard variants (ranging from 15 to 38 s%). For each of the two macro-variables the less frequent variant functions as a distinct marker of speech variety—the s-variant of SI implies standard Swedish while the d-variant of DI implies *Burträskmål*. The more frequent variant of SI or DI does not seem to be a positive signal of either dialect or standard. It is in a sense unmarked for speech variety.

Figure 5 gives a graphic representation of the relationship between the aggregated standard indicator and the aggregated dialect indicator as to s% of 125 speakers' situations, each symbolized by a dot. The remarkable pattern arises from the fact that low s% for DI occurs only with low s% for SI whereas high s% for DI combines with both high and low values for SI. This asymmetry between macro-variables is typical of the implication by which they are related. Using the dialect variant /dɛmm/ implies using the dialect variant /int/, while the reverse is not true. And using the standard variant /inte/ implies using the standard variant /dɔmm/ but not the other way round.

The two macro-variables are thus related in a way which produces *three* distinct speech varieties, *dialect* (D), characterized by d-variants throughout, *standard* (S), characterized by s-variants, and thirdly: an

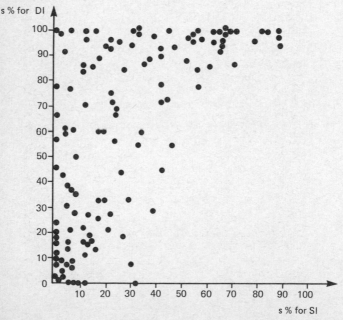

Figure 5

	DI							SI					Speech variety
TV	SV	ARE	THEY	WERE	KV	INF	SC	IT_n	IT_{nn}	NOT	PRES	
d	d	d	d	d	d	d	d	d	d	d	d	D
s	s	s	s	s	s	s	d	d	d	d	d	RS
s	s	s	s	s	s	s	s	s	s	s	s	S

Figure 6

interlanguage which I call *regional standard* (RS), composed of s-variants for dialect indicators and d-variants for standard indicators (see Figure 6). The fact that none of these variants is an unequivocal marker of the interlanguage makes the regional standard stand out as a unique combination of largely non-unique traits. The term regional standard is chosen because its dialect variants have in common a considerable geographic dispersion.

Let us return once more to the question posed at the beginning of my paper. Is the observed mixture of /dɔmm/ and /dɛmm/ for (THEY) due

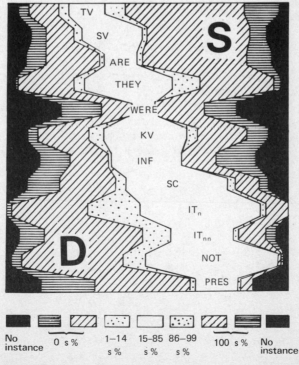

Figure 7

to inherent variability or to a non-homogeneous corpus? Naturally, the corpus is non-homogeneous, being deliberately varied with respect to both speakers and speech situations. A more realistic question would be whether this controlled differentiation can explain the observed variation in its entirety. Judging from Figure 7 the answer is no. The different shades represent various types of categorical and non-categorical usage for each micro-variable in various speakers' situations. The width of the white and the dotted areas corresponds to the proportion of speakers' situations in which *both* standard and dialect variants occur. In approximately one quarter of the speakers' situations this seems to be the case for most variables.

Since the speakers' situation is the lowest level of analysis where extralinguistic factors are under control this residue of variation would appear to be free. However free variation need not invalidate a model of categorical norms since free variation—judging from studies of bilingualism—has its counterpart on the macro-level, usually referred to as non-functional code-switching. For no reason at all a speaker may shift between speech varieties without really mixing. In order to distinguish this kind of code-switching—preserving the notion of separate speech varieties—from code-mixing, we probably have to rely on co-occurrence patterns, as the only observable criteria (Thelander 1976, 1979b: 21–34).

I wish to propose a method of estimating co-occurrence by means of the calculation of *cohesion-coefficients* (KK) at different levels of analysis. KK stands for the total probability of obtaining identical variants in a two-step selection of, first, one unit of analysis among all units available on that level and, second, two specimens of a linguistic variable within each unit. Depending on whether micro-variables or macro-variables are at issue, 'identical' may imply either two tokens of a certain linguistic form or two variants belonging to the same speech variety. With a large material KK can be calculated according to this formula

$$KK = \frac{1}{n} \sum_{i=1}^{n} \left(\frac{x_i}{x_i + y_i} \right)^2 + \left(\frac{y_i}{x_i + y_i} \right)^2$$

where x denotes the frequency of one variant, y the frequency of the other variant and n the number of units (e.g. speakers, utterances etc.) on the chosen level of analysis.

KK for a certain variable becomes interesting only when compared with KK for the same variable on levels defined by successively shorter units. Irrespective of how the speech material is segmented, almost any divergence from inherent variability will result in a relative increase in KK when it is calculated for shorter units. Since this segmentation need not be discontinued on the level where extralinguistic conditions can no longer be controlled, an analysis of KK can prove particularly useful in tracing tendencies of macro-variation which have not yet asserted themselves in the idiolects, due to non-functional code-switching. A simpler method of measuring co-occurrence than the use of KK would no doubt be to calculate the probability of a micro-variable retaining its form from one appearance to the next. However, that probability is likely to correlate with the syntagmatic distance between appearances which in turn depends on the relative frequency of each variable. By looking at variables within syntagmatic units of set length KK avoids this bias and makes comparisons meaningful (cf. also the measure proposed by Jahangiri and Hudson, this volume).

In Figure 8 KK is applied on several levels of analysis to both the model of three speech varieties in Burträsk (upper pair of curves) and the traditional model of only two varieties, dialect and standard (lower pair of curves). To obtain non-broken lines KK has been calculated with a formula incorporating correction for continuity (Thelander 1979b: 32), valuable when each unit contains few instances of the variable. The corpus has been segmented far beyond the level of speakers' situation, testing the hypothesis that non-functional code-switching contributes to the variant mixture within that unit (cf. Figure 7). The increase in KK for these levels indicates that the mixture of variants in speakers' situations is not altogether haphazard. Variants belonging to the same speech variety tend to be organized in sequences.

Moreover Figure 8 demonstrates the superiority of the model of three

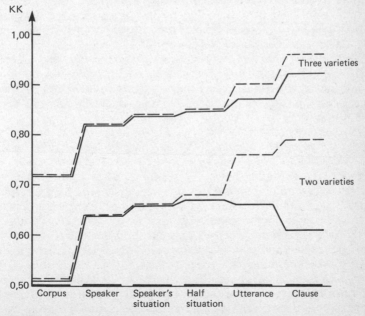

Figure 8

speech varieties over the model of two varieties for discovering macro-tendencies in the speech of Burträskers. The average probability of selecting two variants from only one of dialect, regional standard or standard amounts to approximately 0.9, when the selection is made within an utterance or a clause. It means that only a very small proportion of the variation does not comply with the categorical norms which have been established.

In order to handle a vast body of variation data it may be desirable to synthesize the linguistic characteristics of individual speech samples into some kind of unified index which can then be correlated with various extralinguistic data. In doing this for the Burträsk material I have tried not to lose touch with structured variation or arrive at a measurement which would be a mere statistical artefact. *Language index* (i) is preferably quantitative and can be determined as the mean of s% for SI and s% for DI. One speech sample, for examples, consists of 37 s-variants and 6 d-variants for micro-variables belonging to the dialect indicator. For DI the s% thus equals 86. In the same sample there are 10 s-variants and 57 d-variants for micro-variables belonging to the standard indicator. SI has 15 s%. The mean of 86 and 15 is equal to 51, which is the language index of this sample. Language index may assume any value between 0 and 100. Pure dialect corresponds to index 0, regional standard to index 50 and standard to index 100. Because s%-values of the standard indicator and the dialect indicator do not combine freely (cf. Figure 5) this index in fact provides some qualitative information. As can be seen in Figure 9 an index of 70, for example, can quite reliably be interpreted as being made up of between 80 and 100 s% for DI and between 40 and 60 s% for SI.

Figure 10 gives an example of how this language index can be applied. It shows the relation between age and language index for individual speakers, each represented by a dot. A line through the dot indicates to what extent the speaker exhibits variation in index between the A-situation and the B-situation of the group discussion.

Another measurement was designed to be at least semi-qualitative. I call it *variety classification* and it has only three values: dialect, regional standard and standard. For a certain speech sample the percentage of all d-variants (i.e. for both SI and DI) is compared to the percentage of all s-variants and to the percentage of variants unmarked for speech variety, i.e. s-variants for DI and d-variants for SI. Depending on which of these proportions is largest the language of the speech sample is viewed as dialect, standard or regional standard respectively. In the case used above to demonstrate how language index is calculated, the three ratios to be compared are 63/110, 47/110, 94/110. A majority of unmarked variants implies that this text can best be labelled as regional standard. Figure 11 illustrates the way variety classification relates to language index for each speakers' situation (represented by 125 squares).

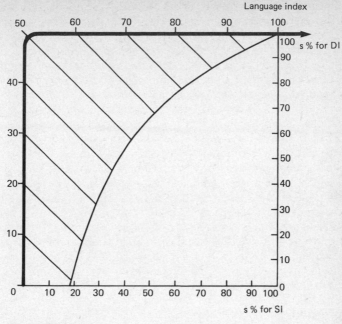

Figure 9

This variety classification allows the basis for categorizing speakers to be reversed. Instead of asking what the linguistic differences between the speech of men and women are, we may pose the question: What are the extralinguistic differences between speakers using dialect and speakers using regional standard in a certain context? That way our possibilities for exploring more complex causes of variation become much greater, which may to some degree compensate for the loss of linguistic subtlety which is of course inevitable at this level of abstraction. In Table 2 all 56 informants are categorized according to speech performance (in terms of variety classification) during the A- and B-situations for the group discussion. Group 1 consists of 18 speakers using dialect in both A- and B-situations. Group 2 comprises 11 speakers with D in A-situations but RS in B-situations. Group 3 is composed of 13 informants speaking RS throughout both situations. Group 4 consists of 6 speakers characterized by the use of RS in the A-situation and S in the B-situation. There is one deviation from the overall pattern; the speech of informant 132 has been classified as standard in the A-situation but as regional standard in the B-situation. She has been assigned to group 5, the rest of which consists of 7 speakers using standard in both situations.

The rest of the table presents on an individual basis some extralinguistic data most of which were touched upon in the above account of the Burträsk material: group composition, alleged purpose of

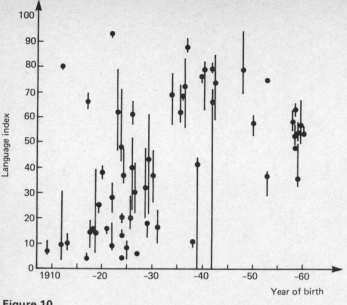

Figure 10

recording, speaker's sex, age and place of birth and finally his or her level of education (I = elementary school, II = secondary school, III = upper secondary school and above). From this overview the sociolinguistic results of the Burträsk investigation can be summarized: The entry of a non-local stranger into a group discussion causes no change of speech variety on the part of two-thirds of the Burträsk informants. Of these, fewer use standard Swedish in both situations than use dialect. It is typical among those speakers who do switch from one speech variety to another to change either from dialect to regional standard or from regional standard to standard. If it is at all justified to speak of bidialectalism in the case of Burträsk, it should obviously be referred to as *relative bidialectalism*.

The least variable and most uniform category of informants is by far the group of 8 school children. They make no distinction between A- and B-situations and use regional standard throughout. A general difference between linguistically stable and variable speakers is associated with the alleged purpose of the conversations. Informants responding to the entry of the stranger by changing speech variety were with few exceptions members of a subject-orientated group. One explanation of this could be that an atmosphere of subject-orientation accentuates the authoritative aspect of the stranger's role, making the feeling of a contrast between the A- and B-situations particularly marked.

Those Burträskers who nowadays use dialect in contexts typified by

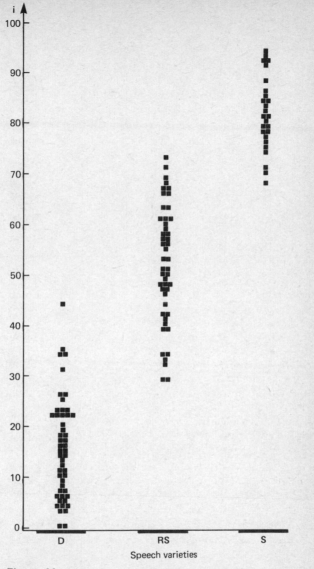

Figure 11

the A-situation are regularly older people who have grown up in rural surroundings and who have no education beyond elementary school level. Persons using regional standard or standard in this situation are typically under 40 years of age and have more than an elementary level of education. Being town-bred may compensate for higher age or lower

Table 2

	Speech variety		Speaker	Speaker's characteristics		place of		Conversation group	
	A-sit	B-sit	no	sex	age	birth	education	composition	purpose
1.	D	D	125	m	51	b	II	closed	language
	D	D	141	m	54	b	I	closed	language
	D	D	142	f	52	b	I	closed	language
	D	D	143	m	55	b	I	closed	language
	D	D	144	f	55	b	I	closed	language
	D	D	153	m	48	b	I	closed	subject
	D	D	154	f	42	b	I	closed	subject
	D	D	161	m	60	b	I	closed	language
	D	D	162	f	49	b	I	closed	language
	D	D	163	m	46	b	I	closed	language
	D	D	164	f	44	b	I	closed	language
	D	D	172	f	35	b	I	closed	subject
	D	D	173	m	49	b	I	closed	subject
	D	D	253	m	49	B	I	open	subject
	D	D	301	m	64	b	I	closed	language
	D	D	302	f	61	b	I	closed	language
	D	D	303	m	56	b	I	closed	language
	D	D	304	f	51	b	I	closed	langauge
2.	D	RS	111	m	34	B	I	closed	subject
	D	RS	112	f	31	b	II	closed	subject
	D	RS	124	f	47	b	I	closed	language
	D	RS	151	m	47	b	I	closed	subject
	D	RS	152	f	44	b	I	closed	subject
	D	RS	171	m	43	b	I	closed	subject
	D	RS	174	f	47	b	I	closed	subject
	D	RS	233	m	49	b	I	open	subject
	D	RS	235	m	44	b	I	open	subject
	D	RS	251	m	54	b	I	open	subject
	D	RS	255	m	53	B	I	open	subject
3.	RS	RS	101	m	14	B	II	closed	language
	RS	RS	102	f	14	B	II	closed	language
	RS	RS	103	m	14	B	II	closed	language
	RS	RS	105	m	14	B	II	closed	language
	RS	RS	113	m	37	B	I	closed	subject
	RS	RS	181	m	14	b	II	closed	language
	RS	RS	182	f	14	b	II	closed	language
	RS	RS	184	f	14	b	II	closed	language
	RS	RS	186	f	14	b	II	closed	language
	RS	RS	212	f	56	n	I	open	subject
	D/RS	RS	222	f	20	b	III	open	language
	RS	RS	224	f	23	b	III	open	language
	RS	RS	254	f	47	B	I	open	subject
4.	D/RS	S	114	f	33	B	II	closed	subject
	RS	S	131	m	39	B	II	closed	subject
	RS	S	133	m	37	B	II	closed	subject
	RS	S	214	f	31	B	II	open	subject
	RS	S	231	m	50	B	II	open	subject
	RS	S	232	f	49	B	I	open	subject
5.	S	S	121	m	61	b	I	closed	language
	S	S	123	m	51	b	II	closed	language
	S	RS	132	f	37	B	II	closed	subject
	S	S	134	f	36	B	II	closed	subject
	S	S	211	m	33	b	II	open	subject
	S	S	213	m	31	B	I	open	subject
	S	S	221	m	20	b	III	open	language
	S	S	223	m	25	b	III	open	language

education in placing a Burträsker in the group speaking regional standard or standard. A person's sex (as well as occupation and present place of residence) is of secondary importance as far as language usage is concerned. Whether an informant was recorded in a closed group or an open group is of little significance for his speech.

What really 'caused' the distribution of (THEY) as 54 per cent /dɔmm/ and 46 per cent /dɛmm/ turned out, to a large extent, to be a non-homogeneous corpus organized in relatively consistent sequences of uni-code speech and, to a lesser extent, inherent variability permitting variants to occur in *free combination*. My aim has been to distinguish the one cause from the other and, as a consequence of the important role played by the former, to bring the analysis of Burträsk speech data beyond the level of merely correlating single linguistic features with extralinguistic factors. With the help of statistical methods the common practice of dismissing all but categorical alternation as isolated micro-variation can be met by the opposite claim: variation that does not comply with the quantitative requirements of inherent variability must bear the stamp of macro-variation. Applying a number of variable rules for single features makes it impossible to reconstruct authentic speech when these rules do not work independently. By overlooking this one runs the risk of leaving the description incomplete (cf. also the papers by J. Milroy and Romaine, this volume). The micro-macro dimension probably constitutes a sliding scale on which few natural speech communities are likely to satisfy the rigorous demands of either extreme. This calls for a combination of analytic approaches.

6

Modelling intonational variability in children's speech

John Local

Introduction

In recent years sociolinguistic variability in the speech of adults has received considerable attention from linguists. However, almost nothing of consequence is known of how children acquire and develop the sociolinguistic skills and patterns of sociolinguistic variability which have been observed and reported for adult speakers.

It is important that these sociolinguistic skills and their acquisition by children should be studied. Firstly such studies can contribute to our understanding of the nature of linguistic variability and of the change of variable systems through time. Secondly such studies are crucial to our knowledge and understanding of the relationships between language, socialization and social behaviour. In addition we require such studies to be able to assess the extent to which children can be considered as constituting a speech community in their own right.

If children are to become competent speakers of their language it is obvious that they must acquire mastery not only of linguistic form and structure, but also of the rules for the appropriate use of that form and structure. They need to become sociolinguistically competent. They need to learn how and when to use which particular variety of their language and to be able to interpret other speakers' use of different varieties of their language; they must learn how to handle competently linguistic variability.

This paper will explore the structure and functioning of linguistic variability in children's speech by focusing on some aspects of non-segmental phonological variation in the speech of a small number of children.

Structure and functioning of non-segmental variability

The importance of non-segmental variability to speakers and hearers in interaction has been well documented. A speaker can use variations in the distribution of non-segmental features to communicate to a hearer his attitudes (Pike 1945; Uldall 1964), to draw a hearer's attention to those stretches of an utterance to which the speaker ascribes particular informational importance (Halliday 1967; Hultzen 1959), and to delimit the syntactic interpretation of an utterance (Crystal 1969; Halliday 1967; Stockwell 1960). Consequently a speaker can marshall the variable resources of non-segmental phonology to frame his utterances (cf. Goffman 1975). That is, prosodic and paralinguistic features can be used to indicate which of a range of speech acts is intended by a speaker at a given point in an interaction; these features encode much of the illocutionary force of utterances (Searle 1969). Non-segmental features thus assist the hearer to recover, in part, speaker intent.

If children are to become sociolinguistically competent it is important that they learn such framing functions of non-segmental systems in order that they may appropriately project their intentions and adequately interpret the intentions of others. Children must thus acquire control over at least one kind of variability exhibited by non-segmental systems—control over what we may call *variability of domain* (cf. Pellowe and Jones 1978). *Variability of domain* refers in a straight-forward way to the location and extent of non-segmental features with respect to other co-occurring (segmental, lexical, syntactic) features of speech. For example, a speaker can choose to produce a tone unit of one word, one clause, or a number of clauses. He may decide that a loudness feature will have as its domain one syllable or twelve syllables. The choices that a speaker makes in the organization of such variability allows him to project the kinds of linguistic, social and affective 'information' referred to above.

As well as exhibiting variability in terms of the domains of realization, non-segmental systems also vary *lectally*. There is a growing literature which indicates clearly that non-segmental systems exhibit regional and social variation which parallels that documented for segmental systems, lexis and syntax. Different varieties (of English, certainly) may, for instance, vary in respect of their inventories of nuclear tone (tone types and relative tone frequencies) and in respect of the co-occurrence of particular non-segmental features with each other and with other levels of linguistic structure (Knowles 1974; Pellowe and Jones 1978; Vanderslice and Pierson 1967; Jarman and Cruttenden 1976). This paper will be concerned with an examination of this latter kind of non-segmental variability (lectal variability) in the speech of children.

I will present and discuss the frequencies and co-occurrence distributions of some of the prosodic features in the speech of a number of children. The emphasis will be on the determination of systems and structure of non-segmental lectal variability in the children's speech *without* primary reference to linguistic function.

As I will show, analysis of the speech data from the children in such terms indicates that it is possible to determine some significant patterns of non-segmental (lectal) variability in their speech. The burden of this paper is exploratory rather than definitive. (Many of the procedures and assumptions rehearsed in this paper derive directly from the work of the Tyneside Linguistic Survey (for details see Pellowe, Nixon, Strang and McNeany 1972).)

Data base; characteristics of speech samples

The primary data which will be discussed here consist of selected episodes of connected speech from six Tyneside children. These episodes were abstracted from a larger corpus collected over the period of about one year. The episodes are all taken from tape-recordings in naturalistic settings in the children's homes.

The episodes were selected from the longer recordings in an attempt to establish comparability across a similar range of interactive situations and a variety of interactants as well as to be representative of the speech of the children.

The episodes chosen for the present purposes of analysis were similar in the following respects: (i) interactant involved—adults, siblings, peers; (ii) settings involved—living-room of child's home, bathroom, child's bedroom. At each of the 'stages' discussed below every effort was

Table 1

Claire	(stage 1)	5.0 yrs	960 Tone Units; mean words per TU 2.3
	(stage 1a)	5.3 yrs	981 TU's; mean words per TU 2.3
	(stage 2)	5.6 yrs	1002 TU's; mean words per TU 2.5
	(stage 2a)	5.8 yrs	1023 TU's; mean words per TU 3.0
	(stage 3)	5.10yrs	993 TU's; mean words per TU 3.0
Angela	(stage 1)	4.11 yrs	897 TU's; mean words per TU 2.0
	(stage 1a)	5.2 yrs	966 TU's; mean words per TU 2.4
	(stage 2)	5.5 yrs	985 TU's; mean words per TU 2.3
	(stage 2a)	5.7 yrs	764 TU's; mean words per TU 2.8
	(stage 3)	5.9 yrs	911 TU's; mean words per TU 2.8
Cath	(stage 1)	4.7 yrs	886 TU's; mean words per TU 2.0
	(stage 1a)	4.10 yrs	1011 TU's; mean words per TU 2.4
	(stage 2)	5.0 yrs	892 TU's; mean words per TU 2.4
	(stage 3)	5.7 yrs	925 TU's; mean words per TU 2.9
Paul	(stage 1)	4.9 yrs	952 TU's; mean words per TU 2.1
	(stage 1a)	5.0 yrs	831 TU's; mean words per TU 2.4
	(stage 2)	5.2 yrs	1061 TU's; mean words per TU 2.3
	(stage 2a)	5.4 yrs	767 TU's; mean words per TU 2.8
	(stage 3)	5.6 yrs	1056 TU's; mean words per TU 2.8
Peter	(stage 1)	5.0 yrs	926 TU's; mean words per TU 2.5
	(stage 1a)	5.2 yrs	703 TU's; mean words per TU 2.5
	(stage 2)	5.4 yrs	901 TU's; mean words per TU 2.5
	(stage 2a)	5.6 yrs	958 TU's; mean words per TU 2.8
	(stage 3)	5.8 yrs	887 TU's; mean words per TU 3.1
James	(stage 1)	5.1 yrs	890 TU's; mean words per TU 2.4
	(stage 1a)	5.3 yrs	1020 TU's; mean words per TU 2.3
	(stage 1b)	5.5 yrs	7787 TU's; mean words per TU 2.6
	(stage 2)	5.7 yrs	853 TU's; mean words per TU 2.9

made to analyse roughly equal amounts of data involving the full range of interactants and variety of settings just outlined. The samples at each stage are composed of approximately equal proportions of talk to parents, to other adults (including investigator), to siblings and peers. All the six children had been born and had lived continuously in the Tyneside area. Details of the six children speakers and some characteristics of the speech samples are given in Table 1. The label 'stage' is used here for convenience of identification only and carries no theoretical weight in this exposition. The stages indicated by digits alone were the first samples to be selected from the total corpus of each child's speech to represent three roughly spaced intervals during the recording period. Those stages designated with digits and letters were later drawn from the corpus to fill out intermediate periods of the child's language development and to check on the directionality of some of the changes which were observed during the analysis of the initial stages.

Analysis of non-segmental features

The system of analysis of non-segmental (intonational) features employed in this paper derives from that devised by Crystal (Crystal and Quirk 1964; Crystal 1969). The essence of this system is that it treats prosodic features as being organized into independent, but interacting systems.

Although the samples of the children's speech were transcribed and analysed in terms of the full range of prosodic and paralinguistic features discussed in Crystal (1969), I shall only be concerned here with an examination of the system of nuclear tone (but see Local 1978; Local, forthcoming).

The system of nuclear tone analysed here is represented by the following basic terms: fall, rise, level, fall-rise, rise-fall, fall plus rise, rise plus fall. Nuclear tones are viewed as kinetic pitch glides/jumps or sustentions (e.g. level tone). Everything else which differs in terms of pitch height may be described by reference to a system of 'pitch-range'.

Structure of non-segmental variation. Variable structure in tonic frequencies. Changes in tonic frequencies through time

In order that the structure of non-segmental variation in the children's speech be clearly understood, we begin by characterizing some of the more important differences between the frequency distributions of nuclear tones in localized Tyneside and non-localized (adult) speech.

Pellowe (1970) and Pellowe and Jones (1978) showed that it is possible to distinguish between variant intonational systems in terms of the gross percentage distribution of particular tone types. Figure 1 pictures such

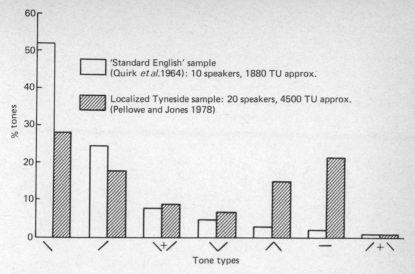

Figure 1: Gross percentage distribution of tones for two samples (adults)

differences and shows the gross percentage distribution of each tone in two samples. Plotted against the frequencies for Quirk *et al*'s (1964) sample are the mean values for the (randomly drawn) Tyneside sample discussed by Pellowe and Jones. This figure reveals that there are considerable differences in the relative frequencies of falls, rise-falls and levels between the two samples. These differences can be regarded as being diagnostic of lectal differences which discriminate between the two types of speech variety.

Figure 2 presents similar gross percentage frequency distributions for the nuclear tones for four samples: the Quirk sample (SA = 'standard speaking' adults); mean values for the sample of six non-localized children (SC = 'standard speaking' children) at the latest stage sampled; mean values for a sample of six localized Tyneside children (TC) at the latest stage sampled; and for the Pellowe and Jones sample (TA = 'Tyneside adults'). The non-segmental transcriptions of the children's speech were all checked and validated by at least one other linguist. Only unambiguously agreed transcriptions are admitted for quantification. A number of points obtrude:

1. There are clear similarities between the non-localized adults and the non-localized children. T-tests performed on these samples indicate that significant differences ($p < 0.001$) are only to be located in the relative proportions of rise plus fall, and fall plus rise tones in the two samples.
2. There are clear similarities between the localized Tyneside adults and localized Tyneside children. T-tests performed on these samples

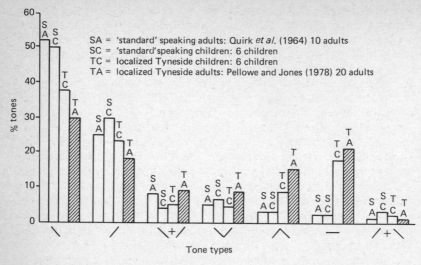

Figure 2: Gross percentage distribution of tones for four samples (adults and children)

reveal that significant differences (p < 0.001) are to be located only in the relative proportions of fall plus rise and rise-fall tones in the two samples. (In addition there is a significant difference (p = .028) between the frequency of rise plus fall tones in the two samples).

3. There are obvious differences between the non-localized and localized Tyneside children in terms of the relative tonic frequencies. T-tests reveal that there are highly significant (p < 0.0001) differences in the relative fractions of falls, rises and levels, levels and rise-fall tones in the two samples.

It is important to note that the differences between the SC and TC samples are not simply to be located in the differences between *absolute* frequencies of particular tones, but also in the ratio of one tone to another. We find, for instance, that there is a significant difference between the SC and TC samples (and also between the SA and TA samples) which can be expressed in terms of the percentage difference between falls and rises in the samples. The Tyneside samples (both children and adults) have a significantly smaller percentage difference between falls and rises than do the S samples (adults p < 0.0001; children p < 0.001). (All samples show a greater frequency of falls than rises.)

These differences and similarities between the children and adult samples provide substantial evidence that the localized and non-localized children are acquiring rather different variant intonational systems.

It is not at all clear what the differences between the respective child and adult samples mean, apart from the fact that they indicate that the children have not yet achieved completely adult-like intonational systems. It is worth noting, however that these differences are to be located in that part of the system of nuclear tone which Crystal (1969) designates 'complex' and 'compound' tone. This may well reflect something about the children's acquisition of particular grammatical constructions and semantic contrasts and the relative frequency of particular syntactic structures in their speech. This issue is further complicated for the localized Tyneside children, however. As will become clear although the proportions of tones in their speech at this latest stage resemble the adult system, the actual *frequency* of particular tones in the speech of individual children is rather different from that of the adults. Before considering in detail the implications of these differences and similarities, it is worth pointing out that although the individual members of each sample show (often considerable) differences of tonic distribution (cf. Table 2 for such details for the Tyneside children), these differences are *not* random.

I turn now to a detailed examination of the significance of some of these differences in tonic frequency in the speech of the Tyneside children. Table 2 presents, in quantified form, the changes which were observed in the relative frequencies of nuclear tone in the Tyneside children's speech over the period studied. From these figures we can identify a number of general trends:

1. The most important changes take place in the relative frequencies of falls, rises, and level tones in the children's speech. (The changes which take place in the frequencies of these tones between the first and third stages sampled, for all the children except James, are highly significant ($p < 0.001$).)
2. For all the children there is a decrease in the frequency of nuclear falls in their speech throughout the period studied.
3. For all the children there is an increase in the frequency of nuclear levels in their speech throughout the period studied.

However, although it is possible to identify these general patterns of change, it is equally clear that the rates of change in relative frequencies of particular tones are not the same for all children, nor are the relationships between tones, or between the rate of change of particular tones.

I will explore the significance of the interactions of various tonic frequencies below, but first it is necessary to deal with one possible objection to the claim that these changes represent movements towards the acquisition of variant localized intonation systems.

One possible explanation for the changes in tonic frequencies presented in Table 2 could be that they are conditioned by changes in the co-occurrent syntactic structures used by the children. It could be argued, for instance, that the increase in rising tones as a proportion of

Table 2: Gross percentage distribution of tones during stages sampled

		\	/	—	∧	/+\	\+/	∨	Miscel-laneous
Claire:	(1)	53	25	5	6	5	3	2	1
	(1a)	50	29	7					
	(2)	48	19	11	7	6	4	4	1
	(2a)	39	35	11					
	(3)	31	39	12	4	2	5	6	1
Angela:	(1)	49	31	6	4	3	2	4	1
	(1a)	40	35	6					
	(2)	37	38	8	5	2	4	5	1
	(2a)	37	40	9					
	(3)	29	41	11	7	1	5	5	1
Cath:	(1)	51	30	8	4	3	2	1	1
	(1a)	44	34	7					
	(2)	42	39	8	4	1	2	3	1
	(3)	57	21	4	5	2	4	5	2
Paul:	(1)	55	25	5	7	5	1	1	1
	(1a)	54	23	6					
	(2)	48	12	15	10	8	3	2	2
	(2a)	44	12	25					
	(3)	35	13	26	9	3	6	5	3
Peter:	(1)	48	24	9	8	5	3	2	1
	(1a)	43	24	10					
	(2)	42	22	13	10	4	5	3	1
	(2a)	38	19	17					
	(3)	39	15	21	11	2	6	5	1
James:	(1)	36	19	25	9	3	3	3	2
	(1a)	35	19	26					
	(1b)	35	18	24					
	(2)	34	16	28	12	2	4	3	1

all other tones in the girls' speech was a direct consequence of an increase in, say, the frequency of a particular kind of interrogative structure. However statistical tests do not reveal significant changes in frequency for four major classes of sentence-type (declarative, imperative, yes/no and tag, wh/other question) in the Tyneside children's speech during the main stages sampled.

In fact, use of declarative structures as questions in interaction does not appear to be a strategy employed by these children. I was only able to identify eight possible occurrences of declarative structures intonationally marked and used as questions in the Tyneside children's speech. Five of these occurred in the speech of Catherine at stage 3 (as I will show below there are good reasons for considering this sample of Catherine's speech to be atypical as part of a sample of localized Tyneside speech). Two possible instances (one with level tone) occurred in the speech of Paul at stage 2. One possible instance (with rise tone) occurred in the speech of Claire at stage 2. By comparison, at the latest stage recorded for the non-localized children there were 26 unambiguous examples of declarative structure realized with a nuclear rise which functioned as questions. This difference is almost certainly a consequence of the rather different status of nuclear rising tone in localized Tyneside and non-localized speech (see further below).

It is necessary to emphasize, moreover, that it does not appear to be the case that this redistribution represents a change in the uses to which particular structures are being put. It is not the case, for instance, that the statements which for the girls are increasingly realized with rises, fulfill the function of questions (i.e. this redistribution is not a consequence of 'speech act' differences in the children's speech). The redistribution is one consequence of the children's acquisition of localized intonational systems.

Figures 3 to 5 explore pictorially the interactions and changing dependencies between the three major classes of tone (fall, rise, level) in the speech of the six Tyneside children.

These figures reveal something of the various courses which the children take to arrive at what resemble the adult-like localized Tyneside varieties pictured by Pellowe and Jones (1978). We can briefly characterize the intonation varieties of these children (and those of a further 12 localized Tyneside children (see Local 1979)) at the latest stage sampled as follows. There are three patterns of frequency distribution (children discussed in this paper are asterisked):

1. Pattern 1: more falls than rises and more levels than rises (Paul,* Peter,* James,* Colin, Robert, Allan)
2. Pattern 2: more falls than rises and more rises than levels (Keith, Derek, Cath,* Eunice, Kate, Judith) (N.B. Cath has many more falls than any of the other children in this group, and considerably fewer levels).
3. Pattern 3: more rises than falls and more rises than levels (Claire,* Angela,* Sheila, Janice, Elaine, Anne).

I presented evidence earlier which showed that the relationship obtaining between the frequency of falling and rising tones might serve to differentiate localized (Tyneside) intonational varieties from non-localized ones. However, on the basis of the patterns of tonic frequency just outlined, it is evident that the relative frequency of falls and rises is also varying significantly *within* localized Tyneside varieties. The most obvious correlate of this 'internal' variation would seem to be the sex of the child-speaker. That is, varieties in which rises are more frequent than falls and levels are realized by girls (Pattern 3). Varieties in which falls are more frequent than rises and levels are also more frequent than rises are realized by boys (Pattern 1). Varieties of the Pattern 2 type are ambiguous in this respect, being realized by both boys and girls. However, there is a trend for the proportion of rises in those varieties of Pattern 2 which are realized by girls to be higher than in the equivalent boy varieties of this pattern. Pellowe and Jones (1978) also found that

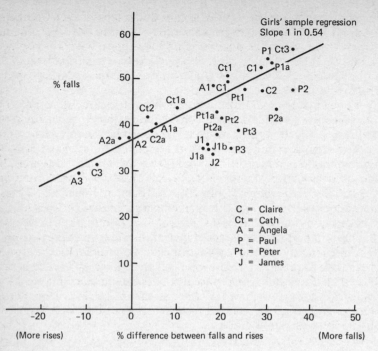

Figure 3a: Plot of %\ on % difference \,/

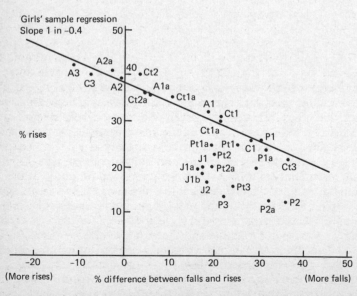

Figure 3b: Plot of %/ on % difference \,/

the percentage difference between falls and rises for adult speakers of localized Tyneside speakers was sex-differentiating. Men were found to have high values on the dimension and women to have low (including negative) ones. The present findings offer confirmation of the sociolinguistic relevance of such non-segmental relationships for Tynesiders.

The various configurations of relationship between falling and rising tones warrants further detailed consideration. To do this I begin with Figures 3a and b, and investigate the dependencies between varying rates of change in falls and rises in the children's speech. These two figures plot the percentage difference between falls and rises against falls and rises respectively. The figures reveal a number of important facts about the relationship of these two tones in localized Tyneside intonational varieties. First, the percentage difference between falls and rises decreases for all children as they get older (Cath 3 is an exception to this and will be discussed later). It is clear, however, that the reasons for this directionality and the rates of decrease are different for the boys and girls taken as groups. For the girls the percentage difference between falls and rises decreases as a consequence of falling tones decreasing and rising tones increasing. For the boys, on the other hand, the narrowing percentage difference is a result of *both* classes of tone-type decreasing, but at different rates.

Second we see that for the girls in the sample there is a very marked dependency between the decreasing frequency of falls in their speech and the ascendency of rising tones as they get older. This trend of association for the girls shows very little deviation from linearity (for falls against percentage difference falls, rises Pearson's $R = 0.96$, significance $p < 0.001$. For rises against the same dimension, Pearson's $R = 0.95$, significance $p < 0.001$). The rank order of the various 'stages' plotted for the girls on y (percentage falls) in Figure 3a is remarkably well-preserved on y (percentage rises) in Figure 3b for Angela and Cath. However, for Claire there are certain rank-order displacements. These are a result of the somewhat anomalous relationship between stages 1a and 2, and 2 and 2a in Claire's speech. Whereas between stages 1 and 1a rises increase (as do levels) and falls decrease, at stage 2 we see that there is a sudden dramatic decrease in the frequency of rises in her speech, although levels keep increasing and falls decreasing slightly. The apparent anomalousness of this tonic patterning (in terms of the girls' sample as a whole) may be explicable in terms of Claire's non-linguistic behaviour at this time. At the time this sample of speech was recorded, Claire was reported (by her parents) to be becoming 'a proper tom-boy' in terms of both her interests and the group of children she associated with. It may well be then that this adjustment of tonic frequencies is a reflection of some kind of network 'convergence' (cf. Milroy and Margrain 1978). For Angela and Cath there is a fairly direct interaction between falls and rises throughout the whole period studied, whereas this interaction for Claire obtains only between stages 1 and 1a, and 2a and 3.

We should note that for some of the other girls studied, but not reported here in detail (Janice, Kate, Anne) rises increase in their speech (a) without falls decreasing significantly or (b) at a faster rate than falls decrease: It seems highly likely that these children are using their increased number of rises to fill out the functions of level tone—they have relatively low percentages of level tone in their speech for localized Tyneside varieties. This relationship may also be true for some of the interstages plotted for Claire, Angela, and Cath. The dependencies between falls and rises which are apparent for the girls do not hold for the boys. The decreasing frequency of rises *does not* co-vary significantly with the decreasing frequency of falls in their speech. This points to a difference in the functional relationship between the two tones in the girls' speech and that in the boys' speech. The relationship obtaining between the acquisition of rises and loss of falling tones in the girls' speech, however, is not a simple one. Consideration of Figures 3a and b shows that the rate of decrease of falls is somewhat faster than the rate of increase of rises in their speech. Thus while it seems clear that rises are taking over some of the distribution of falling tones, it cannot be the case that falls are being entirely replaced by rises. (A look forward to Figures 4a and b suggests that level tone may also be interacting importantly with falling tone in this respect.) In addition it is worth pointing out that the relationship between the gross percentage of falls and rises in the children's speech co-varies with localized realizations at the segmental level. Among the girls those with the lowest (and negative) values on this dimension exhibit the most localized realizations—similarly with the boys. It is not the case, however, that the children with the lowest absolute value on this dimension have the most localized segmental realizations. (All my efforts to locate co-variation between localized segmental variants and indices of socioeconomic class were remarkably unsuccessful.)

Figures 3a and b clarify some of the changing relationships between falling and rising tones in the speech of the girls under consideration. However, if we are to understand the relationship existing between these two tone types in the boys' speech it is necessary to turn attention to the third most frequent tone in the system: level tone. To do this I plot, in Figures 4 and 5, the relative fractions of falls, rises and levels against the percentage difference between levels and falls (Figure 4) and the percentage difference between rises and levels (Figure 5).

These plots give some indication of the important status of level tone in localized Tyneside varieties of English. Pellowe and Jones (1977: 21–2) comment on the characteristics of level tone in adult varieties of Tyneside English:

A very complex perturbation of the tonic system is caused by the formal-functional distinctiveness of level tone in Tyneside varieties compared with level tone in non-localized varieties. . . . In some varieties, the distribution [of level tone] is equivalent to non-localized levels. In some varieties part of the distribution is equivalent to non-localized levels, part to localized rises. In some varieties part of the distribution is equivalent to non-localized levels, part to localized falls. In some varieties parts of the distribution are equivalent to all three (non-localized levels, localized falls, localized rise).

As consideration of Figures 4 and 5 shows, there is good reason to believe that the claims made by Pellowe and Jones for adult varieties are also true for the children's varieties under discussion here.

The first of these plots indicates that for all the children in the sample there is a strong interrelationship existing between the changing fractions of falls and level tones in their speech. (The difference between falls and levels decreases for all the children as they get older (Cath Stage 3 is again an exception).) Significantly we see here that the rates of acquisition of level tone relative to the loss of falls (see also Figure 4b) are different for the boys and girls. Girls lose falls (slope 0.8) faster than they acquire level tone (slope − 0.2). (This offers confirming evidence of the functional omnivorousness of rises in their speech with respect to falls.) The reverse is the case for the boys: they acquire levels (slope 0.54) somewhat faster than they lose falls (slope 0.45). From this we may conclude that there is a rather different relationship obtaining between falls and levels in their speech. That is, levels are not only replacing falls (given the good preservation of rank order on the two independent axes in Figures 4a and b) but are also likely to be acquiring some of the functional distribution of other tones. (For further confirmation of this see Figure 5b.) This relationship between loss of falls and acquisition of levels also holds true of other boys studied (Colin, Robert, Allan).

If we consider the changes in rises plotted against the changing frequencies of falls and levels in the children's speech (not pictured here) we find two markedly different (maximally sex-differentiating) trends. We find (a) boys' varieties where the ascendency of levels over falls co-varies with a decrease in the frequency of rises and (b) the converse for girls (note that the slopes for these two trends are not the same. Girls acquire rises relative to the fractions of falls and levels faster than the boys lose rises). This is a further indication that rise tone has rather different functional and distributional properties in these varieties and that the relationships which nuclear rises contract with other tones yield potential indexical information concerning the sex of the speaker.

Further details of the varying relationships between falls, rises and levels in the speech of these children can be achieved by an examination of Figures 5a and b and a comparison of these figures with Figures 3 and 4. Figures 5a and b plot the changing relationships between rises and levels in the children's speech. These plots add strength to the claims I have been making concerning the rather different status of rise and level tones in the different localized sub-varieties represented here. The most

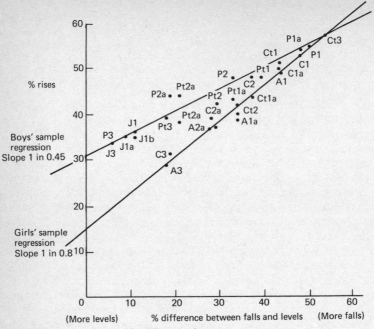

Figure 4a: Plot of %\ on % difference \,—

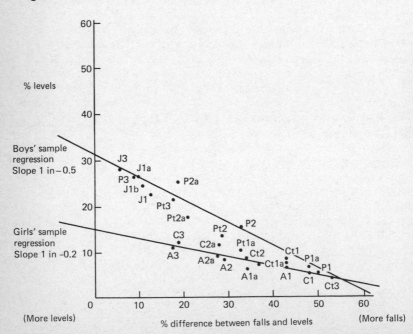

Figure 4b: Plot of %— on % difference \,—

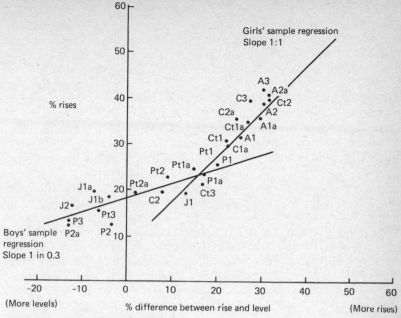

Figure 5a: Plot of %/ on % difference /,—

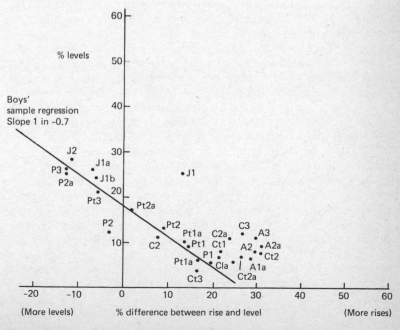

Figure 5b: Plot of %— on % difference /,—

obvious feature highlighted here is the competing trends which are indices of the sex-differentiated varieties. We see (a) those varieties realized by boys in which the percentage difference between rises and levels progressively narrows as they get older and (b) those varieties realized by the girls in which the trend is for the percentage difference between rises and levels to increase. Figure 5a emphasizes the sex-differentiating aspect of these intonational varieties. For the boys a unit decrease in the use of falls in their speech leads to the ascendency of levels over rises by 0.5, whereas for the girls a unit decrease in the use of falls leads to the ascendency of rises over levels by 0.8. These relationships are strongly linear and highly significant ($p < 0.001$ in both cases).

Comparison of Figures 5a and b adds further credence to the claim that levels in the boys' speech take over some of the distributional characteristics of rise tones. There is a highly significant linear relationship between the decreasing percentage difference between rise and level tones in their speech and the increase in level tones. (Again the rank ordering of the stages sampled is well preserved on the independent axes of the graphs.) The interaction between these two tones is not simple, however. There is an asymmetry between the speed of loss of rises in the boys' speech (relative to levels) (slope 0.3) and the speed of acquisition of levels (relative to rises) (slope 0.7). Clearly boys are acquiring levels twice as fast as they are losing rises. Given the above discussion 4–5, it is quite clear that the increase in level tones interacts significantly with the decrease in falls and the decrease in rises. In both cases the rate of acquisition of levels for the boys (as a group) is faster than the loss of these two classes of tone.

Figures 5a and b picture an apparently contradictory state of affairs for relationships in the girls' varieties. Figure 5a shows that there exists a marked linear relationship between rises and the changing relationship between rises and levels (a unit increase in the use of rises results in rises gaining over levels by 1). However, when we examine 5b there is no clear sample regression which would lead us to conclude that levels are determining these tonic relationships. Explanation lies, I think, in the ambiguous status of level tone in the girls' speech. As we have seen rises increase steadily and significantly with respect to all other tones. Levels also increase, though at a much slower rate. I have argued that the larger proportion of these increased rises are filling out the depleted number of falls in the girls' speech. At the same time some of the increased number of levels would seem to be also filling out the distribution of decreasing falls. (This is confirmed by a cursory analysis of the transcripts.) Thus we can argue that lack of sample regression is due to the differing kinds of individual variation (in terms of the roles of rises and levels) exhibited by the children. Close inspection of the relative locations of the *interstages* for the girls plotted in Figure 5b suggests that there may be some stages where increased rises are being used to 'take up the slack' on levels, as well as doing the same for falls. (For example Claire 2–2a; Angela 1–1a; Cath 1a–2.) This is evidenced by the relatively horizontal movement along the plot as they get older. Such facts as these are important in establishing the variable structure of intonational varieties.

So far, in my discussion of Figures 3 to 5, I have been using the directionality and rates of change in tonic frequencies to argue for exchange/replacements relationship between tones in the children's speech. An important feature of these arguments has been the extent to which rank ordering of the stages with respect to the loss or acquisition of one tone was well preserved for the loss or acquisition of another tone. I have shown that for most of the children the directionality and rank order of changing follows roughly similar patterns (I have already indicated some of Claire's stages as exceptions). There is one major exception to these similar trends. In all respects the sample of Cath's speech at stage 3 is wayward in terms of the girls' sample as a whole, and in terms of the early stages plotted for Cath. Up to stage 2 she appears to be acquiring an intonational system (at least in terms of the three major tone classes) which closely resembles that of Claire and Angela. At stage 3, however, there are a number of marked reversals in the trends established by the earlier stages:

1 falls increase
2 rises decrease
3 levels decrease

These reversals are clearly anomalous for Cath (a) as a child acquiring a localized Tyneside intonational variety, and (b) as a Tyneside *girl*. (We should note that the changes observed for Claire stage 2, though odd in some respects, still bear the marks of a localized variety—though the frequency of falls remain high and the frequency of rises drops sharply, the relative frequency of level tones is high (as compared, say, to Cath at stage 3).)

The most plausible explanation to account for these reversals, I think, is to be located in the fact that this sample of speech was recorded some six months after Cath's family had moved from Tyneside to the south of England (Surrey). The relative fractions of falls, rises and levels for Cath at stage 3 are remarkably similar to those pictured for the six non-localized children (Figure 2). We can argue convincingly that the changes in tonic frequency exhibited by Cath at this stage reflect the importance of change of region to Cath as a hearer-speaker. Presumably the family's move from Tyneside, and Cath's mixing with a new peer group having other-localized and/non-localized intonation varieties has exerted considerable influence on the characteristics of her non-segmental realizations. (There are, not unexpectedly, some other changes in Cath's speech when this sample is compared with earlier ones. Very obvious changes occur at the segmental level—most noticeably in the realization of vowels.)

In all the cases discussed the children seem to move from a 'simple' system to a more 'complex' one, Initially falls and rises achieve a considerable amount of work, but gradually the tonal inventory is extended and the functional weight of these tones is redistributed across other tones. (I have, however, heard young (3 to 5 years old) localized Tyneside speakers whose intonational systems did not seem to be so heavily dependent on falls and rises as the children considered here. Clearly more investigation of these changing varieties is required before we can establish their status in the course of the children's language acquisition.)

Conclusion

I have outlined some simple first steps towards the modelling of lectal intonational variability in children's speech. The methods discussed here give us access to a means of monitoring change through time of intonational systems. By examining a number of overlapping representations of tonic frequency distributions it has proved possible to establish significant patterns of variation in the non-segmental systems of a number of children. We have been able to show patterns of development towards localized intonational systems and to indicate some important 'non-linguistic' co-variates of intonational structure. Not all non-segmental dimensions show the same kind of social patterning as do tonic distributions. Differences in mean tone unit length, for instance, do not co-vary with differences between localized and non-localized varieties. They do however show significant relationships with the age of the speaker and with the nature of the talk (see Local 1978).

The patterns of variation revealed for these localized Tyneside children have also been shown to converge on those discussed for localized Tyneside adults by Pellowe and Jones (1978). Some of the relationships discovered between nuclear tones have offered clear evidence that we should not expect intonational varieties to be discrete. Indeed I suspect that such overlapping (Wittgensteinian) similarity between dimensions of linguistic variation is more common than variationists' accounts would suggest. While we can distinguish between varieties with patterns of tonic frequency such as types 1 and 3 (page 93) in non-gradient terms, in varieties where the tonic frequency patterns are similar (Pattern 2 types) distinctions must necessarily be probabilistic. Throughout this paper I have been discussing tone types and tonic distributions relatively independently of their functional properties. It is possible that some investigators might accuse me of ignoring the functions of intonational categories. In fact, it seems to me that the arguments I have been pursuing and the methods of modelling intonational variability I have presented are a crucial first step towards being able to say anything sensible about the functional potential of particular intonational contrasts. It is not possible to delimit (in anything other than an *ad hoc* way) the functions of particular (co-occurrences of) intonational features in a given variety until we have information concerning the distribution and status of those features within those varieties. Intonational 'functions' are achieved primarily by the manipulation of *realizational* variability. However, realizational variability operates against the backcloth of lectal variability. Therefore, we must first determine the structural/distributional characteristics of lectal variability before we can identify the ways in which realizational variability can project 'functions'.

7

An appraisal of the statistical techniques used in the Sociolinguistic Survey of Multilingual Communities

Damian McEntegart and R. B. Le Page

Stage I (Belize) and Stage II (St Lucia)

Summary

McEntegart has worked for the past year checking and evaluating the statistical methods used in the survey, performing his own statistical analyses, and discussing at each stage with Le Page the extent to which they succeeded in modelling or failed to model the hypothesis and riders on which the survey was based. Our purpose here is to give an honest report of the outcome of that appraisal, reporting defects and failures as fully as space permits for the benefit of future research in socio-linguistics. We try to assess the effectiveness of the fieldwork in relation to the quantification of variables, and the usefulness of cluster analysis as a means of studying linguistic focusing and diffusion (as defined in Le Page 1978). We present illustrative results of the statistical analysis, keeping technical terms to a minimum so as to make the problems as generally accessible as possible. For full details and technical treatment we refer to McEntegart (1980).

Outline of the hypothesis, riders and working methods

(see Le Page 1968, 1972, Le Page *et al.* 1974; Le Page 1978; Tabouret-Keller and Le Page 1971)

The hypothesis is that each individual creates for himself patterns of linguistic behaviour so as to resemble those of the group or groups with which from time to time he wishes to be identified (or so as to distance himself from those with which he does not wish to be identified). He is able to do this only to the extent that

(a) he can identify the groups
(b) he has sufficient access to them and the capacity to analyse their systems
(c) his motivation is positive or negative, taking into account the feedback he receives from them of the chances of his being allowed to join them
(d) he is still able to modify his behaviour (e.g. not too old)

A population of children was chosen in each of the territories, straddling the age of puberty. Samples of more formal and less formal speech and of reading were elicited from each. The homes of the children, and the members of the household, were assessed for various non-linguistic (e.g. demographic, cultural, political, economic, religious, geographical) factors. The incidence of a small number of linguistic features, each thought from a pilot survey to be socially marked (i.e. as particularly associated with one or other group in the community) was then quantified in the more formal and less formal speech of each child. Attempts were made to cluster the children according to similarities in their behaviour as determined by these quantities. Membership of such clusters or groups was then tested for its degree of association with the various cultural and socioeconomic indices of the families.

Selection of populations and sampling

Cayo District, Belize and the Eastern Caribbean island of St Lucia were selected in turn because they are post-colonial communities in a state of flux, in search of new identities and new social structures. Cayo District seemed particularly suitable because a new road, running parallel with the Belize River, and linking Spanish-speaking Benque Viejo with Creole-speaking Belize City, had opened up new territory into which people migrated from either end and from the Amerindian lands on either side. St Lucia was chosen partly because of the conservative nature of the French Creole-speaking communities in its relatively inaccessible mountainous interior as contrasted with the port and capital of Castries.

The sampling procedure in Belize was simply to select every fourth child on the school rolls between the ages of 10 and 17 from every school in Cayo District; since school attendance is compulsory, each element in the child population had a known, non-zero, probability of selection. The procedure in St Lucia was less satisfactory since the sample was not random; the best, the worst and a medium-standard school (as classified by the Education Authority) were selected to represent the schools in the capital, in addition to the rural schools of the northern end of the island and one school in the centre felt to represent the East Indian immigrant population. Given this nonrandom sample the population about which inferences could be drawn was not, in St Lucia, clearly defined, as it was in Belize. A problem in both territories was caused by children who for one reason or another did not respond at all or did not provide much speech-data. In Belize this was true of a rather high proportion of the secondary school children, since an unforeseen early end to the term caused them to disperse. In St Lucia difficulties of this kind were anticipated and 150 children included in the initial sample with a view to collecting good data in relation to 100; in Belize there were 280 in the initial sample, but we were never able to use data from more than 200. We cannot be sure of the extent to which these 200 are representative of the 280; it may be, for example, that those who disliked being included in the survey or did not respond well—for example, because they as 'Spanish' children reacted unfavourably to a Jamaican fieldworker (Dr Christie)—formed a high proportion of the absentees. Although efforts were made to make them so, we cannot be sure in St Lucia either how representative the 100 were.

The decision to avoid the procedure followed by Labov (1966, 1972a), Trudgill (1974b) and G. Sankoff (1974), of dividing the population according to pre-established socio-economic categories and then sampling each category, was taken for several reasons. In the first place, such a procedure precludes discovering anything about the emergent social structure other than in terms of these 'imported' and pre-set categories; in the second place, we did not feel we knew enough about the cultural and economic and ethnic stratification of the two societies to arrange our sample in this way; in the third place, it was part of our aim to discover what social mechanisms were at work, what groups were emerging, according to the linguistic symptoms, rather than vice-versa.

Information sampling

The various kinds of information sought have been described in detail in Le Page (1978). We shall refer to the three main kinds as responses to the family questionnaire, the children's language use questionnaire, and the linguistic interview. In the first, a questionnaire was taken to the child's home and the information sought entered on it during the course of discussion with a senior member of the household, often the grandmother or mother. In the second, Dr Christie for Belize and G. Maury for St Lucia, after finishing the child's recorded conversation, story-telling and reading session, asked the child questions about its language use at school and at home, with different age and sex groups and for both jokes and serious talk. The third consisted of the child's recorded conversation, story-telling and reading. Other background information was gained in a variety of ways as described in Le Page (1978).

The design of the *family questionnaires* was less suited to consistent quantification of standard variables than to eliciting as much ethnographic and demographic information as possible. From a statistical viewpoint much of the information collected was unproductive, although it has been productive of a number of case-book studies. Standardized indices concerning e.g. economic status or general family ambitions proved very difficult to construct (see McEntegart (1980) for an attempt using principal components analysis).

The five different fieldworkers used in Belize for the family interviewing varied considerably in the responses they elicited—their own age, sex, ethnic origin and empathies entering into the outcome. The single fieldworker used in St Lucia (M. Diki-Kidiri) again had very variable success from one family to another. It may be that one should try wherever possible to train an 'insider' from the community itself, but in a multi-ethnic community even this would not resolve the problem.

There was an unsatisfactory mix of 'facts' and 'reported opinions' among the answers, although in general it was the latter the team were more interested in (see e.g. Tabouret-Keller 1976 on claims concerning ethnic origin).

The *linguistic interviews* were in each case carried out by one field-worker (P. Christie in Belize, G. Maury in St Lucia). They were designed to range from more formal to less formal topics, and to incorporate some story-telling as a major relaxing device in the middle. A reading passage closed the interview. The fieldworkers had first to surmount very considerable problems about where to record the interview; fieldwork in the tropics is usually unavoidably in noisy surroundings, and the keen curiosity of other children was also a major headache in St Lucia. It was difficult to obtain the very high-quality tapes necessary for the detailed phonological analysis intended. Again, children of different backgrounds and temperaments responded very differently to the fieldworkers. Some were tongue-tied through shyness, some were illiterate, a large proportion were quite unable or unwilling to tell a traditional Anansi story or to talk about ghosts. It is thus extremely difficult to accept the chunks of discourse on which our counts of the linguistic variables are based as truly comparable for this purpose. McEntegart has shown that there is a correlation between e.g. the number of potential loci for nasalization and the percentage incidence of nasalization among the Belize children. One quite probable explanation is that it is the Creole children who responded most readily and relaxed most easily, that their narrative discourse contained many connective 'and's' frequently reduced to [ã], and that we could not find any truly comparable sections of discourse among the non-Creole children. The potential importance of such considerations is discussed below.

The children's *language-use questionnaires* provided the most straightforward information; it is necessary to recognize that what was set down was the claim the child made to the interviewer about the language it used with older and younger generations for serious topics and for jokes, and that what was of interest to us was precisely the implications of the claim made—as also in the case of the family questionnaire. Discrepancies, for example, between the claims made by the children and those made by their elders at home about language use are themselves a source of valuable information, though not one which lends itself easily to quantification.

Some of the defects in research design and field practice were due to inexperience, some to faulty logic; some were inherent in our own background in relation to the nature of the societies we were working in. In the course of our fieldwork and analysis we have certainly learnt a great deal about each society and about language questions generally, but much of it eludes computation and must be the subject of more impressionistic reporting (supported, of course, by detailed case-histories) as in many of our publications to date. A recurring problem in computation has been, how to deal with missing values in particular cells for particular children—e.g., those who did not tell a story, or told one only in Spanish.

Transcription and quantification of linguistic data

It is now well recognized, but was not so well recognized when this survey began, that one difficulty underlying all quantitative linguistics is that of *identity* of the linguistic units to be counted. All systematic linguistics idealizes phonemes, morphemes, syntagmemes and lexemes which retain their identities when the system is manipulated for descriptive purposes. In real life, however, and particularly in contact situations, things are very different. Any lexicographer knows of the arbitrariness of many of the divisions he makes between one head-word and another; in what sense, for example, is *make* in *make the bed* the 'same word' as in *He'll never make it* (i.e. get there in time)? In a fully analytic language like Creole, and to a large extent also in English, part of speech and semantic function are only finally defined by the context of use. To what extent does one end of a diglossic system share the same tense/aspect/mood system or even the same basic divisions of predication (stative/active, inceptive/completive/progressive etc.) as the other? To what extent is the phonology of a broad spoken vernacular based on the same distinctive feature system and the same morpheme-stock as the speech of educated literates in the same society? To what extent can one say in such a society that e.g. Creole /wok/ and Standard < work > are the 'same word' and that both contain a locus for possible r-colouration? If we treat the Creole system as separate, then there is no locus here for possible r-colouration. If we treat it as part of a composite system then there may or may not be a locus depending on whether one regards the underlying system as that represented by the spelling or that represented by some external standard—e.g. r-less RP or r-coloured Standard American English. In real life all linguistic systems are systems of relativities, with no absolute external referents; and it is a methodological question which part of the poly-system (since he cannot possibly take it all) and therefore which type the linguist chooses to relate a token to on any particular occasion. Is a particular occurrence, [ˈwɒʔ], a token of underlying Creole /wok/, General English <work>, British English /wɜːk/ or American /wɝːk/?

In quantitative linguistics we are concerned with variation between *tokens of the same type*, and we try to express the incidence of form A as opposed to form B in terms of percentages of a common denominator representing the total stock of tokens of that type in the corpus. This question of identity in practice raises insuperable problems if we are using lexical types; quite difficult problems if we use syntagmatic types at sentence or clause level; less difficult ones if we use syntagmatic types at morpheme level, less difficult still if like Labov we use sub-morpheme variants, and least difficult if we use phonetic variants of 'the same phoneme'. The more common phonemes in a system are likely to recur so frequently in discourse that we will have no difficulty in having a large denominator to work with. If on the other hand we want to discover the variant terms for a teapot we have to get the informant to talk about teapots and the lexeme may occur very rarely; if we want him to use variants of past punctual we must get him to use narrative in the past tense, and so on. Moreover, all of these types are squishy; there *is* no clear dividing line in practice between past habitual and past punctual; unless the context is very very detailed: 'I worked until ten o'clock' could be either, or sometimes both. There is thus, as both Labov and Trudgill have noted, a strong practical incentive to work with phonological variables. On the other hand, to do so requires very good quality recording and very careful, tedious transcription. There is thus a strong incentive to use a small number of informants, and both Labov and Trudgill have rationalized such a proceeding. We were unable to accept the rationalization, and as a result embarked upon detailed phonetic transcription of many hours of tape. The major part of the Belize transcription was done by Pauline Christie; the next largest part by Le Page; and smaller numbers of informants were transcribed by Douglas Taylor and Kean Gibson. Pauline Christie and Kean Gibson are both 'educated West Indian' speakers; Douglas Taylor and Le Page both 'educated British English speakers'. As hearers, therefore, our perceptions differed (as was clearly demonstrated when e.g. Dr Colville Young, from Belize City, insisted that he could hear nasalized vowels where Le Page was totally unable to hear them, Young for example equating [wã] in [ˈiˈpaˈnowãˈlaiʔ miaˈgɛn] with general Belize Creole future marker /wen/, Le Page probably subconsciously fitting it into the same English syntactic slot as <will>). Although a good deal of time was spent initially by the different transcribers trying to standardize their transcriptions and the mode of counting quantified features, it is now clear, as McEntegart has suggested in his full report, that more rigorous steps should have been taken to reduce the possibility of mismatches between the different transcribers. Moreover, we in turn rationalized using too small a sample of discourse—400 words in each mode.

The selection and quantification of linguistic features

Belize

The five variables selected for Belize were reported on in Le Page (1972): r-colouration as a prestige feature associated with book-learning, its absence with broad Creole; the devoicing of final /-z/ associated with Hispanization; Creole assimilatory vowel-nasalization; and the morphological features associated with Creole past tense and noun-plurals. The linguistic interview was designed to be divided into five sections or 'modes' so that ideally we would have 25 quantities as a specification of the linguistic behaviour of each child. Unfortunately, not only were many scores missing (e.g. where a child did not tell a story) but in many more cases the scores were unreliable being percentages of too few possible loci. Rather than leave out entirely the children with missing scores, we concentrated the statistical analysis on those variables with relatively few missing or unreliable values. The story-telling mode, and the two morphological variables, were therefore left out of our multivariate analysis. Even so, we still had to omit 33 out of a total of 221 transcribed interviews, as containing too many missing scores even on the phonological variables. As these children tend to be the Spanish, Maya and Carib children we must note the consequences for the claimed randomness of the sample.

St Lucia

Because of the enormous time and effort involved in transcribing the Belize tapes for phonological variables, we tried in St Lucia to confine ourselves to morphological variables. These have been enumerated and exemplified in Le Page 1980a. They were selected because in a pilot survey they were found to be realized formally in variants associated with the speech of (a) educated people (b) Anglophone Creole (or 'Bajan'-like, i.e. Barbadian) speakers (c) French patois speakers; or in some cases with both (b) and (c). Severe problems were now encountered in the identification of possible loci (as suggested above), and whereas in Belize semantic criteria had been used (i.e. to define a *past tense* or *noun plural*), in St Lucia M. Diki-Kidiri decided to use only formal criteria for certain variables. Thus where (as reported in Le Page 1977) four forms were available for habitual constructions, each carrying a different social marking, the use of each was expressed as a percentage of the total incidence of the four, and the use of other constructions which might semantically be regarded as habitual, ignored. Some such summations were compounded of more than one feature. For example, 'correct' Standard English past punctual verbs, past habitual verbs, and third person present singular verbs, were all treated as part of one variable, 'correct verb forms', whereas we know that some 'incorrect' forms are more strongly stigmatized than others and we should have dealt with each form separately. (In this respect, the work described by Lesley Milroy in *Language and Social Networks* is of great importance.)

Jean Thomson and Damian McEntegart, successive data analysts, have however re-analysed the St Lucian data from a semantic point of view to establish the supposed loci for the possible occurrence of linguistic variants. It is this revised data which is being referred to in the work which follows for St Lucia, whereas that reported in Le Page 1980a was based on Diki-Kidiri's formal analysis, felt by Le Page to be still reasonably valid.

Internal validation of the linguistic variables

We have already mentioned that Creole children in Belize used more potential loci for nasalization than non-Creole children, as well as using more nasalized forms. This is an example of an unexpected internal correlation for which an explanation had to be sought. It appeared to lie in the greater proclivity of Creole children for extended narrative with 'and' connectives. A number of internal validation tests were carried out on the linguistic data to check their reasonableness in this way, that the variables constructed adequately reflected the hypothesized underlying concepts. Non-parametric correlations between the linguistic variables for both Belize and St Lucia were examined and the relationships in each case seemed intuitively reasonable. A further test however revealed internal correlations which, in the case of the St Lucian data, were more disturbing. In the case of Belize there were, as Table 1 shows, unexpected but significant correlations between feature loci totals and feature scores; an explanation for one of these has already been given, and similar explanations were found for the others. It became evident that one assumption on which the feature counting was based was incorrect, viz: that there could be established (as we previously thought we had established) a size of chunk of discourse within which the incidence of feature loci would be roughly the same for all the children. Beyond this, however, it did not appear that the Belize data was invalid for further analysis. The same unfortunately could not be claimed so readily for the St Lucian data. There is no space here to report in detail the extensive validation enquiry carried out by McEntegart (see McEntegart 1980)—specifically, into what caused the widely-differing incidence among the St Lucian children of various tense and aspect constructions. The most stable evidence here came from examination of the two variables whose distribution made possible the construction of the composite analysis of variance model: the forms used for the habitual present and for the past punctual. Explanatory variables comprised the set of socioeconomic variables culled from the family questionnaire and selected answers

Table 1: Spearman correlation coefficients between feature loci and feature scores for late conversation mode: Belize

% score on

	Loci counts for each child standardized by length of text transcribed for late conversation	Nasalization feature	R colouration feature	Z devoicing feature	Creole past feature	Creole plural feature
1. Nasalization		0.50	−0.31	−0.09	0.42	0.42
2. R colouration		0.02	0.12	0.02	−0.24	−0.13
3. Z devoicing		−0.31	0.44	0.09	−0.63	−0.64
4. Creole past		0.21	−0.23	−0.15	−0.02	0.00
5. Creole plural		−0.13	0.22	0.10	−0.27	−0.26

(163 cases) (163 cases) (162 cases) (111 cases) (159 cases)

Notes:
  i)   All coefficients are Spearman rank correlations.
  ii) As an example for 162 children (cases) then a sample value of 0.129 for the Spearman coefficient would cause the null hypothesis of no association between the two variables to be rejected at the 0.1 significance level for a two tailed test.
  iii) Notice that due to problem of missing values on the feature scores the coefficients are based on different numbers of children. This must be borne in mind.

from the child language use questionnaire. The classificatory analysis of the model (ANOVA) for the habitual present is given in Table 2. The table indicates that several behavioural factors, including the claimed use of English in church services, correlate with a high incidence of habitual present constructions in the child's second interview, in which a major topic was black magic. The transcriptions show that children who attended French Patois-medium church services tended to claim actual personal or family encounters with the devil or black magic, and to narrate the incident in the past tense, whereas children who went to English-medium services tended to speak of the habits of ghosts and spirits in an impersonal way, using the habitual present (textual examples are given in McEntegart 1980).

To summarize the results of this work briefly, we give just three of the many ways in which the data may lead us to classify the St Lucian children spuriously. (It must be remembered that children were allowed to go on talking on any particular topic as long as they wished. A 400-word chunk for one child might therefore cover fewer or more topics than for another child.)

Table 2: Classification analysis of ANOVA model of second interview habitual present usage[1]

Grand mean=0.68

1. Variable and category	2. No. of children	3. Unadjusted deviation from grand mean	4. Adjusted deviation from grand mean
Response to question D[2]			
1. English	16	−0.09	−0.12
2. Patois	61	0.04	0.04
3. Both English & Patois	17	−0.07	−0.04
	94[5]		
Response to question M[3]			
1. Yes	79	−0.02	−0.02
2. No	15	0.12	0.13
Response to question H[4]			
1. English	77	0.04	0.03
2. Patois 1 ⎫			
3. Both English & Patois 16 ⎭	17	−0.17	−0.13
Colour claimed			
1. None	14	−0.12	−0.13
2. Black-negro	35	0.01	0.01
3. Brown-dark	26	0.10	0.09
4. Fair-light	10	0.02	0.03
5. Shabbin-wuz-red	9	−0.15	−0.14

Notes:
1. Usage is standardized by total verb usage.
2. Question D—language children claim they use for insults.
3. Question M—'Do children ever make fun of the way people speak?'.
4. Question H—language used at church child goes to.
5. Six children are not included in the analysis due to missing values on the explanatory variables.

1. Variant selection is influenced by subject matter e.g. the discussion of school topics tends to increase the selection of standard English options, 'black magic' the selection of non-standard options. Thus differential topics between two linguistically identical children can lead to a different set of scores.

2. In the case of St Lucia the habitual present variable has proved to be the only verbal variable surviving rigorous criteria, and thus available as the input to cluster analysis; thus two linguistically identical children, one of whom spends most of the second interview talking about the general habits of ghosts in a non-standard habitual present, the other narrating an experience in the non-standard past, may be clustered differentially if 'non-standard usage' is the criterion. This example can be adapted to illustrate the general case where we are not restricted to one verbal variable.

3. Because of our 'multidimensional space' hypothesis (see Le Page *et al.* 1974) each variant of each variable is regarded as a separate, socially marked dimension; even if both of the variables in (b) are part of the input, the two children will still have different quantitities. This may not

matter for classification if the two quantities are highly correlated. However, our multidimensional model reflects the differential stigmata attached to different variants (see also L. Milroy 1980). If more stigma attaches to non-standard past punctual than to non-standard habitual present, then the variable scores will not accurately compare our two identical children: even though the influence of the topic, 'black magic', may tend to produce non-standard habitual present forms, it may not overcome the countervailing influence of the more powerful stigma attached to non-standard past punctual.

On grounds such as the above, McEntegart's confidence in the St Lucian data as an input to cluster analysis was undermined; his anticipation of lack of success when trying to relate membership of linguistic clusters to background variables was borne out.

To conclude this section: when one takes full account of the almost inevitable constraints placed on a survey in a foreign country by an 'outsider'—constraints of available money, adequate time for training and for a pilot survey, and the unpredictability of responses on the part of different children to the fieldworker—the difficulties of collecting standard and comparable samples of speech for valid statistical analysis appear very great. If one were to learn from the experience of our survey, it would be

(a) to standardize interview settings
(b) to standardize a list of topics and keep one's sample of constant length on comparable topics constraining the respondent's time on each as far as possible, or alternatively, transcribing the whole of each interview.
(c) to standardize the interviewer's lead up to each topic.

Anybody who has done fieldwork where any degree of intimacy is to be established with respondents so that information of value may be gathered will recognize that the above ideals militate strongly against those of achieving eventually a relaxed intimacy. It may well be therefore that one has to choose between statistically comparable but de-humanized 'answers' and linguistically and socially informative conversations (such as have been used in Tabouret-Keller 1980 and Le Page 1980a). A high level of statistical sophistication seems to militate against anything except rather superficial observations.

Cluster analysis: general

This is a technique intended to group data-sets (in our case, giving linguistic profiles of individual children) so that members of one cluster are more 'alike' than they are like members of another cluster. Many problems of definition arise, discussed e.g. in Everitt (1974). Kendall (1966) distinguishes between dissection and classification; the second process searches for true typologies, in which the clusters are clearly discrete, the first makes no such requirement but maps the distribution of the data-sets. Clusters inferred from such maps can be called 'administrative clusters'. We did not expect to find true typologies, clearly discrete clusters, in either Belize or St Lucia, being aware from the outset that we were dealing with societies in a state of flux (indeed, that is why they were chosen) and not with ghetto populations. On the other hand, uses such as the aim of checking membership of linguistic clusters against various socioeconomic factors to create a hierarchy of 'degrees of association' (see Le Page *et al.* 1974) go further than administrative clusters justify, since in the absence of true typologies it is difficult to find criteria for preferring one administrative clustering to another other than the criterion that it yields better socioeconomic associations!

Previous work used the concept of stability of clustering in order to choose the solution for further work. McEntegart has used additional criteria such as:

(i) the replication of cluster solutions with different clustering methods and different distance measures
(ii) internal indicators produced by some methods e.g.
    (a) by hierarchical methods—dendrograms, cophenetic correlation coefficient
    (b) by optimization techniques—criterion plots
(iii) qualitative evaluation
(iv) two- and three- dimensional representations of the data e.g. principal components analysis and non-metric multidimensional scaling.
(v) canonical variate plots
(vi) a random split into two samples to see whether similar clustering solutions are obtained from both samples.

These criteria have to be used in conjunction with each other.

The Belize and St Lucia analyses

The guidelines outlined earlier were applied fully to the Belize and St Lucia data sets. For Belize this consisted of a full set of scores on three phonological variables for early and late conversation and reading modes for 188 children; also, the same set with the omission of the reading mode, since the children had had varying degrees of difficulty in reading. For St Lucia, we used the Standard, Patois and Creole ('Bajan') variants of the habitual present (cf. Le Page 1977) for each interview and the Standard, Creole/Patois and hypercorrection variants of the noun variable, again for each interview, for 100 children. Error categories were not used, so that information was not duplicated.

Applying our criteria, no typological grouping existed in either set. In choosing which, if any, administrative cluster to use the canonical variates plots were particularly helpful. The four-cluster solution produced by Ward's method for Belize was adopted, but none of the St Lucian solutions was sufficiently stable to use.

Various other analyses were performed as described in McEntegart 1980. Here we report only the table of association coefficients between cluster membership and socioeconomic categories. We are not attempting to establish any direct causal relationship between socioeconomic variables and linguistic behaviour. Such relationships have never been part of the hypothesis. Rather we are interested in prediction of linguistic behaviour given the socioeconomic characteristics of the child. In any case McEntegart points out that the sample size is too small relative to the number of explanatory variables to establish any direct effects of the socioeconomic variables. The sample does not permit log-linear modelling or a full series of control tests as required by elaboration analysis.

As in cluster analysis the problem arises of choice from the many coefficients available. Since we are interested in prediction it would appear reasonable to work with coefficients that are interpretable from this viewpoint. This was the motivation underlying the use of Theil's Expected Mutual Information coefficient in Le Page *et al.* (1974). However, as this measure is dependent on the dimensions of the contingency tables its use is not entirely satisfactory. None of the predictive coefficients are totally without problems. For instance both Goodman and Kruskal's lambda coefficient and the SPSS uncertainty coefficient yield misleadingly low values when applied to cross tabulations of variables with skewed distributions. Our data certainly contains variables of this type. Non-predictive measures suffer from the problem that they do not assess the strength of a relationship, e.g. chi-square, or their lack of interpretability, e.g. Cramer's V.

As no one measure is completely satisfactory we used three, chi-square, Cramer's V and the uncertainty coefficient. The latter two have the satisfying property that a minimum of zero indicates lack of association and a maximum of unity denotes complete association. The chi-square measure is fully tested empirically and allows a fairly robust significance test. None of our tables violate the empirically established rules establishing requirements for a valid test.

The results are presented in Table 3. Some tables exclude children due to missing values but the numbers involved are not large enough to give rise to serious concern. As the coefficients are based on a sample the results are of course subject to sampling error. In making any inference about rankings of the coefficients this should be taken into account. Thus the analysis in McEntegart (1980) considers the asymptotic standard deviations of the Cramer's V statistic although for simplicity these are not reported here. It is thus not surprising that the relative order of association strength implied by the two coefficients is not the

Table 3: Association tests between administrative cluster solution membership and socioeconomic categories

Variable	Significance level of chi-squared test	Cramer's V	Uncertainty coefficient
1. Age of child	0.075	0.166	0.031
2. Sex of child	0.71	0.086	0.003
3. School standard of child	0.001	0.219	0.059
4. No. of parent figures	0.82	0.07	0.002
5. Absence/presence of elder siblings	0.94	0.047	0.001
6. Absence/presence of younger siblings	0.339	0.134	0.006
7. Home size	0.314	0.137	0.02
8. Wealth	0.028	0.195	0.031
9. Location of home	0.00	0.295	0.065
10. Religion	0.002	0.284	0.032
11. Politics	0.927	0.056	0.001
12. Claimed language spoken at home	0.000	0.346	0.135
13. Claimed race of family	0.000	0.329	0.134
14. Weekly expenditure per capita of family	0.85	0.11	0.014
15. Father's occupation	0.272	0.147	0.024
16. Incidence of newspaper reading of parents	0.268	0.149	0.008
17. Incidence of cinema going of parents	0.521	0.111	0.004
18. Incidence of meetings with teacher by parents	0.117	0.17	0.022
19. Incidence of radio listening of child	0.02	0.228	0.019
20. Incidence of newspaper reading of child	0.006	0.265	0.027
21. Speech change question	0.885	0.062	0.001
22. Speech ridicule question	0.007	0.262	0.025
23. Child's most natural language	0.000	0.375	0.102
24. Child's desired occupation	0.048	0.205	0.05

same (e.g. school standard compared with religious affiliation). Other factors contributing to such phenomena are the different nature of the coefficients and their performance in the face of skewed variables. Bearing these complications in mind it would appear that the location of a child's home, the religious affiliations of the family, the language claimed to be spoken at home, the claimed race of the family and the child's claimed most natural language are the best predictors of linguistic performance in an interview situation. Less strong but significant associations include school standard, family's wealth, newspaper reading of child, radio listening of child, child's consciousness of speech stigma as measured by his response to the question on speech ridicule and the child's desired occupation. The low values of the coefficients are no cause for concern. We cannot construct a model containing all the variables to arrive at some overall predictive figure. The fact that the maximum uncertainty is 0.135 does not mean that this is the expected reduction in uncertainty for any prediction we make given the full set of socioeconomic data for a child.

A further problem in inferring rankings of association was briefly mentioned earlier. That is, although we have tried to use objective criteria in picking which administrative cluster solution to work with, we cannot claim that the solution we choose is the 'best' or correct one. It is simply one of many useful summaries of the data in the absence of any typologies. This presents two problems for our subsequent contingency tables analysis. From the theoretical viewpoint we cannot say what we are trying to predict. Furthermore, even disregarding this objection, the possibility remains that different solutions will produce different rankings (although we would expect that the majority of rankings that change would be rankings based on the table of coefficients and not inferred population rankings after tests for sampling variation had been carried out). McEntegart's work suggested that these rankings can indeed vary between cluster solutions and that the magnitude of variation is perhaps cause for serious concern. More work needs to be done on this question using a variety of data bases. A final comment is that solutions involving different numbers of clusters and surveys involving relatively small sample sizes may well be particularly susceptible to such effects.

Assessment of the use of cluster analysis in sociolinguistic research

In this section we summarize some points already made and others which brevity has so far forced us to omit.

McEntegart has identified three possible situations with regard to cluster analysis applied to sociolinguistic data. In all these situations cluster analysis can provide divisions of a data set useful for subsequent internal analysis. It is the external analysis using contingency tables which is in question. The situations are:

1. Administrative clusters. This is the most likely outcome of a survey of populations undergoing rapid change. The point has been made that theoretical and practical problems exist with regard to associating membership of such clusters with non-linguistic variables.
2. Discrete separated subtypes of individuals which we establish using the criteria outlined earlier.

This heading embraces two different situations which have different implications for our assessment.

(a) Natural clusters not suitable for association analysis.

An example is given in figure 1 which considers the simple case of just a two-variable input to cluster analysis. The clusters are clearly discernible and yet we have not identified groups of children with very

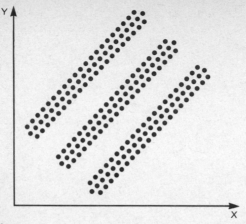

Figure 1

similar speech habits in the sense that children at one extreme of a cluster are relatively distant from children in the same cluster and yet at the other extreme. This is not of course a fault of the cluster analysis. This example is rather extreme but as there is no reason to expect to find spherical clusters such situations could arise.

(b) Well-separated groups suitable for association analysis. In such a situation there are no problems for the survey methodology. The approach brings out different features from Labov's work:

(i) By choosing his sample in a predetermined manner Labov's approach does not allow him to find anything else than the correlation he has set at the beginning of his research.

(ii) Labov is essentially concerned with the social group, and not with the individual, trying to show that what seems to be the inconsistent and chance or accidental behaviour of the individual proves to be consistent and rule governed at the level of the social group. In contrast, the aim of our research is the point of departure of Labov's research—he takes for granted that some groups of people share a common linguistic behaviour and we are looking for empirical evidence of this.

3. Discrete, well separated subtypes which the analysis fails to find.

Several reasons may account for such a situation. We concentrate on problems with input variables. Obviously one must have relevant and discriminating information to find any true divisions in the population. Specifically relevant to this subject is the question of the effects of correlated variables. Highly correlated variables are essentially reporting the same information. The fear is that in calculating the similarities of the observations over such a set of variables a form of double counting takes place. The true nature of the similarity/distance between individuals may be obscured by this double counting. McEntegart agrees with Gower's (1969) argument that where a correlation present is likely to be caused by the existence of the clusters being sought, the information should be retained. It is the duplication of non-essential information that is our present concern.

Consider as an example part of the methodology used in both surveys. We are interested in the direction and magnitude of each child's shift in verbal behaviour as he relaxes, on the assumption that such shifts tell us something about the models at work in the society. If we feed into a cluster programme the data for each mode of behaviour separately, we are duplicating the child's reference position, and this fact can affect the relative magnitude of similarity coefficients. Looking at the procedure one can view a child's data as his reference position and the path formed by his changes of speech. In our clustering we have been giving more weight to the reference point. This is not necessarily desirable and thus McEntegart suggested an alternative procedure. We can calculate the magnitude of change for each child on each variable by subtracting further (to the first) interview or conversation mode scores from the initial set of scores. This gives greater relative weight to the changes.

This operation was carried out on the Belize data. An administrative solution was again adopted. Association tests on this solution would, if taken at face value, give different indications about the degree of association if compared with the previous results. This is probably due to the phenomenon we noted earlier and the fact that we are weighting our information differently.

McEntegart analysed the role of speech changes further. He hypothesized a situation where a typology may exist in the reference positions of the children and/or discrete groups in the speech change paths and yet the data of the two taken together would not reveal clusters. He thus performed further work taking one conversation mode at a time.

Our overall conclusion must be that while cluster analysis may be useful it should be viewed as an exploratory method. Thus the data must not be extracted in such a way to make alternative forms of analysis difficult; e.g. the limited number of variables and their linearly dependent nature (St Lucia) prohibits the use of factor analysis. In our next section we briefly report the further analysis employed for our surveys.

Univariate analysis and significance tests—St Lucia, and some comparison with Belize

By univariate analysis we are referring to the linguistic features extracted from the interview texts. It involves taking each linguistic feature in turn and attempting to relate it to the socioeconomic variables. This procedure is forced on us by the failure to establish truly meaningful clusters—it was hoped that univariate anlaysis would shed some light on the clustering problem. For the most part we use multiple regression/ analysis of co-variance techniques. However, because of the nature of their distributions these techniques are not suitable for the 'Bajan' and 'hypercorrection' variables in each mode. For these variables use of contingency tables was made.

Concerning the latter the situation is as before. The sample of 100 children rules out by its small size the application of full control tests as required by elaboration analysis and it would never be possible to rank the socioeconomic variables in terms of causal importance. As mentioned, however, cause-and-effect relationships between socio-economic factors and linguistic behaviour have never been part of the hypothesis, *but only the individual's perception of groups in his society and his capacities and motivation to model himself on them seen as providing the motivation for his linguistic behaviour.*

The details of the contingency table tests and the reasoning behind their use are set out in McEntegart (1980). Very briefly the results were

First interview 'Bajan' habitual present	No variables significant at 5% per cent level
Second interview 'Bajan' habitual present	Religion and colour significant at 5 per cent level
First interview noun hypercorrection	Sex and location significant at 5 per cent level
Second interview noun hypercorrection	No variables significant at 5 per cent level

The importance to this discussion concerns the paucity of the associations found. If we cannot relate the socioeconomic variables to the individual linguistic variables then it is debatable whether such variables are sufficiently validated to appear in any grouping analysis. With hindsight, it might have been advantageous to assess the validity of the variables in this way earlier, although we did eventually try clustering without them. Reasons for the doubts about these variables are given in McEntegart (1980). The most obvious one is that if an attribute is rare in a population, a higher sample size is needed to estimate the attribute frequency to a given error risk than for a common characteristic. In our case the population is the child's total speech usage, the attribute is the relatively little used Bajan/hypercorrection variable and the sample is the linguistic interview.

We now turn to the other form of 'univariate analysis' employed i.e. linear models. Transformations were applied where necessary—an option not explicitly mentioned by Sankoff and Labov (1979) when expressing their feeling that linear models are often not suitable for linguistic data. The models were fitted with due regard for multicollinearity and specification errors.

We do not feel this paper a suitable place to go into the detailed statistical points involved in the analysis. We will simply outline the major considerations and results of the analysis:

1. The approach is compatible with the survey aims. Multiple regression does not pose questions about which is the most important cause of the dependent variable (unless the explanatory variables are independent). Rather the question is, which would produce the greater expected change in the dependent variable, a unit increase in variable 1, or a unit increase in variable 2 etc.?

2. By constructing composite models we obtain an overall value for the association between a linguistic variable and the socioeconomic variables (although we get one value for each linguistic variable of course). This was not possible in our contingency tables analysis. Unfortunately in this light our results must be considered disappointing although they are perhaps typical of social science data. The highest proportion of variance explained for a St Lucian variable was 31 per cent and the corresponding figure for Belize was 38 per cent. Other variables however were considerably lower with one being zero.

3. Given the poor results of some variables—notably the second interview noun variants for St Lucia—we must again pose the question whether it is sensible to use such variables as the input for cluster analysis.

4. There is little evidence of any hierarchy in the effects (in the sense described) of the explanatory variables. However, the variables appearing frequently throughout the models are location of home, school standard of child, claimed colour and claimed language used at home. Problems of interpretation remain as other variables appear in certain models and not others without any seemingly consistent pattern.

Conclusions

Enough samples of McEntegart's statistical work have been given to suggest:

(a) that the survey was far too ambitious in wishing to take account of all social and psychological factors relating to the linguistic behaviour of the children *at once* (though this is what the hypothesis demands, since it is intended to subsume all factors). Matched samples of children might have been compared to eliminate some of the social variables;

(b) Labov's approach has one distinct advantage over Le Page's, in that by pre-defining the socioeconomic groups he avoids collapsing data across explanatory variables; however, the objection made earlier to assuming that one knows about the stratification of a foreign community, still stands;

(c) even with the best possible data, there are severe limitations on the usefulness of cluster analysis in sociolinguistics. Whatever linguistic variables are selected, if variants are socially marked clustering is bound to pay most attention to those factors that are most strongly marked. Thus, while the apparent relative initial homogeneity of the St Lucian population compared with that of Belize is of interest to the sociolinguist, homogeneity is of no interest to a cluster analysis programme, which is searching for typologies. Sociolinguistic studies typically are concerned with gradience. We are epidemiologists in a multidimensional world where all individuals are more-or-less sick, more-or-less well, rather than where some individuals are sick and some well. We have not yet reached the stage of framing clear-cut and testable hypotheses, since the social variables are far too interdependent to assess causal connections with linguistic behaviour.

(d) The considerations affecting
  (i) the 'linguistic identity' of variables
  (ii) the choice of variables
  (iii) the size of the population and of the speech-sample for each individual to be studied
  (iv) the analysis of the data

contain so many variable and unknown factors that it is difficult to justify working with the small samples used and the kind of data quantified in St Lucia; yet the decisions about St Lucia were forced upon the team by the time and money and personnel available for the work. McEntegart (1980, chapter 11) sets out the case for preferring factor analysis in surveys such as ours where we do not expect a 'ghetto' situation, where there are no sharply discrete linguistic groups in the population (particularly true of St Lucia). However, Comrey (1973) suggests 300 as a good sample size for factor analysis. It may be that both techniques are too demanding for use with sociolinguistic data unless more time for the training of skilled personnel for the carrying out of pilot surveys and trial analyses, and for the ultimate fieldwork and analysis can be allowed for. Certainly continuity in the entire team is a *sine qua non*.

The research in the foregoing paper was supported by the University of York and Université Louis Pasteur, Strasbourg; by the SSRC, London and the CNRS and DGRST in Paris.

8

Networks and sociolinguistic variation in an African urban setting[1]

Joan Russell

The following discussion is rooted in the conviction that people, in their everyday encounters, are largely dependent on others rather than on an abstract society, and that their behaviour is not entirely determined by culture, rules and belief systems. The notion of man 'as an interacting social being capable of manipulating others as well as being manipulated by them' (Boissevain's preface to Boissevain and Mitchell 1973) is at the heart of the network concept, currently being developed and refined within the field of social anthropology, and already made use of in sociolinguistic work, for example by Gumperz (1971 with J.-P. Blom, 1976a, 1976b), Labov (1973a), Milroy (1980), and L. Milroy (this volume).

In this study the method of eliciting linguistic data was based on the notion of social network. Taking such an approach enables the linguist to meet members of the local community as a friend or 'friend of a friend' and ensures a greater degree of informality than is possible in interviews following random sampling. The community in question is fairly cohesive, for a number of reasons to be noted below. In this discussion I will follow Mitchell (1973) in regarding networks and corporate groups as social phenomena at different levels of abstraction and also accept his suggestion that 'networks of relationships are the starting point in the analysis of group behaviour ... they exist as analytical constructs which the observer erects partly by taking the participants' perceptions into account and by fitting together observations not available to the participants themselves.'

The concept 'social network', it must be emphasized, does not in itself

[1]The data referred to in this paper were collected during April–September 1973. I am grateful to the University of York, which granted me study leave, to the Social Science Research Council for financial assistance (Research Project H.R. 2458) and to the Kenya Government for granting me permission to carry out linguistic research in Mombasa. This is an expanded version of a paper presented to the Research Seminar on Sociolinguistic Variation at West Midlands College in 1976 and circulated in mimeo, under the present title, in 1977. I am grateful to Professor R. B. Le Page for commenting on the earlier version.

constitute a theory. Kapferer (1973) points out: 'A concept is one step beyond a description in the sense that it suggests a specified set of rules for organizing human experience. . . . Network and network density when applied to sociological data do not explain anything in themselves. An explanation is provided by a theory.' Kapferer's study and that of van Velzen (1973) both apply exchange theory to network analysis. In the following discussion I shall try to indicate how a model closely related to exchange theory, i.e. the accommodation model, together with Le Page's (1968) 'hypothesis and four riders', may be related to partial networks in order to provide a social explanation of linguistic variation and to help assess the likelihood of this variation constituting potential linguistic change.

Giles and Powesland (1975) give an account of the theory of accommodation and its applicability to linguistic code-choice and code-switching. Briefly:

> The essence of the theory of accommodation lies in the social psychological research on similarity-attraction. . . . This work suggests that an individual can induce another to evaluate him more favourably by reducing dissimilarities between them. The process of speech accommodation operates on this principle and as such may be a reflection of an individual's desire for social approval. In exchange theory terms (Homans 1961), it seems likely that the accommodative act may involve certain costs for the speaker, in terms of identity-change and expended effort, and so such behaviour may be initiated only if potential rewards are available. If one can accept the notion that people find social approval from others rewarding, it would not seem unreasonable to suppose that there may be a general set to accommodate to others in most social situations.

This quotation gives us the general orientation of the theory only. Elaborations and attendant concepts (as well as limitations) are discussed in Giles and Powesland (1975); the concomitant notions of symmetrical and asymmetrical convergence and divergence in dialogues are of particular relevance to the present discussion. The stance of the statement quoted above is strikingly similar to that of Le Page's (1968) hypothesis:

> The individual creates his systems of verbal behaviour so as to resemble those common to the group or groups with which he wishes from time to time to be identified to the extent that:
> (a) he is able to identify those groups,
> (b) his motives are sufficiently clear-cut and powerful,
> (c) his *opportunities* for learning are adequate,
> (d) his ability to learn—that is, to change his habits where necessary—is unimpaired.

The relevance of this hypothesis and that of accommodation theory to my data will be discussed in due course (cf also McEntegart and Le Page, this volume).

The subjects who are to be the focus of the discussion are members of the Swahili-speaking Afro-Arab Muslim community of Mombasa, Kenya's major port. They were all, at the time the linguistic data were collected, resident in the densely-populated Old Town district[2] of Mombasa Island, and all of them had been born in Mombasa. The island forms part of the municipality of Mombasa and is joined to the mainland by two bridges (one of which carries the road and railway to Nairobi), a causeway and two ferries. Ever since missionaries and linguists first directed their attention to the language of the Muslim communities of the East African coast in the middle of the last century, dialectal differences (phonological and morphological and, to a small extent, lexical) have been noted between the speech of Mombasa and Zanzibar and indeed other coastal settlements as far north as the southern end of what is now the Somali Republic.

The standard form of Swahili, which has achieved national language status in Tanzania and Kenya, is an artificial construct based on the form of Swahili used and taught at the UMCA mission in Zanzibar in the final decades of the nineteenth century. (Zanzibar Island is approximately 240 km south of Mombasa by sea, off the Tanzania mainland.) The language engineering required to implement this decision was started in the mid 1920s and continued for the next 30 or 40 years. It is sometimes said that 'Standard Swahili' was based on the Zanzibar town dialect; this is not strictly true, but at the phonological level we are fairly safe in equating 'Standard Swahili' with the Swahili of Zanzibar Town (referred to in dialect descriptions as Kiunguja). However, because the vast majority of people who use Swahili in the countries of East Africa speak it as a second language, there is a great deal of variation at every linguistic level. This variation is, to some extent, controlled by the education system and by radio, and probably to some degree—at least in the major urban areas—by television. Although the medium of education in all urban and many rural primary schools in Kenya is English, Swahili is taught as a subject from the fourth year.

Returning to Mombasa itself, it is important to note that it has been an important sea-port for centuries; Vasco da Gama called there in 1498. It is likely that there has been a settlement on the site of the Old Town district at least since the eleventh century, resulting from the southerly movement of the descendants of Perso-Arabian migrants who had arrived initially—and apparently spasmodically—at the northern end of the East African coast. A north-south movement down the Kenya coast is still discernible today—of young men, particularly from the Lamu area, seeking employment in Mombasa. Mombasans appear to have

[2]The area of the Old Town is approximately 1 sq. km; the population at the time of the 1969 census was 19,959. The choice of this district was influenced by Whiteley's (1955) observations: 'This Afro-Arab group constitutes the core of the Kimvita-speaking community, and is located mainly in the old part of the town overlooking the dhow harbour on the northern shores of the island.'

had for many years a strong sense of identity and a pride in their history—some of the events of which are enshrined in the considerable body of poetry which forms the literary heritage[3] of the northern half of the coastal strip. (The poetry was recorded in a modified form of the Arabic script, which is still in use today, although not taught in the municipal schools, who use the standard Roman orthography.) The poetic tradition appears to have begun in Lamu, in the north, and moved southwards, beginning to flourish in Mombasa in the early part of the nineteenth century. Topographical and economic factors tended to prevent extensive links between Mombasa and the other coastal settlements by land, but there were maritime trading links. This trade was dependent, until the advent of steam propulsion, on the NE and SW monsoon winds. It was these sailing winds which also formed the lands around the Indian Ocean into a trading unit, and was one reason for Mombasans' traditional focus of attention being seawards rather than inland. There were very few links with the interior (compared with those between Zanzibar and the interior) and even those trading links were organized through hinterland middlemen. Mombasa's present ethnic and linguistic heterogeneity dates largely from the early years of this century when the Mombasa-Lake Victoria railway line was completed and a new deep-water harbour was developed on the west side of the island. The economic expansion brought about by both of these undertakings turned the population of Mombasa into a highly cosmopolitan one. The more recent tourist boom has also increased the number of migrant workers from other parts of Kenya, who obtain employment in service and other industries, as well as in government administration. This economic expansion has therefore reduced the proportion of indigenous Swahili-speakers in the population of Mombasa and—at a rough estimate[4]—they now form only approximately 10 per cent of the total population of the municipality. Although members of this community are spread throughout most parts of the town the greatest concentration of them is in the Old Town district. Participant-observation in the Old Town community indicates that the incoming migrant workers (I shall refer to these as 'outsiders') are not

[3]The introduction by Shihabuddin Chiraghdin, to Ahmed Nassir's 1971 collection of poems (see bibliography) sums up very well the sentiments of the Swahili élite towards the poetic tradition and the Mombasa dialect itself.

[4]This estimate is based on the relevant figures for Mombasa Municipality in the 1969 Kenya Population Census. The totals for those groups which are *likely* to be native-speakers of Swahili are combined, thus:

Swahili/Shirazi	3,920
Bajun	5,328
Arab (Kenyan)	13,784
	23,032

The total population of Mombasa Municipality is given in the same census as 247,073.

generally regarded by the 'insiders' as prestigious and their Swahili is certainly not so regarded. 'Standard' Swahili, unless spoken by inhabitants of the southern islands (Zanzibar and Pemba) or by Muslims from the Tanzanian mainland, tends to be associated, especially by older people, with inland non-literary culture and with lack of the sophistication of an Islamic way of life. In the last few years there has been an awareness among the small secondary school educated élite (mostly male teachers and university students) that the Mombasa 'dialect' is in danger of being eroded. One of the manifestations of this recognition is the publication of poems by the foremost local poet. The composition of poetry is still very much a flourishing art and cuts across differences of educational level and occupation. It should also be noted that 'outsiders' do not regard the 'insiders' as a prestige group, but see them as highly conservative and the Old Town as something of a backwater. As far as Swahili is concerned, there is no question in this situation of 'the acquisition of local rules by outsiders moving in' as in the Philadelphia situation referred to by Labov (1973b).

Mombasan Swahili ('Kimvita' in the dialect descriptions—see, for example, Stigand 1915 and Whiteley 1955) is characterized by a number of co-occurring phonological and morphological features (the small number of lexical differences between it and 'Standard Swahili'[5] need not concern us here). Some of these features are shared by the dialects north of Mombasa, and some by the southern group, and it is this which led Whiteley (1969) to refer to Kimvita as one of the 'bridge' dialects in and around Mombasa. Of these features two appear to have become stereotypes in the sense of Labov (1970): 'A small number of sociolinguistic markers rise to overt social consciousness and become stereotypes. There may or may not be a fixed relation between such stereotypes and actual usage.'

When a number of 'insiders' and 'outsiders' were asked to suggest how indigenous Mombasans might be recognized by their speech most of those questioned gave lexical examples to illustrate the difference between 'insider' and 'outsider' speech. The words given all contained the voiced and voiceless dental stop/postalveolar affricate distinction as in:

mtele/mčele	'cleaned rice'	ndia/njia	'road'
kitwa/kičwa	'head'	ndoo/njoo	'come!'
-fita/-fiča (Vb)	'hide'	ndaa/njaa	'hunger'
-teka/-čeka (Vb)	'laugh'	nde/nje	'outside'
-tukua/-čukua (Vb)	'take'	mandano/manjano	'yellow'
-toma/-čoma (Vb)	'burn'	-vunda/-vunja (Vb)	'break'

The dental stop variants were associated by the respondents with

[5] Any discussion of lexical differences between Mombasan and 'Standard' Swahili would, in any case, be hampered by the eclectic nature of the choice of entries for the Standard Swahili Dictionary.

'insider' speech and the affricates with 'outsider' speech. (Note that the voiced variable is prenasalized.) These dental stops are also found in the Kiamu dialect, spoken in Lamu at the northern end of the Kenya coast.

We thus have the variables:

(ṯ/č) and (ṉḏ/nǰ)

The affricate variants are also the 'Standard Swahili' forms. Although 'outsider' Swahili in Mombasa—that is, Swahili used as a lingua franca—is highly heterogeneous, in this one area of the phonology, at least, we may treat 'outsider Swahili' and 'Standard Swahili' as synonymous terms. That is, Mombasan 'outsiders', whether speakers of other Bantu languages (e.g. Kikuyu, Kamba, Luhya) or non-Bantu languages (e.g. Luo), do not replace these affricates by stop consonants—nor by other obstruents, as far as observation indicates. However, in the speech of 'insiders' variation in respect of the stop/affricate alternation is observable, despite the popular image of the stereotypes, and it is this variation which provides the data for our discussion.

As well as expecting some variation in the speech of a community undergoing rapid sociocultural change we should also not be surprised to find that in the speech of a community with a history and geographical position like Mombasa's the identification of the loci of the variables in the lexicon is not a straightforward matter (cf. also McEntegart and Le Page, this volume). For not all occurrences of /ṯ/ and /č/ provide a locus for the voiceless variable. Some items with /ṯ/ in Mombasan speech have alveolar /t/[6] in 'Standard Swahili', e.g.:

ṯaa (Momb)/taa (Std) 'lamp'
-ṯano (Momb)/-tano (Std) 'five'
-ṯaka (Vb) (Momb)/-taka (Vb) (Std) 'want'
ṯu (Adv and Adj) (Momb)/tu /Adv and Adj) (Std) 'simply, merely, just'

Foreign loans with /č/ do not provide a locus for the variable either, e.g. čai 'tea', čerehani 'sewing machine', čaki 'chalk', -čapa (Vb) 'print'. Another set of items with invariable /č/ in both Mombasan and 'Standard' are not obvious loans and so may well be of Bantu[7] origin, e.g.:

[6] Mombasan speech also has alveolar /t/. This and /ṯ/ can both be assigned phonemic status on the basis of a small number of minimal pairs. The voiceless stop and affricate phonemes of the two dialects are thus:

Kimvita	p	ṯ	t	č	k
Kiunguja (Standard)	p		t	č	k

[7] Three of them almost certainly are, i.e. kuča, the infinitive form of -ča (to dawn); -čelewa, a derivative of the same verb-root; and -čače, (see Guthrie 1970, Vol III, Comparative Series 1034 and 1047). The provenance of the others is uncertain.

-čafu	'dirty'	čumvi	'salt'
-čaŋga	'young, newly-born'	čuŋgwa	'orange'
-čemʃa (Vb)	'boil' (trans)	čenza	'mandarin orange'
-čelewa (Vb)	'be late'	kuča	'the whole (night)'

Finally, in connection with the (t̪/č) variable, an environment is not provided by /č/ where it can be shown to be the surface realization of ki+/a/, /e/, /o/ or /u/, e.g.:

ki+aŋgu > čaŋgu, ki+etu > četu, ki+ombo > čombo, ki+uo > čuo.

This rule forces us to omit from consideration a large number of quite common words because 'ki' is the nominal prefix and adjectival and verbal concord-marker of one class of nouns (class 7); these words have /č/ in both Mombasan and 'Standard'.

As far as the voiced variable is concerned only prenasalized forms provide a locus.[8] But there are two small sets of items with such forms which appear to be invariable, and must therefore be discounted as loci. Words in the first set have stop consonants which are dental in Mombasan and alveolar in 'Standard' Swahili, e.g.:

ṇd̪iyo/ndiyo 'it is so', ṇd̪ipo/ndipo 'it is there/then'
    and other inflected forms of ṇd̪i-/ndi-
puṇd̪e/punde (Adv) 'shortly, slightly, recently'
-peṇd̪a/-penda (Vb) 'like, love'.

The second small set of 'exceptions' has an affricate in both Mombasan and 'Standard', e.g.:

nǰema 'very good, certainly'
nǰugu 'groundnuts'[9]

There is space only to mention the major and more obvious ramifications involved in the identification of the environments of the two variables. In attempting to establish these environments I worked from the tape-recorded data first and only used existing grammars, dialect descriptions and dictionaries as corroborative evidence where necessary.

As the dental stop variants seem to be popularly regarded as markers of 'insider' speech I am treating their occurrence in the data as evidence of 'insider' group identity. The data are recorded conversations from 24

[8] This post-nasal voiced segment is in allophonic variation with the implosive palatal stop [ʄ] which occurs in all other environments, i.e. word-initally and intervocalically, in both Kimvita and Kiunguja. The voiced variable, unlike the voiceless one, is thus at the subphonemic level. /ṇd̪/ and /nǰ/ will be shown between slashed lines, however, for ease of reference and to indicate *sociolinguistic* parity with /t̪/ and /č/.

[9] Whiteley (1955) gives also kanǰa 'plaited coconut palm fronds', nǰana 'a kind of fish' and nǰuga 'small bell' as being invariable, but these did not occur in my data.

adults encountered through my host family, the head of which was an influential resident or 'notable' (Gulliver 1971). The speech of members of the network of a prestigious local family might reasonably be supposed to provide at least some information on current linguistic trends. Some of the subjects were encountered during one of their visits to the house. A great deal of neighbourly visiting goes on in this community and talking is a major leisure-time activity. These subjects were then asked to bring along a close friend of similar age on a subsequent occasion. A check was made that the members of each pair fulfilled the three criteria of Mombasan birthplace, Old Town residence and Swahili as mother-tongue; a concomitant attribute was, of course, Muslim religious affiliation.

The natural conversation of peers has been suggested by Labov (1973a) as a possible solution to the 'observer's paradox' and Blom and Gumperz (1972), who make the same point, also make an important statement concerning selection: 'Methodologically, self-recruitment of groups is important for two reasons. It insures that groups are defined by locally recognized relationships and enables the investigator to predict the norms relevant to their interaction.'

The adults fell into two age-groups (i) early 20s to mid 30s, (ii) over 45. (These groups will be referred to as B and C respectively; a group of young adolescents—Group A—will not concern us here.) There were six men and six women in each age-group, and it turned out, not surprisingly, that the members of each single-sex group of six knew each other; not all of them knew the other four as well as they knew their own partner, but they all had at least occasional contact with the others. In addition, the men and women in Group C knew each other, even if only slightly in a few cases. This was only partially true of Group B. In addition, most of the 24 knew one or more members of the host family.

The members of some pairs were linked by a number of role-relationships, e.g. two of the women in Group B were (i) close neighbours (ii) ex-classmates at school (iii) members of the same Muslim women's association. Many-stranded relationships of this kind usually imply frequency of interaction which, together with the fact that rumour and gossip are known to spread rapidly in this district, suggests a situation of the kind which tends to bring about homogeneity of norms and values (Boissevain 1974). The whole group of 24 has a certain homogeneity anyway, since its members form part of one family's network, and live in the central and northern 'mitaa' (small neighbourhoods) of the Old Town district (as well as fulfilling all the criteria noted earlier).

Each person was involved in two kinds of dialogue—a conversation with his or her chosen peer and an interview with me; I spoke 'Standard' Swahili, conforming to the 'outsider' norm of non-accommodation to 'insider' speech. Note that this 'outsider' norm bears out Le Page's

(1968) hypothesis in that 'outsiders' typically do not wish to identify with 'insiders'; in relation to the accommodation model (Giles and Powesland 1975), which relies heavily on exchange theory (Homans *op. cit.*), such non-accommodation could be explained in terms of costs to the speaker, i.e. identity-switch, which he is not prepared to pay. All the subjects, in common with most Old Town residents, have *some* contact with 'outsiders'; those who are in full-time employment have considerable contact, those who are not have much less. But anyone living in Mombasa—or any other urban area of Kenya—is exposed to non-coastal Swahili some of the time. Thus everyone has access to the major features characterizing the two Swahili codes, each of which is associated with particular cultural identities. The reason for calling the conversation with me an 'interview' (apart from ease of reference) is that the use of 'Standard' Swahili implies more formality than the use of Mombasan Swahili, whose use is associated with the home, neighbourhood and an Islamic way of life. Each dialogue consisted of 'informative and evaluative' discussion and personal narrative; all the material in each type of discourse was transcribed, up to a limit of 500 words per type of discourse, per person. (The interview also elicited fictional narrative but this is not relevant to the present discussion.) The topics were all concerned with local and personal matters. The conversation took place either in the house of one member of a pair or in the host family's house; I was not present during the peer-to-peer conversation.

As the loci for the voiced variable are far fewer than those for the voiceless one, it was decided to add the two sets of loci together to give larger totals. This seems justified on the grounds that the variables differ only in voicing and that for the respondents who had provided the original examples they form a 'sociolinguistic natural class'. The results are thus shown as percentages of $/\underline{t}/ + /\underline{n}\underline{d}/$ occurring in the relevant loci. These group percentages are calculated from the individual raw scores.[10]

Putting the two age-groups together, to start with, and simply comparing the men's and the women's scores for $/\underline{t}/ + /\underline{n}\underline{d}/$ we find, in Figure 1, that the popular image of Mombasan speech is most nearly realized in the speech of the women when talking to an 'insider' friend. A comparison of the two discussion scores in the women's speech indicates a difference of 35 per cent, representing a considerable shift in the direction of 'Standard' Swahili when talking to an 'outsider'; the difference in the men's scores here is 23 per cent. Whether the greater convergence of women towards the standard language in the interview is attributable to the interviewer's being a woman or whether this would

[10]The mean number of loci per single-sex age-group of six is as follows:

	Conversation	Interview
Discussion	18	59
Narrative	35	23

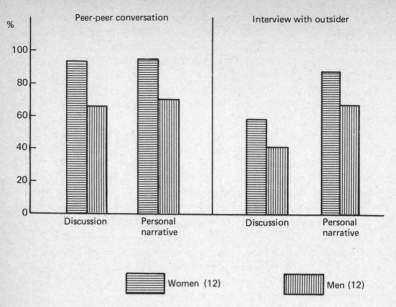

Figure 1: ṭ and ṇḍ by sex

have happened with a male 'outsider' it is not possible to say. Neither do we know whether a Kenyan 'outsider' would have triggered off a lower or higher percentage of Mombasan forms. The important point here is that the subjects were, in varying degrees, able to adjust to the interlocutor's form of speech *if they wanted to*.

A comparison of Figures 2 and 3 provides several important pieces of information not shown up in Figure 1, that is, the very high scores of the younger women in the peer-to-peer conversation and the greater shift towards 'Standard' Swahili of the younger group when talking to the interviewer. Taking the latter point first, we need to look for factors which might account for the greater ability (and willingness?) of the younger group to shift towards 'Standard'. There are certainly educational differences which might account for it. (The only educational factor all the subjects had in common was childhood attendance at Koranic school.) The levels of education achieved by the subjects in Group B at the time of this investigation are shown in Figure 4. Contrast this with group C, in which none of the women and only two of the men had received formal schooling; they are typical of the middle-aged and elderly members of this community who grew up at a time when formal education was very difficult for boys to obtain, and almost impossible for girls. The two men with primary education were both primary school teachers, one of whom had been trained at the large and prestigious teachers' training college in Zanzibar some 25 years earlier.

This difference in educational background between age-groups B and

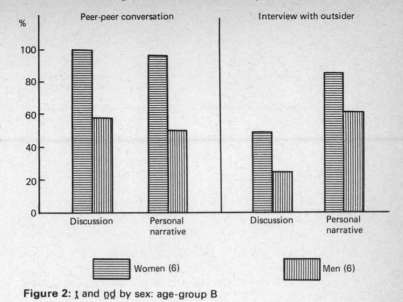

Figure 2: ṭ and ṇḍ by sex: age-group B

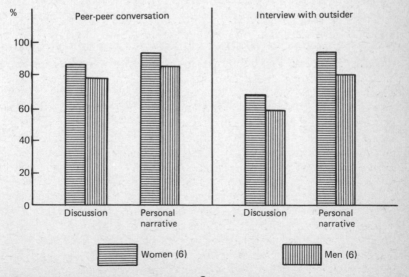

Figure 3: ṭ and ṇḍ by sex: age-group C

Women	Subject no 13	Primary education
	14	No formal education
	15	Primary education +8 months nursery teacher training course
	16	No formal education
	17	4 years secondary education
	18	4 years secondary education
Men	Subject no 19	Primary education
	20	Primary education +2 years army service
	21	4 years secondary education
	22	4 years secondary education
	23	4 years secondary education
	24	3 years secondary education

Figure 4: Educational levels of Group B

C might account for *some* of the difference between their scores in the interview discussion. Obviously, though, formal exposure to 'Standard' Swahili through the education system does not in itself result in widespread use of 'Standard' features by the schooled subjects in all situations. The other notable piece of information gleaned from separating the two age-groups, and already noted above, is the 100 per cent score of the Group B women in the peer-peer conversation; this is a very significant finding. Bearing in mind that four of these women had had formal schooling, two of them having successfully completed a four-year secondary-school course, one would not have been surprised by a much lower score than this. The scores of these women in both types of speech situation are—apart from the discussion in the formal interview—much closer to those of Group C women than one would have expected, given the difference of educational background. This can only support the contention that these women have a much greater sense of 'insider' group identity than the male subjects in the same age-group, and it perhaps also indicates more self-confidence. The fact that the Group C women's scores, although high, nowhere reach 100 per cent underlines the fact that an acquaintance with the education system is not necessary in order to acquire *some* knowledge of 'Standard' Swahili features; simply living in Mombasa—together with access to radio and television and comparatively easy access to Nairobi and other inland towns—is sufficient. One item of interest to emerge from the graphs in Figures 1, 2 and 3 is that in the interview the nature of the discourse in the 'personal narrative' section took precedence over the 'interviewer-interviewee' (or 'outsider-insider') relationship; these narratives were uninterrupted accounts of events in which the subjects had been personally involved.

Taking all the adults together, and making a comparison between schooled and unschooled subjects, we find in Figure 5 that the link suggested above—between the marked shift towards 'Standard' forms in the interview discussion and the acquisition of formal schooling—is now clear. If we are to explore a little further the nature of the difference between the discussion scores in the two dialogues we had better leave out of account the unschooled subjects since their *ability* to shift towards 'Standard' Swahili may be less than that of the schooled group (see Le Page's third and fourth 'riders' above).

So, dealing only with the schooled subjects (eight men and four women) we may ask whether, in the interview, a low score represents convergence to the outside interviewer's speech or a weak sense of 'insider' group identity. Obviously, there is no way of knowing this from the group interview scores alone; we need individual scores, and they will have to be compared with the individual scores achieved in the informal peer-peer discussion. The method employed for the collection of the data was geared towards making eventual statements about group behaviour, and the figures involved, i.e. the *group* scores, are adequate for this. However, the *individual* loci-totals are rather small in some cases, and so any conclusions drawn from the comparison of individual scores must be tentative; I am simply using them to illustrate an approach which seeks an explanation of variation and potential linguistic change at its locus, i.e. the dyadic encounter. The group scores for the discussion and narrative in the peer-peer dialogue turned out to be exactly the same—73 per cent (see Figure 5) and, as the individual loci-totals for the discussion were rather low, it was decided to add to

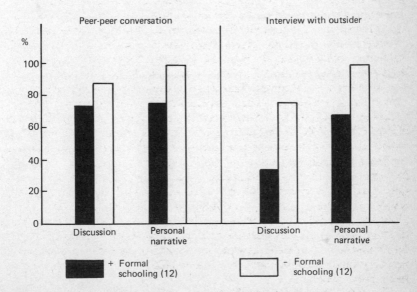

Figure 5: t̪ and n̪d̪ by education

Subject no		Conversation with peer: discussion	Interview with 'outsider': discussion
		%	%
f	13	100	10
f	14 (unsch)	100	
f	15	100	61.5
f	16 (unsch)	100	
f	17	100	37
f	18	87	64
m	19	100	75
m	20	67	100
m	21	0	7
m	22	0	0
m	23	42	54
m	24	75	30
m	31	100	100
m	32	25	13

Figure 6: Comparison of schooled adults' individual /ʈ/ and /ɳɖ/ scores in informal conversation and formal interview discussions

them the individual totals for the narrative when calculating the individual scores; this gave slightly more respectable totals.[11]

Figure 6 shows the individual scores of the schooled adults in the discussion section of both dialogues. (Note that nos. 14 and 16 are unschooled partners and their interview scores are not relevant to the present discussion.) Extracting the low scorers in the interview we find that subjects 13, 17, 21, 22, 24 and 32 all have scores below 40 per cent. Looking now at the peer-peer conversation scores of the pairs of which these subjects are members we find that nos. 13 and 17 were members of convergent pairs each with a high score for (ʈ/ and /ɳɖ/, representing (in the terms I have suggested) a strong feeling of identity with the indigenous Mombasan speech community. Their low score in the interview discussion, that is, their convergence towards the speech of the interviewer, could be interpreted as a willingness to identify temporarily with an outsider, either out of politeness or a general tendency to accommodate to an interlocutor. No. 24 should probably be grouped with these two as his conversation score is fairly high—75 per cent; the pair of which he is a member is only partly convergent.

Contrast these with subjects 21, 22 and 32, where the low interview

[11]The individual totals for both types of discourse in each dialogue range from 23 to 1. The single occurrence of 1 is the 'total' of subject no 31 (one of the Group C men) for the discussion in the peer-peer conversation. He scored 100 per cent in *all* types of discourse (i.e. including the fictional narrative not discussed here); in other—unrecorded—, conversations he was never heard to use 'Standard' forms in these environments. In any case, he, as a high scorer in both dialogues, is not relevant to my final remarks on the carriers of potential linguistic change.

score is matched by a low score in the informal conversation, convergently in the case of 21 and 22 and divergently in the case of 32. The low interview score in these three cases then, appears to be part of a general pattern of 'Standard'-influenced speech and weak group-loyalty; it is *not* evidence of accommodation to the interviewer's speech.

The high scorers in the interview are subjects 15, 18, 19, 20 and 31. Of these 15, 18, 19 and 20 are members of convergent pairs, all with high or fairly high scores, although the convergence of 19 and 20 is not very marked. (Convergence is, of course, what we would expect in this kind of conversation between friends, where no transactional element is involved.) No. 31 is a member of a highly divergent pair.[12] He and his partner, both aged about 50, are the oldest of the schooled adults and it may be that the amount of divergence evident in their scores is the result of the kind of confidence that comes with maturity; each is very much his 'own man'. The five high-scorers look as though they identify strongly with their community, and this sense of identity carries over into dialogue with an outsider. No. 23 has not been mentioned; it does not seem justifiable to group him with the high scorers and we had better leave him where he has placed himself—sitting on the sociolinguistic fence.

From the point of view of the linguistic structure of the 'ways of speaking' along the East African coast which have come to be called 'Swahili' we may, on the basis of the foregoing exploration of variation involving a minute part of that structure, wish to agree with Bickerton (1975): 'The amount of variation in any given language may vary from epoch to epoch, but is always present in some degree, and continually shifts its locus; if the feature that is variable today was often invariant yesterday, it is equally true that today's invariant was yesterday's variable.' We do not know the extent of 'yesterday's' variation in respect of particular phonological or other features of Swahili but there are certainly hints of considerable variation by earlier investigators, e.g. Krapf (1844), who learned Swahili in Mombasa and wrote its first grammar: 'the Sooahelee is so vague and differently spoken by different persons that I frequently was inclined to despair . . .' and Stigand (1915): 'The great bulk of the inhabitants of Mombasa at the present day, talk a language which is neither pure Mombasa nor pure Zanzibar.' However, if we want to discover why what might have been yesterday's invariant has become today's variable we need to observe people talking to a variety of acquaintants, at different points in their personal networks—from their cluster of close friends (Boissevain's 1974 '1st

[12]Nos. 31 and 32 are the two Group C primary-school teachers mentioned earlier. No. 32 is the man who was trained in Zanzibar; he teaches in a school on the mainland (whereas no. 31 teaches in the boys' school nearest to the Old Town district) and has had at least one book of children's stories published—in 'Standard' Swahili. These facts indicate a positive attitude to the 'outside world' and to the standard language, and this is reflected in his speech.

order zone') as well as from their casually encountered and perhaps temporary acquaintances (in the Mombasa context these are likely to be 'outsiders'). The point is that the links in networks are potential communication channels, and an examination (on a larger scale than the one described) of the linguistic behaviour of people linked in this way can help to plot the mechanism of code-switching (used here in the broadest sense of the term) and thus uncover the sources of potential linguistic change in a community.

Subjects 21, 22 and 32, who had low scores in both dialogues, appear to have a general pattern of 'Standard'-influenced speech—a likely indication of a willingness to accept the norms associated with the use of Standard Swahili (which is increasingly identified with government and a non-coastal urban way of life). It is these people and others like them whose total linguistic range is changing, who are the instigators and carriers of potential linguistic change. The linguistic change is the merger of Mombasa /t/ with /č/, thus bringing about congruity with the set of voiceless stop and affricate phonemes of 'Standard' Swahili (see footnote 6) and the merger of Mombasa [d̠] with the [ɟ] allophone of 'Standard' /ʄ/ (see footnote 8). Whether this potential change becomes actual is dependent on a number of social and economic factors and cannot therefore be predicted. It is people like these—men with secondary-school education or post-primary training and a positive attitude to society outside their own speech community—who are the most likely to move away from Mombasa if there are insufficient opportunities for suitable employment there. However, they will only move away if there is congenial employment elsewhere. If this happens and if the southward drift of less-educated and less-skilled men from the Lamu area continues, thus reinforcing the northern features which Mombasan Swahili shares with Lamu speech, then perhaps the existing situation will continue for some time. As far as the present is concerned, if the women in this study are at all representative it certainly looks as though it is women, rather than men, who are preserving the more obvious markers of this speech community.

9

Social network and linguistic focusing

Lesley Milroy

Introduction

The general theoretical notion to which this paper addresses itself is that of a *linguistic norm*—specifically a non-standard or vernacular norm, as opposed to a fully codified standard norm.

Questions concerning linguistic change and variation, which are commonly associated with the Labovian tradition, will not be considered here; for the moment, these phenomena will be taken for granted. On the other hand, it seems clear that some understanding of the opposite phenomenon which is much less frequently discussed and which Le Page has described as 'focusing' is also crucial to sociolinguistic enquiry (cf. McEntegart and Le Page, this volume). A language variety is described as 'focused' when speakers perceive it in some sense as a distinct entity (Le Page 1975). Thus, in the context of the English language, accents such as those of Birmingham, Glasgow, Liverpool and the others described by Hughes and Trudgill (1979), which are all popularly perceived as distinctive and discrete, could be described as relatively focused. On the other hand, the language patterns of geographically or socially mobile persons, which cannot be said to be characteristic of any particular namable accent, but rather a mixture of various social and regional accents, might be said to be relatively *diffuse* (also Le Page's term).

The notion of 'accent' appears to be psycho-social rather than strictly linguistic. Thus, although accents clearly have a psycho-social reality in the sense that speakers show an awareness of their importance as markers of various aspects of social identity, and react correspondingly strongly to them, it is not possible to produce strict 'phonological' definitions of accents any more than 'dialects' can be seen as clear linguistic entities (see Trudgill 1974a for a discussion of this last point and Giles and Scherer 1980 for a recent collection of papers on aspects of the social significance of speech). Nevertheless, the vagueness of the concept of accent should not prevent us from acknowledging that in the relatively recent past the urban accents of many British (and other) industrial cities would not have been perceived as distinct entities meriting a label, far less the degree of codification conferred by the descriptions in a book such as that by Hughes and Trudgill. The characteristic structure of these accents has developed (i.e. linguistic focusing has taken place) along with the development of the industrial cities with which they are associated, many of which are not much more than a century old. Le Page in fact views linguistic focusing as the natural result of a more general cultural process involving the emergence of a distinct sense of group solidarity and identity (1979a: 176).

Belfast is a city of relatively recent development, having undergone its major period of growth (1850–1900 approx.) some 50 years later than comparable English industrial cities. For that reason, Belfast offers an excellent vantage point for examining the phenomenon of focusing in urban speech. One aspect of focusing which we will examine here is the sociolinguistic patterning characteristic of an accent popularly perceived as a relatively homogeneous urban vernacular. In view of this theoretical orientation, it will be clear that although many of the analytic procedures employed are Labovian, the general theoretical orientation is not at all characteristic of Labov.

The data

The argument of this paper is based on data collected in the course of a recent study of Belfast vernacular speech and more fully reported elsewhere (Milroy and Milroy 1978; L. Milroy 1980).

The language of pre-existing social groups in three poor working-class communities—Ballymacarrett, the Clonard and the Hammer—was studied. Although the communities were similar in terms of social status (predominantly unskilled working class) their internal social structure was by no means similar. Ballymacarrett, largely due to its location in the shipyard area, differed from the others in suffering very little from male unemployment. The Clonard and the Hammer suffered unemployment rates of around 35 per cent. This had a considerable effect on informal social relationships in the areas, as Ballymacarrett men tended to work locally and find their entertainment in local pubs and clubs, often interacting almost exclusively within narrow territorial boundaries. Women were much more inclined to look for work outside the locality, and men's and women's activities were sharply polarized. Although the same social patterns may once have prevailed in the Clonard and the Hammer at a time when the traditional linen industry provided local employment, men from these communities now customarily travel to different parts of the city in search of work, often share domestic and child-care duties, and do not contrast so markedly with women in their socialization habits as do their Ballymacarrett counterparts. Despite these local differences, the informal social structure of all three communities corresponded to the dense, multiplex, often kin-based network patterns described by many investigators as characteristic of working-class areas of cities (Young and Wilmott 1962; Fried 1973). This meant that people interacted mostly within a clearly defined territory, tended to know each others' social contacts and were linked to each other in several capacities simultaneously—for example as kin, neighbours and co-employees. Following Bott's arguments (Bott 1971), social anthropologists now generally agree that a social network of this type, which in effect constitutes a bounded group, has the capacity to impose general normative consensus on its members. This point is of great relevance to the argument here, which is fundamentally concerned with the whole notion of a norm. For the moment it is worth recalling Labov's remarks on the capacity of closeknit peer groups to impose consensus on specifically *linguistic* norms upon their members (Labov 1972a: 257).

Although this network structure was generally evident in the Belfast communities, the extent to which *individuals* were linked to local networks varied considerably. Some people for example worked outside the area and had no local kin and no local ties of voluntary assocation, while others were linked to local networks in all these capacities. These differences in personal network structure, which appeared to be the result of many complex social and psychological factors, cut across categories of age, sex and locality; the strongest vernacular speakers however appeared rather consistently to be those whose local network ties were strongest. This observation was treated as a hypothesis, and tested in the manner described in the following section.

Language/network correlations

An individual network score on a scale of 0–5 was calculated for each of the 46 informants. This scale took account of the character of the individual's network ties in the sectors of work, kin, neighbourhood and voluntary association (see Cubitt 1973 for a discussion of the general importance of these particular network sectors). The score assigned to each individual provided a means of reflecting differences in multiplexity and density of personal networks without using corporate group constructs based on, for example, status as a means of differentiating individual speakers.

An informant's network score was calculated by assigning him one point for each of the following conditions he fulfilled:

1. Membership of a high density, territorially based cluster (i.e. any identifiable bounded group).
2. Having substantial ties of kinship in the neighbourhood. (More than one household, in addition to his own nuclear family).
3. Working at the same place as at least *two* others from the same area.

4. The same place of work as at least two others of the same sex from the area.
5. Voluntary association with workmates in leisure hours.

Condition one is designed as an indicator of density, and reflects Cubitt's (1973) insistence on the importance of taking account of the density of specific clusters in considering networks (as we are here) as norm enforcement mechanisms. (A cluster is defined as a portion of a personal network where relationships are denser internally than externally). The Jets, Cobras and T-Birds described by Labov (1972a) form clusters; many of the young men in the Belfast communities belong to similar clusters; some of the middle-aged women belong to clusters of six or seven individuals who meet frequently to drink tea, play cards and chat. Some individuals on the other hand avoid association with any group of this kind.

Conditions two, three, four and five are all indicators of multiplexity; if they are all satisfied, the proportion of the individual's interactions which are with members of the local community is very high. Three and four are intended to reflect the particular capacity of an area of homogeneous employment to encourage the development of dense, multiplex networks; four also reflects the fact that polarization of the sexes usually occurs when there is a large number of solidary relationships in a specific neighbourhood.

It may appear at first sight that multiplex ties of the kind reflected in conditions three, four and five are usually contracted by men, and that men would, therefore, automatically score higher on the network strength scale. In fact, since both the Hammer and the Clonard are areas of high *male* unemployment, individual women frequently score as high as or higher than men.

The scale is capable of differentiating individuals quite sharply. Scores range from zero for someone who fulfils none of the conditions, (although a zero score is rare) to five for several informants who fulfil them all. Such individuals must be considered extremely closely integrated into the community in the sense that their kin, work and friendship ties are all contracted within it; additionally, they have formed particularly close ties with a corporate group (such as a football fans' club) or a less formal group based in the area. The defined territorial base associated with the kind of network structure which interests us here is reflected in conditions one and two. This is very important, for geographical mobility appears to have the capacity to destroy the structure of long established networks (Turner 1967; Wilmott and Young 1962).

It is important to emphasize that the network strength scale is designed fundamentally as a tool for measuring differences in an individual's level of integration into the local community. It is not claimed that this scale is the *only* means of doing so; for example attitudinal factors are likely also to be good indicators. However, the major advantage of the scale adopted here is that the indicators are *based on an explicit set of procedures* for analysing social relationships. Further, they can be observed directly and are subject to checking and verification (see Boissevain 1974 for a full account of network theory and Milroy 1980 for a discussion of its relevance to sociolinguistic method and theory).

Scores for each individual speaker on eight separate phonological variables were calculated (using the methods developed by Labov 1966) and a large number of rank order correlation tests carried out as a means of testing the hypothesis that network patterns were related to patterns of language use. When all subjects were considered together, significant results were obtained for five of the eight variables. This result appears to confirm the hypothesis that the strongest vernacular speakers are those whose network ties are strongest. Of those eight variables, only the significant ones are considered here.

Before proceeding further, it is necessary to explain the relevant phonological features associated with these variables. This account is necessarily brief and partial; a fuller description of the complexities of this urban vernacular phonology can be found in Milroy (1981) and to a more limited extent in L. Milroy (1980) and Hughes and Trudgill (1979).

1 (a)   Index scores are used, measuring degrees of retraction and back-raising in items of the /a/ /ɑ/ class (e.g. *hat*, *man*, *grass*). A five point scale is used, ranging from one for tokens with [æ] to five for tokens with [ɔə] with intermediate variants of [a], [ä] and [ɑ]. Scores are based on 60–80 tokens per speaker.

2 (th) Percentage scores measure deletion of intervocalic [ð] in a small lexical set (e.g. *mother*, *brother*). Since the lexical distribution of this variable is limited, scores are based on only 856 tokens for all speakers—approximately 16–20 tokens per speaker.

3 (ʌ)   Percentage scores measure frequency of [ʌ] variant in a small lexical set which alternates between the /ʌ/ and /ʊ/ word-classes: e.g. *pull*, *shook*, *foot*. Altogether, 1500 tokens are considered. An account of this word class and its importance for theories of lexical diffusion and linguistic change can be found in J. Milroy (1980).

4 (ε¹) (ε) Percentage scores measure frequency of low vowel [æ] (as opposed to a mid-vowel [εə] in items of the /ε/ class (*peck*, *bet*, *went*). This analysis is restricted to monosyllables closed by a voiceless obstruent or by a voiceless obstruent preceded by a liquid or nasal.

5 (ε²) *Percentage* scores measure frequency of the same low vowel in di-and polysyllables.

The correlations between individual scores for these five variables and individual network scores are presented in Table 1. This significant relationship between network structure and language use was further explored by dividing the informants into sub-groups based on sex, age and area and again correlating linguistic scores with network scores. It is the results which emerged when the sub-groups were divided according to area which are of particular interest to us here.

In fact, it is only in Ballymacarrett that many phonological variables correlate significantly with personal network structure. Five of the eight give statistically significant results in Ballymacarrett, one in the Hammer and none in the Clonard (see Table 2).

We may arrive at a plausible interpretation of these results by referring back to the variant network patterns in the three communities. In Ballymacarrett *male* networks seemed more closeknit largely as a result of local employment patterns and contrasted sharply with the relatively looseknit *female* network pattern. This contrast between the sexes was not apparent in other areas. A series of analysis of variance

Table 1: Correlations between network scores and linguistic variable scores for all subjects. N refers to the number of subjects tested for a given variable

Variable	r	t	N	Level of Significance
(a)	0.529	3.692	37	$p < .01$
(th)	0.485	3.591	44	$p < .01$
(Λ^2)	0.317	2.142	43	$p < .05$
(ε^1)	0.255	1.709	44	$p < .05$
(ε^2)	0.321	2.200	44	$p < .05$

Table 2*: Correlations between network scores and linguistic variable scores calculated separately for three areas. B = Ballymacarrett, H = Hammer, C = Clonard

Variable		r	t	N	Level of Significance
(a)	B	0.930	8.360	13	$p < .01$
	C	0.345	2.287	15	$p > .05$
	H	−0.344	2.286	9	$p > .05$
(th)	B	0.816	4.679	13	$p < .01$
	C	0.011	0.039	15	$p > .05$
	H	0.346	1.379	16	$p > .05$
(Λ^2)	B	0.426	1.560	13	$p > .05$
	C	−0.042	0.151	15	$p > .05$
	H	0.247	0.920	15	$p > .05$
(ε^1)	B	0.771	4.016	13	$p < .01$
	C	−0.118	−0.429	15	$p > .05$
	H	0.053	−0.199	16	$p > .05$
(ε^2)	B	0.719	3.433	13	$p < .01$
	C	0.027	0.098	15	$p > .05$
	H	0.096	0.361	16	$p > .05$

*One further variable ($_1$), showed a significant relationship to network scores only in the Hammer.

tests was carried out to check on significant differences in the distribution of *network* scores by age, sex and area (see L. Milroy 1980 for details). Although many significant differences and interactions emerged, the important result for our purpose here is that *only in Ballymacarrett* are male and female network scores significantly different (means = 3.9583:1.3333). These may be compared with the Hammer (2.125:1.875) and the Clonard (2.750:2.875). Considered overall, network scores did not vary significantly simply according to area; the variables of network and sex were apparently connected in a subtle and complicated way.

The main points of the argument so far may be summarized in the following way. Of the three lower working-class areas studied, only in Ballymacarrett do patterns of language use correlate with personal network structure when individual scores on those two sets of variables are compared. In the same area the difference between the network structures of the two sexes also emerges as very much sharper than in either the Clonard or the Hammer. We now move on to examine differences in *patterns of language use* between the sexes. This is of course quite a different matter from the *correlations between the language scores and the network scores* of individuals which have already been discussed.

Linguistic sex grading in the communities

The simplest initial way of examining patterns of sex grading in the communities is to refer to the graphic patterns presented in Figures 1–4. These represent scores on the four variables (th) (ε^1) (a) and (Λ) calculated in accordance with the methods outlined by Labov (1966). All four of these phonological elements have emerged as sharp sex-markers in working class Belfast (Milroy and Milroy 1978; L. Milroy 1980) and in Ballymacarrett the difference between male and female speech is in all cases much sharper and more consistent across two generations of speakers than in the other two areas.

This is particularly clear if (ε^1) is considered; there appears to be a tendency in *all* areas for this phonological element to function[1] as a sex marker; but the tendency is sharpest in Ballymacarrett. Some of the figures on which Figure 1 are based are given in Table 3. These reveal that in Ballymacarrett the low centralized variant of (ε^1) seems to be categorical amongst males, but used only just over half the time by

---

[1] The term *function* is used here and elsewhere in much the same manner as the Prague School linguists: that is, a phonological element may be said to function within the sociolinguistic system, if it is possible to point to a job it does in relation to other elements. To say that an element functions as a sex marker, for example, does not then in any way imply that speakers are conscious of this function (although in fact, subjective reaction tests reveal their general awareness of sociolinguistic markers) any more than Mathesius's use of the term implies that speakers are conscious of the functional significance of theme and rheme (cf. O'Kane 1977). I am indebted to Suzanne Romaine and Philip Smith for drawing my attention to possible misunderstandings of the term *function*.

Table 3: Mean scores for (ε^1) of both sexes in three areas

	Male	Female
Ballymacarrett	100.000	50.9421
Clonard	92.9763	78.8200
Hammer	93.5625	75.7138

Mean scores for (ε^1) of both sexes in 3 areas.

females. Men and women in the other two areas differ less in respect of their use of (ε^1), although men still use the low centralized variant much more than women.

A similar pattern emerges with (th); sex differentiation patterns are *sharpest* in Ballymacarrett, although they are still very clear elsewhere. Mean differences between male and female scores for both (ε^1) and (th) are in fact significant at 0.01 level when all areas are considered together.

The character of the contrast between the (a) and (Λ) patterns in *Ballymacarrett* as opposed to the other areas is rather different. It is not simply a matter of the sex differentiation being *sharper* in Ballymacarrett; rather, only in Ballymacarrett are patterns of sex-differentiation with respect to these elements *stable over two generations*. In the case of (a) there is only a tiny and insignificant difference between the sexes in the Hammer while in the Clonard the *young women* (but not the older women) use backed variants of (a) at a particularly high level. In fact, this irregular pattern reflects statistically significant interaction effects (area by sex: $F = 5.7593$, $p < 0.01$; sex by age: $F = 6.0003$, $p < 0.05$). If we examine the (Λ) graph, we see that in both the Hammer and the Clonard, but particularly in the Clonard, the older women use the unrounded variant at unexpectedly high levels. Again, this pattern reflects a statistically significant sex by age interaction effect: ($F = 16.8535$, $p < 0.001$). The notion of statistical interaction and the importance of taking interaction effects into account in interpreting sociolinguistic data are discussed in L. Milroy 1980.

One plausible conclusion to be drawn from these patterns however is that when we consider two important variables, (a) and (Λ), only in Ballymacarrett does there seem to be clear agreement on their social function as sex markers across two generations. On the other hand there seems to be agreement across generations on the function of (th) and (ε^1) in all three areas; but the patterns of sex differention are consistently sharpest in Ballymacarrett. Thus, it seems reasonable to suggest that in Ballymacarrett the linguistic norms of the community can be most clearly observed; there is apparently very consistent agreement on what constitutes appropriate speech for males and females. Moreover, as we would expect from other urban studies, females generally favour variants characteristic of high-status social groups. The subjective responses of males and females to these same variants are very sharply

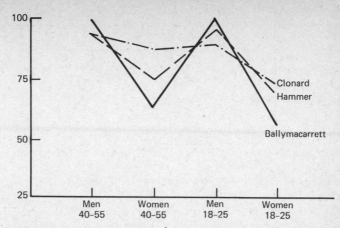

Figure 1: percentage low vowel for (ε¹) in variable monosyllables and prefixed and inflected disyllables

different, but as expected reflect the patterns of Figures 1–4. The subjective reaction tests on which these responses are based are discussed in O'Kane 1977.

Interestingly, sharp sex grading in Ballymacarrett appears to go along with this clear tendency of all speakers to use phonological variables extremely consistently. Thus, the fact that a norm appears to have emerged in Ballymacarrett by no means implies linguistic uniformity or denies the existence of the regular patterns of variability which we have come to expect in a real (as opposed to an imaginary) community. On

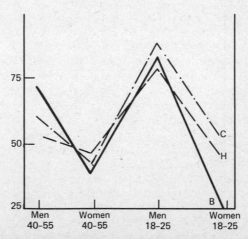

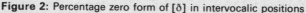

Figure 2: Percentage zero form of [ð] in intervocalic positions

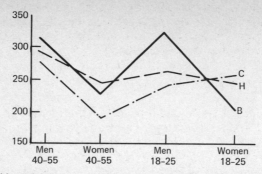

Figure 3: Backing of /a/ in the three communities: (a) index score

the contrary, it is the very *regularity* of these patterns of variability (as opposed to their irregularity in the Clonard and the Hammer) which might be said to constitute the linguistic norm.

In fact, if we view variable language behaviour as parallel, in important respects, to other types of variable social behaviour we might predict a pattern rather like that revealed in Figures 1–4. For much of the literature on traditional closeknit working-class communities of this type has emphasized polarization of the sexes as an important characteristic (see Bott 1971 for a review). This seems to be generally true of low-status closeknit communities, although on the whole only broad social reflexes of this polarization (such as allocation of tasks and responsibilities) have been considered, rather than specifically linguistic reflexes. However, from our point of view, we may conclude that an

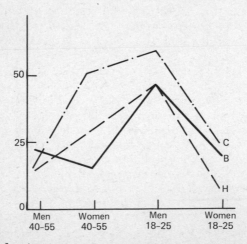

Figure 4: % [ʌ] variant in the three communities

important sociolinguistic reflex of *focusing* (or the emergence of an agreed norm) may be the presence of clear linguistic sex-grading, without complications being introduced into the pattern by, for example, age or area interaction effects.

Conclusion

A large amount of social and linguistic data has been adduced in this paper, and the same set of data has been analysed in more than one way. It will be helpful at this point to pull the main strands of the argument together, and relate them to the central concern of the paper.

First, we saw that only in Ballymacarrett was there a clear and consistent correspondence between a person's network structure and his (or her) degree of use of vernacular phonological variants. It was further noted that social conditions in Ballymacarrett were favourable to the emergence of a closeknit network structure of the type commonly found in traditional low-status communities. It was suggested that these language/network correlations in Ballymacarrett were associated with the capacity of a closeknit network to impose normative consensus on its members. This point is not a new one; it has already been made by Labov (1972a) in his discussion of the consistent relationship between a speaker's place in the adolescent peer group structure and the extent to which vernacular features are evident in his speech.

However, a second point is that the relationship between group structure and language is not as simple as the correlations shown in Tables 1 and 2 imply. A closeknit network structure is not observable in Ballymacarrett independent of other social variables. When individual *network* scores for all three areas are considered, Ballymacarrett differs from the others in that males and females have sharply different network patterns, with males scoring high on the network strength scale and females scoring low. It appears from the anthropological literature that in communities of this type the polarization of the sexes reflected by these scores is rather general.

The third point may be related to the second. Sex grading in language (as well as in network structure) is very much sharper in Ballymacarrett than in the other two areas. Furthermore, in Ballymacarrett more clearly than elsewhere, speakers reveal in their patterns of language use the existence across two generations of an agreed set of linguistic norms.[2] Paradoxically, this agreement on a set of norms does not involve a simple reduction in variability, or in any sense a move towards linguistic uniformity, since sex grading in Ballymacarrett is, as we have seen, particularly sharp. Rather, it involves the emergence of regularity

---

[2]I use the term 'sociolinguistic norm' here to refer to an element which displays regular distributional patterns in the community of the kind we have been discussing.

in the patterning of these variable elements and the development of a clear social function to which that regularity might be related.

Taking all these points together, I would suggest that if we wish to examine the social mechanisms which encourage linguistic focusing we must view the variables of sex and network structure as working together in a particularly intimate way. At the moment we are not able to characterize this relationship very precisely.

The relationship between group structure and the emergence of a linguistic norm has already been discussed by Le Page (1979 *et passim*), who makes very similar points to some of those raised here. In particular, he suggests that the emergence of a closeknit group, a sense of solidarity and a feeling of shared territory are all conditions favouring focusing (cf. also Cheshire, this volume). However, he does not use the concept of social network as an analytic procedure to examine the sociolinguistic reflexes of focusing, as I have tried to do in this paper. In fact, the set of procedures which are used in social network analysis appears to have very powerful implications for sociolinguistic research (cf. also Russell, this volume). Network analysis is designed fundamentally to reflect the character of an individual's relationship to the informally constituted groups with which he is associated. From the point of view of the linguist, the technique can be seen as a useful tool for the purpose of characterizing the manner in which persons adapt their language to the language of the various groups to which they may be said to belong. To describe, at a satisfying level of linguistic and social detail, the relationships between individual and collective linguistic behaviour must surely be the most important ultimate goal of those engaged in the study of language variation.

10

Linguistic variation and social function

Jenny Cheshire

The fact that linguistic variation is correlated with a wide range of sociological characteristics of speakers has been extensively documented over the last 15 years by the many studies that have been inspired by the work of William Labov. It is well established, for example, that the frequency with which speakers use non-standard linguistic features is correlated with their socioeconomic class. More recently, studies involving speakers from a single socioeconomic class have been able to reveal some of the more subtle aspects of sociolinguistic variation. It has been found, for example, that the frequency of use of non-standard phonological features in Belfast English is correlated with the type of social network in which speakers are involved (see Milroy and Margrain 1980). This paper will show that the frequency with which adolescent speakers use many non-standard morphological and syntactic features of the variety of English spoken in the town of Reading, in Berkshire is correlated with the extent to which they adhere to the norms of the vernacular culture. It will also show that linguistic variables often fulfil different social and semantic functions for the speakers who use them.

The paper will consider nine non-standard features of Reading English:

1. the present tense suffix with non 3rd person singular subjects
   e.g. we *goes* shopping on Saturdays
2. *has* with non 3rd person singular subjects
   e.g. we *has* a little fire, keeps us warm
3. *was* with plural subjects (and singular *you*)
   e.g. you *was* outside
4. multiple negation
   e.g. I'm *not* going *nowhere*
5. negative past tense *never*, used for standard English *didn't*
   e.g. I *never* done it, it was him
6. *what* used for standard English *who*, *whom*, *which*, and *that*
   e.g. there's a knob *what* you turn
   Are you the boy *what*'s just come?

7 auxiliary *do* with 3rd person singular subjects
  e.g. how much *do* he want for it?
8 past tense *come*
  e.g. I *come* down here yesterday
9 *ain't*, used for negative present tense forms of *be* and *have*, with all
  subjects
  e.g. I *ain't* going
    I *ain't* got any

Many, though not all, of these features function as markers of vernacular loyalty for adolescent speakers in Reading, though some are more sensitive markers than others. *Ain't*, in particular, is able overtly to symbolize some of the important values of the vernacular culture. Furthermore, some features are markers of loyalty to the vernacular culture for adolescent boys but not for adolescent girls, and vice-versa.

The data

The analysis is based on the spontaneous, natural speech of three groups of adolescents, recorded by the method of long-term participant-observation in adventure playgrounds in Reading. The aim was to record speech that was as close as possible to the vernacular, or most informal style, of the speakers. Thirteen boys and twelve girls were recorded over a period of about eight months.

Some of the speakers were subsequently recorded at school, by their teacher, with two or three of their friends. The fieldwork procedures are discussed in detail in Cheshire 1979.

The vernacular culture index

Labov (1966) maintains that the use of non-standard features is controlled by the norms of the vernacular subculture, whilst the use of standard English features is controlled by the overt norms of the mainstream culture in society. Any analysis of variation in the occurrence of non-standard features needs to take this into account, for it means that an adequate sample of non-standard forms is more likely to be found where speakers conform more closely to vernacular norms than to the overt norms of the dominant mainstream culture. The speakers who were chosen for the present study were children who often met at the adventure playgrounds when they should have been at school, and the boys, in particular, were members of a very well-defined subculture. In many respects this culture resembled a delinquent subculture (as defined, for example, by Andry 1960; Cohen 1965; Downes 1966; Willmott 1966 and many other writers). Many of the boys' activities, for example, centred around what Miller (1958) calls the 'cultural foci' of *trouble, excitement, toughness, fate, autonomy* and *smartness* (in the American English sense of 'outsmarting').

Since the vernacular culture was in this case very clearly defined, it was possible to isolate a small number of indicators that could be used to construct a 'vernacular culture index', in the same way that socioeconomic indices are constructed. It seemed reasonable to assume that those aspects of the peer-group culture that were sources of prestige for group members and that were frequent topics of conversation were of central importance within the culture. Six factors that met these requirements were selected. Four of these reflect the norms of trouble and excitement; three directly, and one more indirectly. *Skill at fighting, the carrying of a weapon* and *participation in minor criminal activities,* such as shoplifting, arson, and vandalism, are clearly connected with trouble and excitement. Though interrelated, they were treated as separate indicators because not all boys took part in all the activities to the same extent. The job that the boys hoped to have when they left school was also included as a separate indicator, for the same reason. Again, acceptable jobs reflect the norms of trouble and excitement, though perhaps more indirectly here, and the job that the boys hoped to have when they left school (or, in a few cases, that they already had) was an important contributing factor to the opinion that they formed of themselves and of other group members. Some jobs that were acceptable were slaughterer, lorry driver, motor mechanic, and soldier; jobs that were unacceptable were mostly white-collar jobs. A fifth indicator was 'style': the extent to which dress and hairstyle were important to speakers. Many writers stress the importance of style as a symbolic value within adolescent subcultures (see, for example, Cohen 1972; Clarke 1973), and for many of the boys in the group it was a frequent topic of conversation.

Finally, a measure of 'swearing' was included in the index, since this appeared to be an extremely important symbol of vernacular identity for both boys and girls. Swearing is, of course, a linguistic feature, but this does not affect its use as an indicator here, since it involves only a few lexical items which could not be marked for any of the non-standard features of Reading English.

The behaviour of the boys with regard to each of these factors could be shown on a Guttman scale. The coefficient of reproductability was 0.97, which confirms that the data are scalable (see Pelto 1970, Appendix B).

The boys were then given a score for each of the indicators, and were divided into four groups on the basis of their total score. Group 1 consists of those boys who can be considered to adhere most closely to the norms of the vernacular culture, whilst group 4 consists of boys who do not adhere closely to vernacular norms. Groups 2 and 3 are intermediate in their adherence, with group 2 adhering more closely than group 3.

Linguistic markers of adherence to the vernacular culture

Table 1 shows the frequency of occurrence of the nine nonstandard features in the speech of the four groups of boys.

The features are arranged into three classes, which reflect the extent to which they mark adherence to the vernacular culture. Class A contains four features whose frequency is very finely linked to the vernacular culture index of the speakers. The most sensitive indicator is the non-standard present tense suffix, which occurs very frequently in the speech of those boys who are most firmly immersed in the vernacular culture (group 1), progressively less frequently in the speech of groups 2 and 3, and rather infrequently in the speech of boys who are only loosely involved in the culture (group 4). This feature, then, functions as a powerful marker of vernacular loyalty.

The features in Class B (non-standard *never* and non-standard *what*) also function as markers of vernacular loyalty, but they are less sensitive markers than the features in Class A. Significant variation occurs only between speakers in Group 1 and speakers in Group 4, in other words, between the boys who adhere most closely to the vernacular culture, and the boys who adhere least closely. This type of sociolinguistic variation is not unusual: Policansky (1980) reports similar behaviour with subject-verb concord in Belfast English, where significant variation is found only between speakers at the extreme ends of the social network scale (cf. also Jahangiri and Hudson, this volume).

The fact that there is some correlation between the vernacular culture index and the frequency of use of Group B features can be clearly seen if the speakers in Groups 2 and 3 are amalgamated into a single group.

Table 1: Adherence to vernacular culture and frequency of occurrence of non-standard forms

		Group 1	Group 2	Group 3	Group 4
Class A	nonstandard -*s*	77.36	54.03	36.57	21.21
	nonstandard *has*	66.67	50.00	41.65	(33.33)
	nonstandard *was*	90.32	89.74	83.33	75.00
	negative concord	100.00	85.71	83.33	71.43
Class B	nonstandard *never*	64.71	41.67	45.45	37.50
	nonstandard *what*	92.31	7.69	33.33	0.00
Class C	nonstandard aux. *do*	58.33	37.50	83.33	—
	nonstandard *come*	100.00	100.00	100.00	(100.00)
	ain't=aux *have*	78.26	64.52	80.00	(100.00)
	ain't=aux *be*	58.82	72.22	80.00	(100.00)
	ain't=copula	100.00	76.19	56.52	75.00

NB   Bracketed figures indicate that the number of occurrences of the variable is low, and that the indices may not, therefore, be reliable. Following Labov (1970) less than 5 occurrences was considered to be too low for reliability.

Table 2: Frequency indices of group 1, groups 2 and 3, and group 4

	Group 1	Groups 2 & 3	Group 4
nonstandard *never*	64.71	43.00	37.50
nonstandard *what*	92.31	18.00	0.00

Table 2 shows that non-standard *never* and non-standard *what* now show regular patterns of variation. These features, then, do function as markers of vernacular loyalty. But they are less sensitive markers than the features in Class A, showing regular patterning only with rather broad groupings of speakers.

Features in class C, on the other hand, do not show any correlation with the speakers' vernacular culture index. For the most part, figures are completely irregular. All these features, however, are involved in other, more complex, kinds of sociolinguistic variation, and this could explain why they do not function as straightforward markers of vernacular loyalty. There is convincing evidence, for example, that non-standard auxiliary *do* is undergoing a linguistic change away from an earlier dialect form towards the standard English form (see Cheshire 1978. See also Aitchison, 1981, for some interesting ideas concerning the mechanism of the change). Some forms of *ain't* appear to function as a direct marker of a vernacular norm, as we will see. We will also see that the use of non-standard *come* bears an interesting relation to the sex of speakers: it functions as a marker of vernacular loyalty for adolescent girls, but for boys it is an invariant feature, occurring 100 per cent of the time in their speech, irrespective of the extent to which they adhere to the vernacular culture.

Stylistic variation

We will now consider what happens to the frequency of occurrence of these linguistic features when the boys are at school. The Labovian view of style shifting is that formality–informality can be considered as a linear continuum, reflecting the amount of attention that speakers give to their speech. As formality increases, the frequency of occurrence of some non-standard linguistic features decreases (see Labov 1972b, chapter 3). This approach has been questioned by a number of scholars. L. Milroy (1980) and Romaine (1980), for example, found that reading, where attention is directly focused on speech, does not consistently result in the use of fewer non-standard features. And Wolfson (1976) points out that in some situations speakers will monitor their speech carefully to ensure that they use *more* non-standard features, in order to produce an appropriately informal speech style.

The present study also found difficulties in applying the Labovian approach to the analysis of style, for the ability of some linguistic features to signal vernacular loyalty affects the frequency with which they occur in different speech styles.

The recordings made at school were clearly made in a more formal setting than the recordings made in the adventure playgrounds. The speakers were in school, where the overt norms of mainstream society are maintained (see, for example, Moss 1973), the teacher was present, the speaker knew that he was being recorded, and there had been no 'warm-up' session with the tape-recorder before the recording was made. On the other hand, the speaker did have two (at least) of his friends present. This was in an attempt to stop him 'drying up', as he may have done in a straightforward interview situation, and although the intention was to make the situation somewhat more relaxed, it nevertheless clearly represents a more formal setting than the adventure playground.

Unfortunately only eight of the thirteen boys could be recorded at school. Four boys had recently left school, and the fifth was so unpopular with the teacher that she could not be persuaded to spend extra time with him.

Table 3 shows the frequency of occurrence of the nonstandard linguistic features in the vernacular style and in the school style of these eight speakers. We can see that those features that are sensitive markers of vernacular loyalty (class A) all occur less often in the boys' school style than in their vernacular style, though the difference in frequency is very small in the case of non-standard *was*.

Non-standard *never*, in class B, also occurs less often in the school recordings. Non-standard *what*, however, does not decrease in frequency; instead, it increases slightly in occurrence. The remaining features in the table do not decrease in frequency in the school style, either. Non-standard *come* remains invariant, and *ain't* increases in frequency by quite a large amount. (There were no occurrences of third person singular forms of auxiliary *do* in the school recordings).

So far, of course, this is quite in accordance with the Labovian view of

Table 3: Stylistic variation in the frequency of occurrence of non-standard forms

		vernacular style	school style
Class A	nonstandard *-s*	57.03	31.49
	nonstandard *has*	46.43	35.71
	nonstandard *was*	91.67	88.57
	negative concord	90.70	66.67
Class B	nonstandard *never*	49.21	15.38
	nonstandard *what*	50.00	54.55
Class C	nonstandard *do*	—	—
	nonstandard *come*	100.00	100.00
	ain't=aux. *have*	93.02	100.00
	ain't=copula	74.47	77.78

the stylistic continuum. Labov classifies linguistic variable
'indicators' and 'markers', which differ in that indicators show r
variation only with sociological characteristics of speakers, wh
markers also show regular correlation with style. We could, therei◡ɪe,
class the linguistic variables in class A, together with non-standard
never, as markers in Reading English, and class the other variables as
indicators. But this would be oversimplistic. As we will see, there are
some more complex factors involved in stylistic variation, which only
become apparent if we compare the linguistic behaviour of individual
speakers, rather than of groups of speakers.

Table 3 expressed the frequency of occurrence of the non-standard
features in terms of group indices; in other words, the speech of the eight
boys analysed together, as a whole. There are many practical advantages
to the analysis of the speech of groups of speakers, particularly where
morphological and syntactic variables are concerned. One advantage is
that variables may not occur frequently enough in the language of an
individual speaker for a detailed analysis to be made, whereas the
language of a group of speakers will usually provide an adequate
number of occurrences of crucial forms (cf. also the discussion in
J. Milroy, this volume).

The school recordings consisted of only about half an hour of speech
for each boy. This did not provide enough data for an analysis in terms
of individual speakers, and in most cases it did not even provide enough
data for a group analysis. There was one exception, however. Present
tense verb forms occur very frequently in speech, so that even within a
half hour recording there were enough forms for an analysis of their use
by individual speakers to be made. This enables us to investigate some of
the more subtle aspects of sociolinguistic variation, that would be
overlooked in a group analysis.

Table 4 shows the frequency of occurrence of non-standard present
tense verb forms in the speech of each of the eight boys, in their
vernacular style and in their school style. Noddy, Ricky and Perry are
Group 1 speakers, with a high vernacular culture index; Kitty, Jed and
Gammy are group 2 speakers, and Barney and Colin are in group 3.

There are considerable differences in the use of the non-standard
forms by the different speakers. Noddy's use of the non-standard form,
for example, decreases by only 3.22 per cent in his school style, whereas
the other group 1 speakers (Ricky and Perry) show a much greater
decrease. Jed (a group 2 speaker) does not use the non-standard form at
all in his school style, although the other group 2 speakers (Kitty and
Gammy) continue to use non-standard forms, albeit with a reduced
frequency. Colin, like Jed, does not use the non-standard form in school
style; Barney's use of the form, on the other hand, actually increases, by
quite a large amount.

Present tense verb forms are sensitive markers of vernacular loyalty,
as we have seen; and a group analysis of their occurrence in different

Table 4: Frequency of occurrence of non-standard present tense verb forms

	vernacular style	school style
Noddy	81.00	77.78
Ricky	70.83	34.62
Perry	71.43	54.55
Jed	45.00	0.00
Kitty	45.71	33.33
Gammy	57.14	31.75
Barney	31.58	54.17
Colin	38.46	0.00

speech styles showed that they were also sensitive to style. We saw that the feature could be classed as a marker, in the Labovian sense. Individual analyses, however, reveal that two speakers do not show the decrease in frequency that we would expect to find in their school style: Noddy, as we have seen, shows only a slight decrease, unlike the other boys in his group, an Barney's frequency actually increases. Their linguistic behaviour does not seem to be related to the vernacular culture index, for Noddy is a group 1 speaker, showing strong allegiance to the peer-group culture, whilst Barney is a group 3 speaker. One factor that could explain Noddy's behaviour is age: Noddy was only 11, whilst the other boys were aged between 13 and 16. Noddy may, therefore, have simply not yet acquired the ability to style shift. Labov (1965) suggested that children do not acquire this ability until the age of about 14, and there is some empirical evidence to support this (see Macaulay, 1977). Other recent studies, however, have found evidence of stylistic sensitivity at a rather younger age (see Reid 1978; Romaine 1975) , so that we cannot conclude with any certainty that this is a relevant factor here. In any case, Barney's behaviour cannot be explained this way, for he was 15, and old enough to show some signs of stylistic sensitivity. We need to explore further, then, to discover an explanation for this irregular behaviour.

Barney was recorded with Noddy and Kitty, by their teacher. The teacher was asking them about their activities outside school, and the boys were talking about a disco that they were trying to organize. The teacher was making valiant efforts to understand the conversation, but was obviously unfamiliar with the kind of amplifying equipment and with the situation that the boys were telling him about. It is worth noting that Barney and Noddy hated school and made very derisory remarks about their teachers. Barney had only just returned to school after an absence of a whole term, and Noddy attended school only intermittently. Kitty, on the other hand, attended school more regularly—his father was very strict, and he did not dare to play truant as often as his friends did.

These factors suggest an explanation for the boys' linguistic behaviour. A great deal of insight into linguistic behaviour has been gained from recent research by social psychologists, working within the framework of speech accommodation theory. It has been shown that speakers who are favourably disposed towards each other and who are 'working towards a common goal' adjust their speech so that they each speak more like the other, whereas speakers who are not working towards a common goal may diverge in their linguistic behaviour. One way in which speech convergence is marked is the frequency of occurrence of certain linguistic variables (see Thakerar, Giles and Cheshire, forthcoming).

An explanation along these lines gives some insight into the behaviour of Noddy, Kitty and Barney in the school situation. Kitty knows the teacher, attends school fairly regularly, and we can imagine that he accepts the constraints of the situation. As a result his speech converges towards the teacher's, and he uses fewer non-standard linguistic forms than he does normally. Noddy, on the other hand, hates school and dislikes the teacher; as a result he asserts his allegiance to the peer-group culture rather than to the school, by refusing to acknowledge the situational constraints. The frequency with which he uses the non-standard form, therefore, does not change (or changes only slightly). Barney, who has only recently returned to school, asserts his total independence and hostility to the school by using more non-standard forms than he does usually. This is a very clear example of speech divergence. As we saw earlier, Barney is not closely involved in the vernacular culture, and this is reflected in his speech by a relatively low use of non-standard present tense forms. When he wants to assert his independence from the school culture, however, he is able to exploit the resources of the language system, by choosing to use a higher proportion of non-standard forms than he does usually.

Can an explanation in these terms account for the linguistic behaviour of the other boys in this study? For at least three of the boys, it seems that it can.

Ricky, Perry and Gammy were recorded together, by a teacher that they knew and liked. He had taken them on camping and fishing weekend expeditions, with some of their classmates. The conversation was initially about one of these weekends, and then moved on to racing cars and motorbikes, subjects that interested both the teacher and the boys. Speech accommodation theory would predict that in this situation the linguistic behaviour of the boys would converge towards that of their teacher (and, of course, vice-versa). This is precisely what happens—all three boys use a lower proportion of non-standard present tense forms here than they do in their vernacular speech style. The fact that they continue to use *some* non-standard forms, however, means that they are still able to show their allegiance to the vernacular subculture.

Jed and Colin behave rather differently from the other boys, for in their school recordings they do not use any non-standard forms at all.

This is surprising, particularly in the case of Jed, who is a Group 2 speaker, like Kitty and Gammy. There are, however, some striking similarities between the linguistic behaviour of these two boys, and the situations in which the school recordings were made. They were recorded at different times, with a different speaker, but both recordings were made in a classroom situation, with about 20 pupils and the teacher. Both Jed and Colin participated a great deal in the discussions, partly because the teacher had purposely chosen topics on which they had strong views (football hooliganism, in Jed's case, and truancy, in Colin's case), and partly because they were encouraged to take part by the teacher. It is possible, though, that the situation was so drastically different from the situation in the adventure playground that the overall formality overrode the option of displaying linguistically their allegiance to the vernacular culture. Or perhaps the fact that no other members of the peer-group were present meant that the boys were more susceptible to the pressures of the norms of the school culture.

It seems, then, that a simple analysis in terms of the formality or informality of the situation cannot fully explain stylistic variation here. A better explanation can, perhaps, be achieved if we think in terms of situational constraints on exploiting the resources of the linguistic system. The non-standard present tense suffix is a powerful indicator of vernacular loyalty, and in some cases this function overrides other situational constraints on linguistic behaviour (as in the speech of Noddy and Barney, for example) In other cases, (as with Jed and Colin), the situational constraints exclude the possibility of using the feature in this way.

The linguistic behaviour of adolescent girls

Many surveys of non-standard English have found that female speakers use nonstandard speech forms less frequently than male speakers do. Table 5 shows that an analysis of the use of non-standard forms by girls and by boys confirms this pattern of behaviour.

Only non-standard auxiliary *do* is used more often by girls than by boys. As we have seen, this feature is involved in an on-going linguistic change, and has several irregular characteristics. The other non-standard features are all used less often by girls than they are by boys. In some cases the difference in frequency is very small (non-standard present tense verb forms, for example), but for most features the difference in frequency is more striking.

This kind of analysis, however, again conceals the ways in which linguistic features function as symbols of vernacular identity.

It was not possible to construct a vernacular culture index for the girls, as it was for the boys. The girls did not form structured peer-groups in the way that the boys did and, partly as a result of this, the norms of their

Table 5: Linguistic variation and sex differences

	Frequency indices for nonstandard features in boys' speech	Frequency indices for nonstandard features in girls' speech
nonstandard -*s*	53.16	52.04
nonstandard *has*	54.76	51.61
nonstandard *was*	88.15	73.58
negative concord	88.33	51.85
nonstandard *never*	46.84	40.00
nonstandard *what*	36.36	14.58
nonstandard *do*	57.69	78.95
nonstandard *come*	100.00	75.33
ain't=aux *have*	92.00	64.58
ain't=aux *be*	74.19	42.11
ain't=copula	85.83	61.18

vernacular subculture were less well-defined. It was possible, however, to divide the girls loosely into two groups, for three of the girls were clearly different from the others. They did not swear, steal, or set fire to the playground. They attended school regularly, and their parents did not approve of the adventure playground, because the children that their daughters met there were 'common' and 'rough'.

Table 6 shows the frequency of use of the nine non-standard features in the speech of these three girls, and also in the speech of the other girls in the group. This division of speakers is, of course, not ideal, since we are comparing the speech of a group of only three speakers with the speech of a group of nine speakers, but it can, nevertheless, give us an idea of the different ways in which linguistic features can function as markers of vernacular loyalty.

It can be seen from the table that some linguistic features appear to mark adherence to the vernacular culture, in that they are used less often by the 'good' girls than by the others. Other features, however, do not behave in this way. And if we compare Table 6 with Table 1, which showed those features that mark vernacular loyalty in the boys' speech, some interesting differences emerge.

Table 6: Use of non-standard features by 'good' girls and by other girls

	Frequency index: 'good' girls	Frequency index: other girls
non-standard -*s*	25.84	57.27
nonstandard *has*	36.36	35.85
nonstandard *was*	63.64	80.95
negative concord	12.50	58.70
nonstandard *never*	45.45	41.07
nonstandard *what*	33.33	5.56
nonstandard *come*	30.77	90.63
ain't=copula	14.29	67.12

(There are no data for non-standard auxiliary *do*, nor for *ain't* as auxiliary *be* or as auxiliary *have*.)

Features 1–4, for example, (non-standard -*s*, non-standard *has*, non-standard *was* and negative concord) all function as sensitive markers of vernacular loyalty for boys. Three of these features function in the same way for girls, as Table 6 shows. Non-standard *has*, however, is used with approximately the same frequency by both 'good' girls and the other girls. This feature does not, therefore, function as a marker of vernacular loyalty for girls.[1]

Non-standard *never* and non-standard *what* functioned only loosely as markers of vernacular loyalty for the boys. For girls, they do not appear to fulfil any symbolic function at all: the 'good' girls use them, in fact, more often than the other girls.

On the other hand, non-standard *come* and *ain't* appear to function as markers of vernacular identity for girls, although they do not for boys. Non-standard *come* is an invariant feature of the dialect for boys, occurring 100 per cent of the time in the speech of all speakers, in both speech styles (including those speakers who adhere only loosely to the norms of the vernacular culture). 'Good' girls, however, use non-standard *come* relatively infrequently (30.77 per cent of the time), whilst the other girls use it much more often (90.63 per cent of the time). Similarly, *ain't* is used much less often by the 'good' girls than it is by the other girls.

We can conclude, then, that male and female speakers in Reading exploit the resources of the linguistic system in different ways. Some linguistic features are markers of vernacular loyalty for both sexes (non-standard present tense verb forms, non-standard *was*, and negative concord). Some features function in this way for boys only (non-standard *never* and nonstandard *what*). And others fulfil this function only for girls (non-standard *come* and *ain't*).

The direct reflection of vernacular norms

Non-standard features can sometimes reflect vernacular norms in a more direct way; not just in terms of the *frequency* with which different speakers use the non-standard forms, but also in terms of the specific *form* of a variable that speakers choose to use (cf. also the papers by J. and L. Milroy, this volume).

For example, *ain't* has a number of different phonetic realizations in the speech of the adolescent groups. These include [ɪnt], [ænt] and [eɪnt], and can be divided into two main groups—those approximating to *ain't*, and those approximating to *in't*. It is reasonable to expect that [ɪnt] would correspond to standard English *isn't*. This is not the case, however: [ɪnt] forms are used with all subjects, and they are used when the verb is auxiliary *have*, as well as when it is *be*.

The use of *ain't* forms rather than the corresponding standard English

---

[1]As L. Milroy (1980) points out.

forms is subject to a linguistic constraint in Reading English: *ain't* occurs more often in a tag question than it does in any other syntactic environment. The usual function of tag questions is to seek confirmation or corroboration from the hearer for the proposition expressed in the main sentence (see Stockwell, Schachter and Partee 1973). Some tag questions, however, are used by the adolescent groups in a way that does not seek confirmation, but that expresses instead feelings of aggression and assertion. These tags do not require an answer from the hearer, and in most cases the hearer would be unable to provide one.

An example can be found in the interchange below. The boys were going to be taken on a camping weekend by the social worker who was in charge of the adventure playground, and all boys aged 16 and over were supposed to help put up the tents. I was having trouble understanding whether Roger was going on the trip or not, and he was getting impatient:

1	*Jenny*:	Aren't you going to help, though?
2	*Roger*:	No, I ain't going. I ain't going to help. Bugger that!
3	*Jenny*:	Are you staying here?
4	*Roger*:	Eh?
5	*Jenny*:	Are you staying here?
6	*Colin*:	No, he's going camping.
7	*Roger*:	No, I'm going, mate, *in I?*
8	*Jenny*:	You're going, but you're not going to help?
9	*Roger*:	No, I'm not going to help. Bugger that.
10	*Jenny*:	Aren't you over 16, though?
11	*Roger*:	Yeah, I'm 17.

The effect of Roger's tag question (line 7), which was addressed specifically to me, was (intentionally) to make me feel that I had asked a foolish question, and the general impression was one of aggression. I did not know the answer to his question; in fact, I had been trying to obtain the answer from him.

Another example occurs in the interchange below, between Colin, Puvvy and Roger:

1	*Roger*:	He might be taking Britt, he says.
2	*Colin*:	Oh, what a thrill. What a name, Britt.
3	*Puvvy*:	Who started calling her it?
4	*Roger*:	It's her proper name, *in it?*

Again, the effect of Roger's tag question (in line 4) is aggressive: he conveys the impression that Puvvy is foolish not to know that 'Britt' is a real name; and he is *telling* him that it is her proper name, rather than asking for confirmation.

Assertion and aggression, of course, are important elements in the vernacular subculture. Street fights, swearing, shouting and stealing are all aggressive acts. It is significant, therefore, that those tag questions that contain a negative present tense form of *be* or *have* and that are assertive and aggressive in meaning are marked linguistically by the categorical use of the form *in't*. Other phonetic realizations of *ain't* never occur in these tag questions; nor do the corresponding standard English forms. *In't* is used with all subjects, and as both *be* and *have*. In other kinds of tag question, however, *in't* occurs variably with *ain't* and the standard forms.

A full discussion of the use of *ain't* in Reading English can be found in Cheshire (forthcoming). It should be clear, though, that this is an example of a non-standard form that can overtly reflect the norms of the vernacular culture. The use of *in't* in a tag question, then, can fulfil a semantic function for speakers of Reading English.

Conclusion

This paper has focused on the social function of linguistic variation in the speech of adolescent peer-groups. We have seen that non-standard linguistic features function in a number of different ways. Some are very sensitive markers of vernacular loyalty, showing a regular correlation in frequency with the extent to which speakers adhere to the vernacular culture. Others are less sensitive markers of vernacular loyalty. We have also seen that the social function of non-standard features can vary with the sex of the speaker, and that this social function can sometimes override the constraints imposed on speakers by the formality of the stituation. Finally, in one case at least, linguistic variation is able to fulfil a semantic function, in that a speaker's choice of a variable form can directly reflect some of the values of the vernacular culture.

References

AITCHISON, J. 1981: *Language change: progress or decay?* London: Fontana.

ANDRY, R. G. 1960: *Delinquency and parental pathology*. London: Methuen.

BEEMAN, WILLIAM O. 1976a: Status, style and strategy in Iranian interaction. *Anthropological Linguistics*, 305–22.

—1976b: *The meaning of stylistic variation in Iranian interaction*. University of Chicago PhD dissertation.

—1977: The hows and whys of Persian style: a pragmatic approach. In Ralph W. Fasold and Roger W. Shuy, eds, *Studies in language variation*, Washington, DC: Georgetown University Press, 269–82.

BERDAN, ROBERT 1975a: *On the nature of linguistic variation*. University of Texas, PhD thesis.

—1975b: The necessity of variable rules. In Ralph W. Fasold and Roger W. Shuy, eds, *Analyzing variation in language*, Washington, DC: Georgetown University Press, 11–26.

—1978: Multidimensional analysis of vowel variation. In Sankoff, ed, 149–61.

BICKERTON, D. 1975: *Dynamics of a Creole system*. Cambridge: Cambridge University Press.

—1971: Inherent variability and variable rules. *Foundations of Language* 7, 457–92.

BLOM, J.-P. and GUMPERZ, J. 1972: Social meaning in linguistic structures: code-switching in Norway. In Gumperz, J. and Hymes, D., eds, *Directions in Sociolinguistics*, New York: Holt, Rinehart and Winston, 407–34.

BLOOM, L., LIGHTBOWN, P. and HOOD, L. 1975: *Structure and variation in child language*. Monographs of the Society for Research in Child Language Development 160.

BOISSEVAIN, J. 1974: *Friends of friends: networks, manipulators and coalitions*. Oxford: Blackwell.

BOISSEVAIN, J. and MITCHELL, J. C., eds, 1973: *Network analysis: studies in human interaction*. The Hague: Mouton.

BOTT, E. 1971: *Family and Social Network* (rev. edn). London: Tavistock.

CHESHIRE, J. 1978: Present tense verbs in Reading English. In Trudgill, ed., 52–69.

—1982: *Variation in an English dialect: a sociolinguistic study*. London: Cambridge University Press, forthcoming.

—(forthcoming): Variation in the use of *ain't* in an urban British dialect. *Language in Society*

CHOMSKY, N. and HALLE, M. 1968: *The sound pattern of English*. New York: Harper.

CLARKE, J. 1973: *The skinheads and the study of youth culture.* Occasional paper, Birmingham: Centre for Contemporary Cultural Studies.

COHEN, A. K. 1955: *Delinquent boys.* New York: The Free Press.

COHEN, P. 1972: *Subcultural conflict and working-class community.* Working papers in cultural studies, 2, Birmingham: Centre for Contemporary Cultural Studies.

COMREY, A. L. 1973: *A first course in factor analysis.* London: Academic Press.

CORDER, S. PIT. 1973: *Introducing applied linguistics.* Harmondsworth: Penguin.

CRAWFORD, BARBARA E. 1976/7: The earldom of Caithness and the kingdom of Scotland, 1150–1266. *Northern Scotland* 2, 97–117.

CRYSTAL, D. 1969: *Prosodic systems and intonation in English.* London: Cambridge University Press.

—1979: Prosodic development. In Garman, M. and Fletcher, P., eds, *Language Acquisition,* Cambridge: Cambridge University Press.

CRYSTAL D. and DAVY, D. 1969: *Investigating English Style.* London: Longmans.

—1970: *Advanced conversational English.* London: Longmans.

CRYSTAL, D. and QUIRK, R. 1964: *Systems of prosodic and paralinguistic features in English.* The Hague: Mouton.

CUBITT, T. 1973: Network density among urban families. In Boissevain and Mitchell, eds, 67–82.

DECAMP, DAVID 1971: Toward a generative analysis of a post-Creole speech continuum. In Hymes, D., ed, *Pidginization and creolization of languages.* London: Cambridge University Press, 349–70.

DORE, J. A. 1973: *The development of speech acts.* City University of New York, PhD dissertation, unpublished.

DORIAN, NANCY C. 1977: The problem of the semi-speaker in language death, *International Journal of the Sociology of Language* 12, 23–32.

—1978: *East Sutherland Gaelic.* Dublin: Dublin Institute for Advanced Studies.

—1980: The maintenance and loss of same-meaning structures in language death. *Word* 31, 39–45.

—1981: *Language death: the life-cycle of a Scottish Gaelic dialect.* Philadelphia: University of Pennsylvania Press.

DOWNES, D. 1966: *The delinquent solution.* London: Routledge & Kegan Paul.

EVERITT, B. S. 1974: *Cluster analysis.* London: Heinemann.

FASOLD, R. 1978: Language variation and linguistic competence. In Sankoff, D., ed, 85–95.

FERGUSON, C. A. and FARWELL, C. B. 1975: Words and sounds in early language acquisition. *Language* 51, 419–39.

FILLMORE, CHARLES J. 1979: On fluency. In Charles J. Fillmore, Daniel Kempler and William S.-Y. Wang, eds, 85–101.

FILLMORE, C., KEMPLER, D. and WANG, W. 1979: *Individual differences in language ability and language behavior.* New York: Academic Press.

FILLMORE, K. L. 1976: *The second time around: cognitive and social strategies in second language acquisition.* Stanford University, PhD dissertation.

FISHMAN, J. 1968: Some contrasts between linguistically heterogeneous and linguistically homogeneous polities. In Fishman, J., Ferguson, C. and Das Gupta, J., eds, *Language problems of developing nations.* New York: Wiley, 53–68.

—1971: The sociology of language. In Joshua A. Fishman, ed., *Advances in the sociology of language,* vol. I, The Hague: Mouton, 217–404.

FRIED, M. 1973: *The world of the urban working class.* Cambridge, Mass.: Harvard University Press.

GARVEY, C. and DICKSTEIN, D. E. 1972: Levels of analysis and social class differences in language. *Language and Speech* 15, 375–84.

GAUCHAT, L. 1905: L'unite phonetique dans le patois d'une commune. In *Aus Romanischen Sprachen und Literaturen: Festschrift Heinrich Morf.* Halle: Max Niemeyer, 175–232.

GILES, H. and POWESLAND, P. E. 1975: *Speech style and social evaluation.* New York: Academic Press.

GIMSON, A. C. 1980: *Introduction to the pronunciation of English,* 3rd edn, London, Longmans.

GOFFMAN, E. 1975: *Frame analysis.* London: Penguin.

GOWER, J. C. 1969: A survey of numerical methods useful in taxonomy. *Acaralogia* 11, 357–76.

GULLIVER, P. H. 1971: *Neighbours and networks.* California: University of California Press.

GUMPERZ, J. 1968: The speech community. In *International encyclopaedia of the social sciences.* New York: Macmillan, 381–6.

—1971: The speech community, reprinted in Anwar S. Dill, ed, *Language in social groups: Essays by John J. Gumperz.* Stanford: Stanford University Press.

—1972: Sociolinguistics and communications in small groups. In Pride, J. B. and Holmes, J., eds, *Sociolinguistics. Selected readings.* Harmondsworth: Penguin, 203–224.

—1976a: *Social network and Language shift.* In Working Paper 46, Language Behavior Research Lab., Berkeley: University of California, unpublished.

—1976b: *The sociolinguistic significance of conversational code-switching.* In Working Paper 46, Language Behavior Research Lab., Berkeley: University of California.

GUTHRIE, M. 1970: *Comparative Bantu* vol. III. Farnborough: Gregg Press.

GUY, G. 1974: *Variation in the group and the individual: the case of final stop deletion.* Pennsylvania Working Papers on Linguistic Change and Variation. Vol. III, 4.

—1977: A new look at -t, -d deletion. In Fasold, R. and Shuy, R., eds, *Studies in language variation,* Washington, DC: Georgetown University Press, 1–2.

HALLIDAY, M. A. K. 1967: *Intonation and grammar in British English.* The Hague: Mouton.

—1975: *Learning how to mean—explorations in the development of language.* London: Edward Arnold.

HARRIS, J. and MILROY, J. (forthcoming) *Variation in 'the short /ɔ/' system in Belfast.* Report to SSRC.

HEATH, C. D. 1980: The pronunciation of English in Cannock, Staffordshire. *Publications of the Philological Society* xxix, Oxford: Basil Blackwell.

HERMANN, E. 1929: Lautveränderungen in den Individualsprachen einer Mundart. *Nachrichten der Gesellschaft der Wissenschaften zu Göttingen.* Philosophisch-Historische Klasse II, 195–214.

HOMANS, G. C. 1961: *Social Behaviour.* New York: Harcourt, Brace & World.

HUDSON, RICHARD A. 1980: *Sociolinguistics.* Cambridge: Cambridge University Press.

HUGHES, A. and TRUDGILL, P. 1979: *English accents and dialects*. London: Edward Arnold.

HULTZEN, L. S. 1959: Information points in intonation. *Phonetica* 4, 107–20.

HYMES, DELL 1964a: Introduction: Towards ethnographies of communication. In John J. Gumperz and Dell Hymes, eds, *The ethnography of communication*, American Anthropologist Special Publication 66, 6, part 2, Menasha, Wisconsin: American Anthropological Association, 1–34.

—1964b: Directions in (ethno-) linguistic theory. In A. Kimball Romney and Roy Goodwin D'Andrade, eds, *Transcultural Studies in Cognition*, American Anthropologist Special Publication 66, 3, part 2, Menasha, Wisconsin: American Anthropological Association, 6–56.

—1967: Models of the interaction of language and social setting. *Journal of Social Issues*, 23, 8–28.

—1971: Sociolinguistics and the ethnography of speaking. In Edwin Ardener, ed, *Social Anthropology and language*, ASA Monographs 10, London: Tavistock, 47–93.

—1974: *Foundations in sociolinguistics*. Philadelphia: University of Pennsylvania Press.

IRVINE, J. 1978: Wolof noun classification: the social setting of divergent change. *Language in Society* 7, 37–65.

JAHANGIRI, NADER 1980: *A sociolinguistic study of Persian in Tehran*. University of London, PhD thesis.

JAKOBSON, R. 1941: *Kindersprache, Aphasie und allgemeine Lautgesetze*. Uppsala.

JARMAN, E. and CRUTTENDEN, A. 1976: Belfast intonation and the myth of the fall. *Journal of the International Phonetics Association* 61, 4–12.

JESPERSEN, O. 1984: *Progress in language with special reference to English*. London: Swan Sonnenschein & Co.

KAPFERER, B. 1973: Social network and conjugal role in urban Zambia: towards a reformulation of the Bott hypothesis. In Boissevain and Mitchel, eds, 83–110.

KAY, P. 1978: Variable rules, community grammar and linguistic change. In Sankoff, D., ed, 71–82.

KENDALL, M. G. 1966: Discrimination and classification. In P. R. Krishnaiah, ed, *Multi-variate analysis*, New York: Academic Press.

Kenya Population Census, vol, I 1969: Kenya Ministry of Finance and Economic Planning (Statistics Division).

KNOWLES, G. 1974: *Scouse: the urban dialect of Liverpool*. University of Leeds, PhD thesis, unpublished.

—1978: The nature of phonological variables in Scouse. In Trudgill, ed, 80–91.

KRAPF, L. 1844: Copy of letter to R. P. Waters, US Consul in Zanzibar. Mombasa, 2 September 1844, Folio 27 of File CA5/016 (Krapf's correspondence with CMS headquarters.) London: CMS archives, Church Missionary House.

LABOV, W. 1963: The social motivation of a sound change. *Word* 19, 273–309.

—1965: Stages in the acquisition of Standard English. In Shuy, R., ed., Social dialects and language learning. Proceedings of the Bloomington, Indiana, Conference, 1964. Champaign, Ill.: National Council of Teachers of English.

—1966: *The social stratification of English in New York City*. Washington, DC: Center for Applied Linguistics.

—1969: Contraction, deletion and inherent variability of the English copula. *Language* 45, 715–62.

—1970: The study of language in its social context. *Studium Generale* 23, 66–84.

—1972a: *Language in the inner city*. Philadelphia: Pennsylvania University Press.

—1972b: *Sociolinguistic patterns*. Philadelphia: Pennsylvania University Press.

—1973a: The linguistics consequences of being a lame. *Language in Society* 2, 1, 81–115.

—1973b: Where do grammars stop? *23rd Annual Round Table Meeting on Linguistics and Language Studies*. Washington: Georgetown University Press, 43–88.

—1975: Empirical foundations of linguistic theory. In Austerlitz, R., ed, *The scope of American linguistics*. Lisse: The Peter de Ridder Press, 77–135.

LABOV, W., COHEN, P., ROBINS, C. and LEWIS, J. 1968: *A study of the non-standard English of Negro and Puerto Rican speakers in New York City*. Final Report, US Office of Education Cooperative Research Project No. 3288, vols I and II, Washington, DC: Office of Education.

LABOV, W., YAEGER, M. and STEINER, R. 1972: *A quantitative study of sound change in Progress*. Philadelphia: US Regional Survey.

LAFERRIÈRE, M. 1977: Boston short *a*: social variation as historical residue. In Shuy and Fasold, eds, 100–108.

LASS, R. 1980: *On explaining language change*. London: Cambridge University Press.

LE PAGE, R. B. 1968: Problems of description in multilingual communities. *Transactions of the Philological Society*, 189–212.

—1972: Preliminary report on the sociolinguistic survey of Cayo District, British Honduras. *Language in Society* 1, 1, 155–72.

—1977: *Decreolization and recreolization: a preliminary report on the sociolinguistic survey of multilingual communities, stage II, St Lucia*. York Papers in Linguistics 7, 107–28. University of York: Department of Language.

—1978: *Projection, focusing and diffusion, or steps towards a sociolinguistic theory of language, illustrated from the sociolinguistic survey of multilingual communities, stages I: Belize (British Honduras) and II: St Lucia*. Society for Caribbean Linguistics Occasional Paper 9, Mimeo. School of Education, University of the West Indies, St Augustine, Trinidad. Reprinted in York Papers in Linguistics 9, University of York: Department of Language.

—1979: Review of *Dell Hymes—Foundations in sociolinguistics and Norbert Dittmar—Sociolinguistics. Journal of Linguistics* 15, 168–79.

—1980a: Hugo Schuchardt: In K. Lichem and H. J. Simon, eds, *Schuchardt symposium 1977 in Graz*, 114–46. Vienna: Osterreichischen Akademie der Wissenschaften, Veröffentlichungen des Kommission für Linguistik und Kommunikationsforschung, Heft 10.

—1980b: Theoretical aspects of sociolinguistic studies in pidgin and creole. In A. Valdman and A. R. Highfield, eds, *Theoretical Orientations in Creole Studies*, New York: Academic Press, 331–69.

LE PAGE, R., JURDANT, B., WEEKES, A. and TABOURET-KELLER, A. 1974: Further report on the survey of multilingual communities. *Language in Society* 3, 1–32.

LE PAGE, R. B., TABOURET-KELLER, A., MAURY, G., DIDI-KIDIRI, M., and WEEKS, A. J. 1977: *Report to DGRST, Paris, on the sociolinguistic survey of multilingual communities, stage II: St Lucia.* University of York: Department of Language, mimeo.

LEWIS, M. M. 1936: *Infant speech: a study of the beginnings of language.* London: Routledge & Kegan Paul.

LOCAL, J. K. 1978: *Studies towards a description of the development and functioning of children's awareness of linguistic variability.* University of Newcastle-upon-Tyne, PhD thesis, unpublished.

—(forthcoming) *On the interpretation of linguistic variability in children.*

LONGMIRE, B. J. 1976: *The relationship of variables in Venezuelan Spanish to historical sound changes in Latin and the Romance languages.* Georgetown University, PhD thesis.

MACAULAY, R. K. S. 1977: *Language, social class and education: a Glasgow study.* Edinburgh: Edinburgh University Press.

MCENTEGART, D. 1980: *Final report and appraisal of the collection and analysis of the data in the sociolinguistic survey of multilingual communities, stages I (Belize) and II (St Lucia).* London: SSRC.

MARTHLEW, M., CONNOLLY, K., and MCCLEOD, C., 1978: Language use, role and context in a five year old. *Journal of Child Language* 5, 1, 87–99.

MILLER, W. B. 1958: Lower-class culture as a generating milieu of gang delinquincy. Journal of Social Issues 14 (3), 5–19.

MILROY, J. 1976: *Length and height variations in the vowels of Belfast vernacular.* Belfast Working Papers in Language and Linguistics 1, 3.

—1977: *Speech community and language variety in Belfast, A report to the Social Science Research Council.*

—1978: *Lexical alternation and diffusion in vernacular speech.* Belfast Working Papers in Language and Linguistics 3, 100–115.

—1980: Lexical alternation and the history of English. In Traugott, ed.

—1981: *Regional accents of English.* Belfast: Blackstaff.

MILROY, J. and MILROY, L. 1978: Belfast: change and variation in an urban vernacular. In Trudgill, ed, 19–37.

MILROY, L. 1980: *Language and social networks.* Oxford: Blackwell.

MILROY, L. and MARGRAIN, S. 1978: *Vernacular language loyalty and social network.* Belfast Working Papers in Language and Linguistics 3, 1–59.

MILROY L. and MARGRAIN, S. 1980: Vernacular language loyalty and social network. *Language in Society* 9, 43–70.

MITCHELL, J. C. 1973: Networks, norms and institutions. In Boissevain and Mitchell, eds, 15–35.

MONTGOMERY, M. 1979: *The development of intonation as a communicative resource.* Mimeo.

MOSS, M. H. 1973: *Deprivation and disadvantage?* Open University Course Book E 262:8. Milton Keynes: The Open University Press.

NASSIR, A. S. CHIRAGHDIN, ed., *Malenga wa Mvita.* Nairobi: Oxford University Press.

NICHOLLS, C. S. 1971: *The Swahili coast: politics, diplomacy and trade on the East African littoral 1798–1856.* London: Allen & Unwin.

O'KANE, D. 1977: *Overt and covert prestige in Belfast vernacular speakers: the result of self-report tests.* Belfast Working Papers in Language and Linguistics 2, 54–77.

PATTERSON, D. 1860: *The provincialisms of Belfast pointed out and corrected.* Belfast: Mayne.

PAUL, H. 1920: *Prinzipien der Sprachgeschichte.* Halle: Niemayer.

PELLOWE, J. 1970: *Establishing some prosodic criteria for a classification of speech varieties.* Newcastle: University School of English, mimeo.

PELLOWE, J., NIXON, G., STRANG, B., and MCNEANY, V., 1972: A dynamic modelling of linguistic variation: the urban (Tyneside) linguistic survey. *Lingua* 30, 1–30.

PELLOWE, J. and JONES, V. 1977: *On intonational variability in Tyneside speech*: Newcastle: University School of English, mimeo.

—1978: On intonational variability in Tyneside speech. In Trudgill, ed., 101–22.

PELTO, P. J. 1970: *Anthropological research: the structure of inquiry.* New York: Harper & Row.

PIKE, K. L. 1945: *The intonation of American English.* University of Michigan Publications in Linguistics 1. Ann Arbor: University of Michigan Press.

PINE, L. G. 1959: *Burke's peerage.* London: Burke's Peerage Ltd.

POLICANSKY, L. 1980: *Verb concord variation in Belfast vernacular.* Paper delivered to the Sociolinguistics Symposium, Walsall.

POLOME, E. C. 1967: *Swahili language handbook.* Washington: Center for Applied Linguistics.

POPPER, K. 1961: *The poverty of historicism.* London: Routledge & Kegan Paul.

PRINS, A. H. J. 1967: *The Swahili-speaking peoples of Zanzibar and the East African coast.* London: International African Institute.

QUIRK, R., SVARTVIK, J., DUCKWORTH, A. P., KUSIECKI, J. P. L. and COLIN, A. J. T. 1964: *Studies in the correspondence of prosodic to grammatical features in English.* Proceedings of the IXth Congress of Linguistics, Boston 1962. The Hague: Mouton.

REID, E. 1978: Social and stylistic variation in the speech of children: some evidence from Edinburgh. In Trudgill, ed., 158–73.

ROMAINE, S. 1975: *Linguistic variability in the speech of some Edinburgh school-children.* University of Edinburgh, M Litt. thesis.

—1978: Postvocalic /r/ in Scottish English: sound change in progress? In Trudgill, ed, 144–58.

—1979a: The social reality of phonetic descriptions. *Northern Ireland Speech and Language Forum Journal* 5, 21–36.

—1979b: *On the non-decisiveness of quantitative solutions: or why Labov was wrong about contraction and deletion of the copula.* Work in Progress, Department of Linguistics, University of Edinburgh, 12, 10–17.

—1980: Stylistic variation and evaluative reactions to speech: problems in the investigation of linguistic attitudes in Scotland. *Language and Speech* 23, 3, 213–32.

—1981: The status of variable rules in sociolinguistic theory. *Journal of Linguistics* 17, 93–121.

SACLEUX, C. 1909: *Grammaire des dialectes Swahilis.* Procuré des pp. du Saint-Esprit, Paris.

SALIM, A. I. 1973: *Swahili-speaking peoples of Kenya's coast 1895–1965.* Nairobi: East African Publishing House.

SANKOFF, DAVID and LABERGE, SUZANNE 1978: Statistical dependence among successive occurrences of a variable in discourse. In Sankoff, David, ed., 119–27.

SANKOFF D. ed. 1978: *Linguistic Variation. Models and methods.* New York: Academic Press.

SANKOFF, D. and LABOV, W. 1979: On the uses of variable rules. *Language in Society* 8, 189–222.

SANKOFF, D. 1979: *Ordering variable rules.* Paper given to the LSA meeting, Los Angeles, California.

SANKOFF, G. 1974: A quantitative paradigm for the study of communicative competence. In R. Bauman and J. Sherzer, eds, *Explorations in the ethnography of speaking.* London: Cambridge University Press, 18–49.

SAPIR, E. 1921: *Language.* New York: Harcourt, Brace & World.

SCHERER, K. R. and GILES, H. 1979: *Social markers in speech.* Cambridge: Cambridge University Press.

SEARLE, J. 1969: *Speech acts. An essay in the philosophy of language.* London: Cambridge University Press.

SCHLEICHER, A. 1863: *Die Darwinsche Theorie und die Sprachwissenschaft.* Berlin.

SHATZ, M. and GELMAN, R. 1973: *The development of communication skills: modification in the speech of young children as a function of the listener.* Monographs of the Society for Research in Child Development 38.

SHUY, R. and FASOLD, R., eds, 1977: *Studies in language variation.* Washington, DC: Georgetown University Press.

SLAVIKOVA, M. and BRYAN, M. A. 1973: The case of two Swahili dialects. *African Language Studies,* 53–81.

SPSS 1975: *Statistical package for the social sciences*—manual by N. H. Nie, C. Hadlai Hull, J. G. Jenkins, K. Steinbrenner and D. H. Bent. New York: McGraw-Hill.

Standard Swahili-English dictionary. 1939: London: Oxford University Press.

STIGAND, C. H. 1915: *A grammar of dialectic changes in the Kiswahili language.* Cambridge: Cambridge University Press.

STOCKWELL, R. P. 1960: The place of intonation in a generative grammar of English. *Language,* 36, 360–7.

STOCKWELL, R. P., SCHACHTER, P. and PARTEE, B. H. 1973: *The major syntactic structures of English.* New York: Holt, Rinehart & Winston.

STROSS, B. 1975: *Variation and natural selection as factors in linguistic and cultural change.* Lisse: The Peter de Ridder Press.

TABOURET-KELLER, A. 1976: Ethnic names and group identity in British Honduras. *Rassegna Italiana di Linguistica Applicata* 8, 2–3, 191–201.

—1980: Psychological terms used in Creole studies: some difficulties. In Valdman and Highfield, eds, Bloomington: Indiana University Press, 313–31.

TABOURET-KELLER, A. and LE PAGE, R. B. 1971: L'enquête sociolinguistique à grande echelle; un exemple. Sociolinguistic Survey of Multilingual Communities, part I, British Honduras survey. Paris: *La Linguistique* 6, 103–18.

THAKERER, J. N., GILES, H., and CHESHIRE, J. (forthcoming) Psychological and linguistic parameters of speech accommodation theory. In Fraser, C. and Scherer, K. R., eds, *Advances in the social psychology of language.* Cambridge: Cambridge University Press.

THELANDER, MATS 1976: Code-switching or code-mixing? In Nordberg, B., ed, *Sociolinguistic research in Sweden and Finland. International Journal of the Sociology of Language* 10, 103–123.

—1979a: Språkliga variationsmodeller tillämpade på nutida Burträsktal 1. Models of linguistic variation applied to present speech in Burträsk. Part 1: presentation of material and analysis on the level of linguistic variable. *Studia Philologiae Scandinavicae Upsaliensia* 14, 1, Uppsala. (English summary in part 2).

—1979b: Språkliga variationsmodeller tillämpade på nutida Burträsktal 1. Models of linguistic variation applied to present speech in Burträsk. Part 2: theoretical premises and analysis on the level of linguistic variety. *Studia Philologiae Scandinavicae Upsaliensia* 14, 2. Uppsala. (With a summary in English.)

TRAUGOTT, E. *et al.*, eds, 1980: *Papers from the Fourth International Congress in Historical Linguistics.* Amsterdam: Benjamins.

TRUDGILL, P. 1974a: *Sociolinguistics.* Harmondsworth: Penguin.

—1974b: *The social differentiation of English in Norwich.* London: Cambridge University Press.

—ed, 1978: *Sociolinguistic Patterns in British English.* London: Edward Arnold.

TURNER, C. 1967: Conjugal roles and social networks. *Human Relations* 20, 121–30.

ULDALL, E. T. 1964: Dimensions of meaning in intonation. In D. Abercrombie *et al.*, eds, *In honour of Daniel Jones.* London: Longmans, 271–9.

VANDERSLICE, R. and PIERSON, L. S. 1967: Prosodic features of Hawaiian English. *Quarterly Journal of Speech* 53, 2, 156–66.

VAN VELZEN, H. U. E. THODEN 1973: Coalitions and network analysis. In Boissevain and Mitchell, eds, 219–250.

WASHABAUGH, W. 1975: *Variability in decreolization on Providence Island, Colombia.* Wayne State University, PhD thesis.

WATSON, JOSEPH, 1974: A Gaelic dialect of N.E. Ross-shire. Lochlann 6, 9–90. (*Norsk Tidskrift for Sprogvidenskap,* supplementary vol. vi, Oslo: Aschehoug.

WEINREICH, U. 1966: *Explorations in semantic theory.* The Hague: Mouton.

WEINREICH, U., LABOV, W. and HERZOG, M. 1968: Empirical foundations for a theory of language change. In Lehman, W. P. and Malkiel, Y., eds, *Directions for historical linguistics.* Austin: University of Texas Press, 95–189.

WHITE, GEOFFREY H., ed, 1953: *The Complete peerage.* London: St Catherine Press.

WHITELEY, W. H. 1955: Kimvita: an enquiry into dialectal status and characteristics. *Journal of the East African Swahili Committee* 25, 10–39.

—1969: *Swahili: the rise of a national language,* London: Methuen.

WILLMOTT, P. 1966: *Adolescent boys of East London.* London: Routledge & Kegan Paul.

WOLFRAM, WALTER A. 1969: *A sociolinguistic description of Detroit Negro speech.* Washington, DC: Center for Applied linguistics.

WOLFSON, N. 1976: Speech events and natural speech: some implications for sociolinguistic methodology. *Language in Society* 5, 2, 189–211.

YOUNG, M. and WILMOTT, P., 1962: *Family and kinship in East London:* London: Penguin.

Index

sampling, 35n, 42 – 3, 106 – 9, 111, 115, 117, 119, 120, 122, 123 – 5.

semi-speaker, 3 – 4, 26 – 33.

sex differentiation: and education, 57 – 8; and intonational varieties, 93 – 101; and network, 9, 142 – 52; and norms, 61 – 3, 70 – 3, 79 – 83, 133 – 40; and peer group, 154 – 66; and social class, 2 – 3, 9, 43 – 4.

simplification, 22 – 3, 38, 46.

social class/status, 2, 8 – 9, 20 – 1, 37, 49, 50, 57, 148, 153. *See also* social hierarchy.

social (class) hierarchy, 21, 32, 36 – 9, 42.

social network, *see* network.

sociolinguistic methodology, *See* methodology.

sociolinguistic patterns, 1 – 3, 9, 85, 142.

sociolinguistic theory, 1, 6, 23 – 4, 145.

sociolinguistic variable, *See* variable.

solidarity, 9, 51n, 56, 142.

speech act, 86, 93.

speech community: adults *vs* children as members of 6 – 7, 85 – 6; diglossic, 15, 109; grammars of, 7, 15, 18, 20 – 4; homogeneous *vs* heterogeneous, 15, 65 – 83 *passim*, 124; membership in, 4, 8, 26 – 7, 30 – 1; New *vs* Old World, 1 – 2; shape/structure of, 1, 3, 35, 39 – 40, 45 – 6; and social evaluation, 29, 32 – 3. *See also* competence, norms.

standard: *vs* creole, 109 – 116, 122; *vs* non-standard, 2, 9 – 11, 15, 51 – 4, 57, 59, 62, 109, 153. *See also* dialect, vernacular.

standardization, 40, 42, 46 – 7. *See also* dialect, standard, vernacular.

statistical significance, 43 – 5, 54 – 5, 60, 62, 89 – 92, 95 – 100, 112 – 24, 147 – 8, 155.

stereotype, 32, 129. *See also* indicator, marker.

style: and formality, 7, 40, 105, 108, 133, 157, 162; shifting, 13, 19, 51; and situation, 50 – 1, 56 – 7, 65, 68 – 83; and stylistic continuum, 159 – 60; and vernacular culture, 155.

Tehran (Persian), 3, 5, 8, 11, 49 – 63 *passim*.

tokens, 5, 6, 53, 70, 76, 110 – 11, 145. *See also* variable.

tone, 86, 88 – 103 *passim*.

topic, 56, 69, 114 – 5, 133.

Tyneside, 85 – 103 *passim*.

univariate analysis, 121 – 3.

variability of domain, 86.

variable (sociolinguistic): bimodal distribution of, 8, 16; binomial, 37 – 8; complex, 35 – 7; constraints on: 5, 16; function of, 57 – 60, 102 – 3, 147 – 52 *passim*, 153 – 66 *passim*; lexical input/loci/word class membership for, 9, 36, 39, 42, 51, 108, 111, 130 – 3, 145; macro- *vs* micro-, 5, 66 – 83 *passim*; quantification of, 2, 35 – 7, 42 – 6, 57 – 63, 65 – 83 *passim*, 105 – 9, 112 – 24 *passim*; semantic, 53 – 7, 111 – 12; social evaluation of, 9, 31 – 2, 38, 46, 149; syntagmatic relations of, 53 – 5, 77, 110. See also indicators, markers, stereotypes.

variable rule: and change, 20 – 3; constraints on, 19 – 20, 37 – 8, 67, 165; and grammar, 3 – 4, 6, 19, 23, 49, 83. *See also* speech community, probabilistic model, variable.

vernacular: change in, 22, 39 – 41, 46, 141 – 3; culture, 141 – 52 *passim*, 153 – 66 *passim*; loyalty, 14. *See also* dialect, norms, peer group, standard.

Wolof, 23.